RELIGIOUS PERSPECTIVES AND PROBLEMS

An Introduction to The Philosophy of Religion

Allen V. Eikner

UNIVERSITY
PRESS OF
AMERICA

190818

Library of Congress Catalog Card Number: 80-67265

This book is dedicated to:

Steve Bennett
David Clohessy
Steve Highfill
Lucie Juneau
Karin Kilpatric
Scott Martin
Susan Turnbull

who found the philosophie way.

CONTENTS

IV. EXISTENTIAL THEISM

V. NEW DIRECTIONS

TOPICAL CONTENTS

PREFACE

This book of readings is arranged and edited with the beginning student in the philosophy of religion in mind. It does not deal with certain technical and highly specialized problems which are of interest to the advanced student. The articles have been chosen because of their deep insight into some of the more basic and general problems in the philosophy of religion and because of their clarity of explanation.

There are two fundamental ideas which have guided the editor. One is that religion needs to be understood in terms of the way in which it answers basic philosophical questions. The most basic of such questions for religion are: how can religious Reality be known? what is the nature of that Reality? how can human language symbolize transcendent Reality? how can transcendent Reality be experienced? These questions are pursued in each of the perspectives under the problems of "The Existence of God" and "The Nature of Religious Experience."

The other guiding idea is that basic religious assumptions regarding the existence of God and religious experience should be seen in perspective. The full meaning of religious experience cannot be grasped until its relation to other basic experiences is understood. These other basic experiences have been categorized as "Science," "Morality," and "Human Destiny." Thus a full understanding of religion should not only include an understanding of God and how one comes to that understanding, but also the implications of that understanding for how one shall relate himself to the non-human world, other human beings and the purposes of human history.

A category of "Religion and the Problems of Human Society" is added to each perspective in order that the student may see how the problems of human society are assessed from the standpoint of different religious perspectives. In these articles the perspectives are largely assumed rather than explained. They should not only aid in the understanding of the perspective but also in showing how an analysis of social problems can be made from basic religious assumptions.

The four religious perspectives drawn together here are "live" options in the contemporary world. Their basic differences are centered in different assumptions regarding human nature and knowledge which can be clearly understood. The perspectives are broad enough to embrace differing traditional religious views and people of differing backgrounds and interests. When such perspectives are brought into dialogue with each other it should encourage not only the seeking of a meaningful religious synthesis but also motivation towards self-thinking.

Though the editor has organized these articles on the problems of religion into perspectives, they can be used so that the primary emphasis is on the problems. In that case the organization presented under the topical contents should prove helpful.

Allen V. Eikner
Drury College
June, 1980

PART ONE

HUMANISM

Paul Kurtz
Sidney Hook
Erich Fromm
Julian Huxley
Max Otto
Algernon D. Black
David E. Willcox

1

I. INTRODUCTION

Humanism as it is defined by the writers which follow is largely a twentieth century development. While it has fostered humanistic associations and publications participation in these institutions is not essential to being a humanist. While humanists may appear within varying types of institutions, or none at all, and may disagree about many political beliefs and social questions, they do share some concerns, beliefs and convictions in common. These have been characterized by one humanist as "a concern for humanity, a belief that moral values must be removed from the mantle of theological dogma, and a conviction that our moral ideals must be constantly re-examined and revised in the light of present needs and social demands."[1]

There have been three general qualifications of contemporary Humanism which represent compelling interests within the whole movement. These are the scientific, ethical and religious:

> The particular charge of scientific Humanism is to give us our most reliable knowledge of how things happen in the continuity of man and nature. It is our strongest resource for effective operations. Its connection with naturalism bars an impoverishing concentration on man in isolation from the rest of the world. It also enforces the moral discipline of thorough inquiry and objective thinking.
>
> Ethical Humanism has a focal interest for integrity and justice in the treatment of persons and groups. It is not wedded to a fixed moral code, but is concerned with the development of standards in these

---

[1]Paul Kurtz, "Humanism and the Moral Revolution," THE HUMANIST ALTERNATIVE, Paul Kurtz, ed. (Buffalo: Prometheus Books, 1973), p. 49.

matters; in a world of suffering it would extend an
ethic of compassion. It seeks constructive paths towards non-exploitive relations and toward freeing
people for mutually supportive growth.

Religious Humanism primarily means a dedication to
Humanist values and a nurturing of faith in them. It
may also include an interest in worthy celebration of
life's crises and triumphs. Beyond these points it has
a tendency toward a cosmic range of feeling, appreciation and apprehension. It wants its sense of human
greatness to be in keeping with a sense of 'other'
greatness whether in nature or in imagined ideal
realism. Such experience may be intensely mystical.[2]

Not all humanists have all three of these compelling interests. Indeed some would not subscribe to the term Religious
Humanism at all. Whether or not they claim to be religious
humanists, however, they all believe that human values have
their origin in human experience and not in supernatural realities
or authoritarian dogmas. The HUMANIST MANIFESTO written in
1933, and signed by 34 prominant humanists expressed the need to
establish a religion which was opposed to supernaturalism but
expressed a commitment to human values in its affirmation of
individual and social life as the highest good. One of the signers
of that Manifesto still insists that "humanism is a certain religious temper" in that it "involves an attitude toward, and an
appraisal of, the nature and possibilities of man and his essential
needs. This temper is religious because it involves a "faith in
man himself--in man's infinite possibilities. . . . faith in intelligence and in man. . . ."[3]

---

[2]Horace L. Friess, "Humanistic Responsibilities," Ibid.,
p. 41.

[3]John Herman Randall, Jr., "What is the Temper of
Humanism?" Ibid., p. 58.

4

Whether the humanist characterizes himself as scientific, ethical or religious, it is possible to synthesize these various emphases in a perspective which can properly be called religious. The principal assumptions which form the basis of such a humanistic perspective are as follows:

(1) The limitations of human knowledge make it impossible to know any supernatural reality; therefore, we must either give up "God talk" or redefine the terms so it is clear that they refer to some dimension of human experience only.

(2) The experience of the realization of the highest human ideals is an authentic religious experience.

(3) Religion and science do not conflict with each other as long as religion is defined within the boundaries of knowledge set by science.

(4) Morality is the use of intelligence to bring about the good life through the realization of human possibilities. The vision which recognizes the value of those possibilities and the temperament which prompts us to pursue them can properly be called religious.

(5) The goodness of life is an end in itself. It does not have to be justified by eternal rewards.

The article by the distinguished humanist Paul Kurtz, which follows, indicates most of the emphases of Humanism outlined above. It stresses the central emphasis upon a scientific understanding of human life and how religious values, when based upon that ideology, are able to offer rich possibilities for a good life amidst inevitable futilities, including death.

The Condition of Man

Paul Kurtz

The tragic element implicit in human existence--over and beyond our instrumental effectiveness--is apparent to all who are willing to reflect on its nature, and it is especially revealing to all who are willing to reflect on its nature, and it is especially revealing to all who have divested themselves of their cultural myths, whether those of the ancient god of Immortality or, in our contemporary scene, those of the gods of Love, Success, or Progress. These religious myths may serve psychological and sociological functions; they may provide a balm, peace of mind guaranteed, and social cohension. These functions are lost to the literal scientific man who takes these myths (especially the theistic) for literal nonsense, although he himself may worship at his own mythological altars, whether of Determinism, Progress or some other ideal.

The truly religious man is one who dares to face the nature of life and death with courage, the man who has a sense of both the rich possibilities and the inevitable futilities of life--and few of the devotees of organized religions are religious in this sense. It is a mistake to think that theism has a monopoly on religion. On the contrary, humanism is capable of a deeper and fuller understanding of the conditions of man. The true religious response is a response to the demands of the external world. It develops usually when men come to realize in full shock, and usually in times of crisis, the flux of human existence, and when they recognize that, though the fondest human dreams may be realized, alas, "vanity, O vanity," they rest upon quicksand. In the words of the author of Ecclesiastes: "All go unto one place, all are of the dust, and all return to the dust again."

From DECISION AND THE CONDITION OF MAN, by Paul Kurtz, pp. 283-286, 288. Copyright 1965, by University of Washington Press, and reprinted by their permission.

The tragedy of the temporal historicity of life, the death of each human being, the fact that all men are unclothed, naked, and alone--this is the awesome bedrock fact that confronts the sensitive religious consciousness. The existentialists were not the first to discover this fact of nature and life or the pathos of suffering and dread. Yet all too few men are willing to see life and death for what they really are; they put death out of their minds, and, like the other animals, ignore it, or they think that it is a problem only for the old to worry out. We see others die, not ourselves. Yet life and civilization are mere mortal events which will pass like all else.

Along with this awareness of the transcience of life--and it takes true courage to face it--there is another fact to be faced: the recognition that there are powers and forces external to and independent of us, the recalcitrant given. There is a source of our being that we cannot control, but that we can only come to terms with and accept. Some mistakenly call this "God," or attribute its power to mysterious demons and mythological entities. Others attribute it to "causal law" and to the fact that we are only a small part of vast systems of events. In any case, some recognition of our dependence upon the tide of events and the limitations of our powers is present in the religious response, and this usually leads to some stoic resignation and perhaps a degree of "natural piety."

These facts of life and death, of transience and dependence, I think that all can accept. They are easily confirmable by scientific observation, and they are as true for the atheist as for the theist. And these facts do not disappear by claiming that the whole problem is a "pseudo problem" or cognitively meaningless. True, there may not be a solution, but there is still a "real" predicament that we face. Yet men frequently do not wish to face their transience and impotence. They cover it up or disguise it. The cares of society and culture dominate our consciousness. Civilization builds symbolic worlds, and we are taken up by new events. We are concerned about making a living, getting married, writing a sonnet, playing the stock market, investigating the causes of disease, supporting the party, contributing to economic growth, to democracy, or to world government. And, in our haste, we frequently overlook our brute animal existence.

The "existential" condition of man is often not faced; it is usually forced upon us in times of extreme crisis or change. When it is faced, and faced hard, the truth may chill us, and so we construct false mythologies to avoid it: the immortality myth of the good life promised later on, or the utopian myth of the good life on earth for mankind now. But the scientific method can confirm neither, nor can it guarantee that our vain hopes are inscribed in the womb of nature. The assertions of traditional theistic religions, that God exists or that there is an immortal soul, are at best expressive or imperative utterances that have not been verified and are unverifiable. And the messianic promises of social reformers or psychological therapists that unlimited social progress or psychological happiness is just around the corner awaiting us with certainty are also seen to be idle chatterings in the wind.

We huddle together in society and create smoke screens for the protection of life against the cold wind and death. Nature cannot sustain them--and with the dust they will eventually vanish. As we open the frontiers of space new challenges will confront the human species. Our organic existence will be given new dimensions as we learn to travel in a wider universe. But the new discoveries awaiting us cannot alter the ultimate condition of man or the impermanence of life. There are some things we can ameliorate and change, and there are many problems we can resolve-- but who except the completely self-deluded can believe in their final solution or in our ultimate salvation? . . .

I do not wish to seem overly pessimistic. I have said throughout that it is important for us to unify our scientific knowledge, particularly our knowledge of man. I have persistently asserted that a science of man is both possible and necessary, and that there are no unalterable or a priori obstacles, as far as I can see, to the understanding of human nature. Neither the appeal to motive, historical, or teleonomic explanations as special kinds of explanation, nor the fact of free intension or decision, nor any alleged "mind-body dualism" can invalidate the scientific explanation of human nature. The fact is that man is a teleonomic animal capable of decision and action, and science can trace the conditions of such behavior. Moreover, this knowledge, and I have

8

argued, enables us to improve our practical know-how and our power for making decisions. Our prescriptions and rules are more effective if based on descriptive knowledge. Science itself is not purely descriptive, but has a prescriptive basis. But this does not undermine its claims or make it totally unlike other human interests. It merely places it in its proper valuational locus.

Moreover, scientific ideology is probably the most effective value system and ideology available in the world today, and it is one that we should be committed to, individually and socially, for the good life. It provides the best means for individual happiness and social progress, and it is particularly the hope of the vast mass of underdeveloped humanity in the twentieth century . . . .

All that man has is life. What he makes of it, or what it makes of him is all that counts. Society and culture have emerged in part to facilitate our animal desires, but they can also be a mask for deception. Man has knowledge. Through knowledge he may discover what he is, what he needs, what he desires, and the desire of life; yet life ultimately ends in death. Life while lived can be good and bountiful: love, devotion, kindness, knowledge, achievement, success, well-being, happiness, economic growth, and social betterment are all possible within limits. But all good things must pass, and life has its bitter end . . . .

2. THE EXISTENCE OF GOD

The problems which humanists have with the concept of a transcendent God are clearly explained by Sidney Hook. Not only does our knowledge of the world fail to discover the existence of such a God but the concept of it is incomprehensible. How can a human concept express the meaning of a God who is transcendent to human experience? If God is unique a unique language would be required to express this fact, but there is no such language. To claim that God is "uniquely unique" is to claim that the word has no understandable meaning. All words symbolize human experience. When we try to have them symbolize that which is transcendent to human experience it is only anthropomorphism in disguise. Hook recognizes that some humanists use the word "God" as a symbol of the highest human ideals, but because of possible confusion he does not do so.

Modern Knowledge and the Concept of God

Sidney Hook

Many years ago in a discussion with Jacques Maritain he remarked that anyone who was as keenly interested in arguments for the existence of God as I seemed to be was not beyond hope of redemption. One can with equal justification observe that strong concern with the validity of the arguments for God's existence threatens the integrity of belief in him. Some believers have become agnostic when they discovered that the chain of argument which was the anchor of their faith had defective links.

From THE QUEST FOR BEING, by Sidney Hook (New York: Dell Publishing Co., 1963). Copyright by St. Martin's Press, Inc., and reprinted by their permission.

I owe it to the reader to indicate that the point of view from which I shall develop my position is that of a still unredeemed, "skeptical God-seeker. " I call myself a "God-seeker" because I am willing to go a long way, to the very ends of reason itself, to track down every last semblance of evidence or argument which promises fulfillment of the quest. I call myself a "skeptical God-seeker" because I have so far returned from previous expeditions empty-handed. Since I am prepared to undertake the quest anew, I have not embraced any of the final negations of traditional disbeliefs which would forever close off further objective inquiry by metaphysical fiat.

This freedom from question-begging commitment is all the more appropriate because I am primarily concerned with "the concept of God" and only secondarily concerned with the question whether that of which we form or have the concept exists. It is of the utmost importance that we abide by this distinction. Who would dispute for long about whether "snow men" exist or whether a "hippogriff" exists without first defining or indicating in a rough way what the meaning of these terms is ? Such definitions or concepts do not have to be very precise, but they cannot be so vague that we are unable to distinguish them from definitions and concepts of quite different terms altogether. The least we must know is what we are to count as "snow man" or "hippogriff" before looking for it.

Although this initial demand for clarity is regarded as legitimate in the analysis of most concepts, there is an extraordinary resistance to following the same procedure in connection with the term "God. " Many people will heatedly discuss the question whether God exists--without displaying any concern over the fact that they are encompassing the most heterogeneous notions in the use they make of the word "God. " After such discussion, one is tempted to say, "God only knows what 'God' means. "

Now this expression "God only knows what 'God' means" is perfectly good theology, for it can be taken as a way of saying that "Only God has complete or perfect knowledge of God. " Unfortunately, however, not only "complete or perfect knowledge" of the meaning of God is denied us by some theologians, but even <u>adequate</u> knowledge. According to these theologians, the concept of God refers to something "unique," and therefore it is impossible to describe him in terms which are applicable to other things. Otherwise God would merely be another item in the catalogue of common things. But he is <u>sui</u> <u>generis</u>. Father Copleston, the able Jesuit philosopher, puts the point explicitly: "God by hypothesis is unique; and it is quite impossible to describe Him adequately by using concepts which normally apply to ordinary objects of experience. If it were possible, He would not be God . . . this must be so, owing to the finitude of the human intellect . . . ."

Now I believe it can be shown that this conclusion is false. The finitude of the human intellect is no bar to adequate knowledge of other things, even of things which are not finite; for example, we can give an adequate account of an infinite series of integers. Nor can our inability to describe God adequately flow from the presumed uniqueness of God because there are unique things in the world which we can describe adequately in terms that apply to other things. If there was a first man in the world, then by definition he is or was certainly unique. There couldn't be two first men. Nevertheless, we have a rather adequate understanding of what it would mean for anything to be the first man.

What must be intended by Father Copleston and those who share his views is that God is uniquely unique. In order to understand why God is considered uniquely unique, we must recognize the second of the difficulties that are said to be involved in getting an adequate knowledge of God. This is that the concept of God refers to something or someone that necessarily exists. What does it mean to say that something necessarily exists? It means that our knowledge of its existence cannot be the conclusion of an empirical or inductive argument, for such can only lead to a probability judgment. Nor can our knowledge be the conclusion of a formal deductive argument--unless the premises are taken as absolutely or necessarily true, which is never the case even with propositions in geometry. The only test which is at all plausible of the necessary truth of an assertion concerning the existence of anything is that the denial of this assertion is self-contradictory. There are enormous difficulties here, the upshot of which is that at most and at best the only assertions which fulfill this requirement are the laws of logic. Everything else which is given or discovered in the world can be otherwise. Now if the laws of logic are taken as formal conditions of discourse they cannot establish the existence of anything (including God) as necessary. If they are taken as statements about things then they produce an embarrassing richness of necessary existences. Those who accepted them would be under the intellectual compulsion of finding a way to distinguish between God and other necessary existences. This makes it impossible for believers to use the laws of logic alone, for since they generally assume that the existence of other things depends upon God, they cannot accept any method of argument which leads to the conclusion that there are other necessary existences as well. Such a conclusion would entail that God's power is limited. If, for example, we assert that the world necessarily exists, it would be self-contradictory to bring in God as its necessary creator or sustainer.

It should now be clear why those who talk about the concept of God, especially in traditional terms, have such difficulties, and why their arguments keep breaking down. In intellectual fairness we must recognize that they have embarked upon a project of belief which forces them to use the language of paradox and analogy. What exacerbates their difficulty is that the language of paradox and analogy cannot be the same as the ordinary models of paradoxical or analogical discourse. To do justice to the theologians, imagination must give wings to our understanding and broaden the perspective of our vision. But we must also remain within the horizon of intelligibility or of what makes sense.

If the term "God" has meaning, we must be able to say what it is. If we say what God is, we must be able to describe him in certain distinct combinations of words and sentences, and therefore we must find some principle which controls our statements. No one who regards the term God as meaningful will admit the propriety of any statement about God, but at the very least he must recognize degrees of appropriateness with respect to language. And the problem with which we are wrestling breaks out

13

all over again when we ask: what principle determines the appropriateness of the language? For example, the reflective believer in God knows that the epithet "person" or "father" cannot be literally applied to God, that God isn't a person like other persons or a father like other fathers. Nonetheless he finds no difficulty in praying to "Our Father in Heaven." He would, however, deem it singularly inappropriate for anyone to refer to God in prayer as "Our Nephew in Heaven." Why?

The most plausible answer, based upon a study of the names of God and the attributes predicated of him, suggests that the principle which controls the appropriateness of our utterances is derived from the language of human ideals, in their anthropological and ethical dimensions. The conclusion is incontestable that in some sense every intellectual construction of man will reflect his nature. Nor does this fact necessarily entail subjectivity. For even science (which next to mathematics is most frequently taken as a paradigm of objectivity) can be considered a human enterprise whose propositions are constructions of, or inferences from, the data of ordinary experience, and describable in language either continuous with ordinary language or constructed from terms which are ultimately so derived, no matter how technical. But the great difference between God as an object of religious belief, and the objects of scientific belief, is that assertions about the latter are controlled by familiar rules of discourse, understood by all other investigators, that they are related by logical steps to certain experimental consequences, and that those consequences can be described in such a way that we know roughly what counts as evidence for or against the truth of the assertions in question. Now this is not the case with respect to those statements which affirm the existence of God. Certain observable phenomena will sometimes be cited as evidence for the truth of the assertion, but it will not be shown how this evidence follows from God's existence; nor will there ever be any indication of what would constitute evidence against its truth . . . .

This brings us back to a consideration of the principle which controls the appropriateness of our utterances about God. The most fruitful hypothesis about this principle seems to me to have been formulated by Ludwig Feuerbach, that greatly neglected figure of the nineteenth century, who declared after a study of the predicates attributed to God that they were projections of human needs--not the needs of the understanding but the needs of the heart, not of the human mind but of human feeling: emotions, hopes, and longings. What Feuerbach is saying, as I interpret him, is that the principle which controls the appropriateness of our utterances about God is man's idealized conception of himself, and that the predicates of God, particularly those which make him an object of reverance, worship, and aspiration are objectifications of man's highest ethical ideas . . . .

If the concept of a transcendent God is incomprehensible, it is difficult to see what difference it makes whether we declare that he created the earth in six days or six million years, whether he created man in one operation out of dust or through a long series of evolutionary changes. At the Darwin Centennial celebration at the University of Chicago last year, Sir Julian Huxley denied that our earth and its inhabitants were created, and he presented anew the evidence for believing that both evolved out of earlier forms. To which Father J. Franklin Ewing, professor of anthropology at Fordham University, replied in somewhat the same way as other distinguished theologians replied to Huxley's grandfather: "God is the creator of man--body and soul. Whether he used the method of evolution for the preparation of the human body or created it from unorganized matter is not of primary importance. In either case he is the Creator . . . God created not only all beings but also all potentialities for evolution."

In short, no matter what the findings of science are, they cannot affect the truths of religion. And it is significant that in his address to the Vatican Academy of Sciences on November 22, 1951, Pope Pius XII without any embarrassment accepted the findings of modern astronomy about the age and evolution of the universe. This withdrawal in advance from any possible conflict with the claims of science to true knowledge of the physical universe makes it difficult to understand the intense warfare waged by religion and theology against science in the past. If it really is the case that the domains of scientific inquiry and religious beliefs do not touch at any point, and therefore cannot conflict, then it becomes hard to explain why the advance of science should in fact have weakened religious belief and produced periodic crises of faith. Whatever the present situation may be, science was not in the past given such autonomy either by religion or theology.

Feuerbach's interpretation of these periodic crises of belief is that they are nodal points in human consciousness when men become dimly aware that their statements about God are not the same kind of thing as their statements about ordinary matters, but are expressions of need and hope for an absolutely secure source, a power or an Ideal, beyond Nature, yet not foreign to human nature, on which to rely for protection against all the evils that beset them in their precarious careers on earth. "The Creation, like the idea of a personal God in general, is not a scientific, but a personal matter," he writes, "not an object of the free intelligence but of the feelings . . . ." If God is awesome and tremendous and mysterious it is because he has unlimited power over nature--and therefore unlimited Will which is related to human will. God defies rational analysis because his "existence" is postulated not by any imperative of thought but by the anguished feelings of finite, suffering man, who wishes to preserve his "personality of subjectivity" against the forces which reduce him to the level of matter. For him "the belief in God is nothing but the belief in human dignity . . . and the true principle of creation the self-affirmation of subjectivity in distinction from Nature." Religion must find a form in which the dignity of men cannot be destroyed by discoveries about Nature whose creatures men are . . . .

This brings me to the . . . conception of God, according to which God is neither a supernatural power nor a principle of immanent structure, but a symbolic term for our most inclusive moral ideals. The "divine" refers to that dimension in human life which is not reducible merely to the physical, the social and the psychological, although it emerges from and affects them. It is a dimension which is experienced whenever ideal ends, justice, compassion for all suffering creatures, dedication to truth, integrity, move men to change the world and themselves. This is the humanist conception of God. It is what Feuerbach's God becomes when men grow aware of the mechanisms of transference and projection by which their needs create the objects of ideal allegiance.

16

The humanist conception of God, which is suggested by John Dewey's phrase, "the effective union of the ideal and actual, " is fundamentally opposed to any notion of a supernatural power as the source of human morality or even as the justification of morality, although it admits that belief in such a power can serve as a support of human morality . . . .

I wish to conclude with a few observations about the humanist conception of God. The great problem which Humanism as a religion must face is not so much the validity of its conception of God but how to justify its use of the term "God. " The defense can be made briefly. All large terms in human discourse are historically variable in meaning or actually ambiguous in use: "atom, " "substance, " "experience, " "reason, " "love, " even "man"--all show this variation in meaning. Each term stands for a family of meanings (like a term "game" in Wittgenstein's analysis) which resemble one another but are nevertheless not completely consonant. Consequently, it is argued that if the same penumbral complex of attitudes (intellectual humility, piety, reverance, wonder, awe, and concern) are manifest in a use of the term "God" which designates no thing or person but our highest ethical commitment, no legitimate objection can be raised--providing, of course, we make it clear that the new use or meaning is different from the old.

The criticism can be made just as briefly. The new use always invites confusion with the old use, and there is, after all, such a thing as the ethics of words. By taking over the word "God" as the religious humanists do, the waters of thought, feeling, and faith are muddied, the issues blurred, the "word" itself becomes the object of interest and not what it signifies . . . .

Is, then, the religion of Humanism justified in using the term "God" for its conception of the moral enterprise ? John Dewey answered the question affirmatively. I answer it negatively. Each one of my readers must answer it for himself.

17

3. THE NATURE OF RELIGIOUS EXPERIENCE

Erich Fromm uses his psychoanalytical powers to distinguish humanistic religion from authoritarian religion. Authoritarian religion, which is based upon a supposed need for superhuman power, actually results in the impoverished condition of self-denial. Humanistic religion, which is based upon the realization of real human possibilities, results in joy, confidence, humility and strength. Religious experience is that experience of self-acceptance and confidence which results in self-realization. It is both individualistic and social in that the need to love other human beings is based on the fact that human beings are dependent upon each other. We do not, however, need to relate ourselves to a superhuman being. God is simply a symbol which expresses our need to love each other.

What is Humanistic Religion?

Erich Fromm

What is the principle of authoritarian religion? The definition of religion given in the Oxford Dictionary, while attempting to define religion as such, is a rather accurate definition of authoritarian religion. It reads: "(Religion is) recognition on the part of man of some higher unseen power as having control of his destiny, and as being entitled to obedience, reverance, and worship."

Here the emphasis is on the recognition that man is controlled by a higher power outside of himself. But this alone does not constitute authoritarian religion. What makes it so is the idea

---

From PSYCHOANALYSIS AND RELIGION, by Erich Fromm. Copyright 1950, by Yale University Press, and reprinted with their permission.

that this power, because of the control it exercises, is entitled to "obedience, reverance, and worship." I underline the word "entitled" because it shows that the reason for worship, obedience, and reverance lies not in the moral qualities of the deity, not in love or justice, but in the fact that it has control, that is, has power over man. Furthermore it shows that the higher power has a right to force man to worship him and that lack of reverance and obedience constitutes sin.

The essential element in authoritarian religion and in the authoritarian religious experience is the surrender to a power transcending man. The main virtue of this type of obedience, its cardinal sin is disobedience. Just as the deity is conceived as omnipotent or omniscient, man is conceived as being powerless and insignificant. Only as he can gain grace, or help from the deity by complete surrender can he feel strength. Submission to a powerful authority is one of the avenues by which man escapes from his feeling of aloneness and limitation. In the act of surrender he loses his independence and integrity as an individual but he gains the feeling of being protected by an awe-inspiring power of which, as it were, he becomes a part . . . .

Humanistic religion, on the contrary, is centered around man and his strength. Man must develop his power of reason in order to understand himself, his relationship to his fellow men, and his position in the universe. He must recognize the truth, both with regard to his limitations and his potentialities. He must develop his powers of love for others as well as for himself and experience the solidarity of all living beings. He must have principles and norms to guide him in this aim. Religious experience in this kind of religion is the experience of oneself in oneness with the All, based on one's relatedness to the world as it is grasped with thought and with love. Man's aim in humanistic religion is to achieve the greatest strength, not the greatest powerlessness; virtue is self-realization, not obedience. Faith is certainty of conviction based on one's experience of thought and feeling, not assent to propositions on credit of the proposer. The prevailing mood is that of joy, while the prevailing mood in authoritarian religion is that of sorrow and of guilt . . . .

The distinction between authoritarian and humanistic religion not only cuts across various religions, it can exist within the same religion . . . .

That early Christianity is humanistic and not authoritarian is evident from the spirit and text of all Jesus' teachings. Jesus' precept that "the kingdom of God is within you" is the simple and clear expression of nonauthoritarian thinking. But only a few hundred years later, after Christianity had ceased to be the religion of the poor and humble peasants, artisans, and slaves (the Amhaarez) and had become the religion of those ruling the Roman Empire, the authoritarian and humanistic principles in Christianity never ceased. It was the conflict between Augustine and Pelarius, between the Catholic Church and the many "heretic" groups and between the various sects within Protestantism. The humanistic, democratic element was never subdued in Christian or in Jewish history, and this element found one of its most potent expressions in the mystic thinking within both religions. The mystics have been deeply imbued with the experience of man's strength, his likeness to God, and with the idea that God needs man as much as man needs God; they have understood the sentence that man is created in the image of God to mean the fundamental identity of God and man. Not fear and submission but love and the assertion of one's own powers are the basis of mystical experience. God is not a symbol of power over man but of man's own powers.

Thus far we have dealt with the distinctive features of authoritarian and humanistic religions mainly in descriptive terms. But the psychoanalyst must proceed from the description of attitudes to the analysis of their dynamics, and it is here that he can contribute to our discussion from an area not accessible to other fields of inquiry. The full understanding of an attitude requires an appreciation of those conscious and, in particular, unconscious process occurring in the individual which provide the necessity for and the conditions of its development.

While in humanistic religion God is the image of man's higher self, a symbol of what man potentially is or ought to become, in authoritarian religion God becomes the sole possessor of what was originally man's: of his reason and his love. The more

20

perfect God becomes, the more imperfect becomes man. He projects the best he has onto God and thus impoverishes himself. Now God has all love, all wisdom, all justice--and man is deprived of these qualities, he is empty and poor. He had begun with the feeling of smallness, but he now has become completely powerless and without strength; all his powers have been projected onto God. This mechanism of projection is the very same which can be observed in interpersonal relationships of a masochistic, submissive character, where one person is awed by another and attributes his own powers and aspirations to the other person. It is the same mechanism that makes people endow the leaders of even the most inhuman systems with qualities of superwisdom and kindness. . . .

When man has thus projected his own most valuable powers unto God, what of his relationship to his own powers? They have become separated from his and in this process he has alienated from himself. Everything he has is now God's and nothing is left in him. His only access to himself is through God. In worshipping God he tries to get in touch with that part of himself which he has lost through projection. After having given God all he has, he begs God to return to him some of what originally was his own. But having lost his own he is completely at God's mercy. He necessarily feels like a "sinner" since he has deprived himself of everything that is good, and it is only through God's mercy or grace that he can regain that which alone makes him human. And in order to persuade God to give him some of his love, he must prove to him how utterly deprived he is of love; in order to persuade God to guide him by his superior wisdom he must prove to him how deprived he is of wisdom when he is left to himself.

But this alienation from his own powers not only makes man feel slavishly dependent on God, it makes him bad too. He becomes a man without faith in his fellowmen or in himself, without the experience of his own love, of his own power of reason. As a result the separation between the "holy" and the "secular" occurs. In his worldly activities man acts without love, in that sector of his life which is reserved to religion he feels himself to be a sinner (which he actually is since to live without love is to live in sin) and tries to recover some of his lost humanity by being in touch with God. Simultaneously, he tries to win forgiveness by emphasizing his own helplessness and worthlessness. Thus the attempt to obtain forgiveness results in the activation of the very attitude from which his sins stem. He is caught in a painful dilemma. The more he praises God, the emptier he becomes. The emptier he becomes, the more sinful he feels. The more sinful he feels, the more he praises his God--and the less able is he to regain himself.

Analysis of religion must not stop at uncovering those psychological processes within man which underlie his religious experience; it must proceed to discover the conditions which make for the development of the authoritarian and humanistic character structures, respectively, from which different kinds of religious experience stem. Such a sociopsychological analysis goes far beyond the context of these chapters. However, the principal point can be made briefly. What people think and feel is rooted in their character and their character is molded by the total configuration of their practice of life--more precisely, by the socio-economic and political structure of their society. In societies ruled by a powerful minority which holds the masses in subjection, the individual will be so imbued with fear, so incapable of feeling strong or independent, that his religious experience will be authoritarian. Whether he worships a punishing, awesome God or a similarly conceived leader makes little difference. On the other hand, where the individual feels free and responsible for his own fate, or among minorities striving for freedom and independence, humanistic religious experience develops. This history of religion gives ample evidence of this correlation between social structure and kinds of religious experience. Early Christianity was a religion of the poor and down-trodden; the history of religious sects fighting against authoritarian political pressure shows the same principle again and again. Judaism, in which a strong anti-authoritarian tradition could grow up because secular authority never had much of a chance to govern and to build up a legend of its wisdom, therefore developed the humanistic aspect of religion to a remarkable degree. Whenever, on the other hand, religion allied itself with secular power, the religion had by necessity to become authoritarian. The real fall of man is his alienation from himself, his submission to power, his turning against himself even though under the guise of his worship of God.

From the spirit of authoritarian religion stem two fallacies of reasoning which have been used again and again as arguments for theistic religion. One argument runs as follows: How can you criticize the emphasis on dependence on a power transcending man; is not man dependent of forces outside himself which he cannot understand, much less control?

Indeed, man is dependent; he remains subject to death, age, illness, and even if he were to control nature and to make it wholly serviceable to him, he and his earth remain tiny specks in the universe. But it is one thing to recognize one's dependence and limitations, and it is something entirely different to indulge in this dependence, to worship the forces on which one depends. To understand realistically and soberly how limited our power is is an essential part of wisdom and of maturity; to worship it is masochistic and self-destructive. The one is humility, the other self-humiliation.

We can study the difference between the realistic recognition of our limitations and the indulgence in the experience of submission and powerlessness in the clinical examination of masochistic character traits. We find people who have a tendency to incur sickness, accidents, humiliating situations, who belittle and weaken themselves. They believe that they get into such situations against their will and intention, but a study of their unconscious motives shows that actually they are driven by one of the most irrational tendencies to be found in man, namely, by an unconscious desire to be weak and powerless; they tend to shift the center of their life to powers over which they feel no control, thus escaping from freedom and from personal responsibility. We find furthermore that this masochistic tendency is usually accompanied by the very opposite, the tendency to rule and to dominate others, and that the masochistic and the dominating tendencies form the two sides of the authoritarian character structure. Such masochistic tendencies are not always unconscious. We find them overtly in the sexual masochistic perversion where the fulfillment of the wish to be hurt or humiliated is the condition for sexual excitement and satisfaction. We find it also in the relationship to the leader and the state in all authoritarian secular religions. Here the explicit aim is to give up one's own will and to experience submission

under the leader or the state as profoundly rewarding. Another
fallacy of theological thinking is closely related to the one concerning dependence. I mean here the argument that there must be a
power or being outside of man because we find that man has an in-
eradicable longing to relate himself to something beyond himself.
Indeed, any sane human being has a need to relate himself to others; a person who has lost that capacity completely is insane. No
wonder that man has created figures outside of himself to which he
relates himself, which he loves and cherishes because they are not
subject to the vacillations and inconsistencies of human objects.
That God is a symbol of man's need to love is simple enough to
understand. But does it follow for the existence and intensity of
this human need that there exists an outer being who corresponds
to this need? Obviously that follows as little as our strongest
desire to love someone proves that there is a person with whom
we are in love. All it proves is our need and perhaps our capacity . . . .

4. THE RELATION OF RELIGION AND SCIENCE

The biologist <u>Julian Huxley</u> believes that while a supernaturalistic God hypothesis may have served some useful purpose in ancient cultures when scientific knowledge was scarce it is no longer needed. Indeed progress in almost every field of endeavor has been made by replacing such superstitions with naturalistic belief systems based upon scientific knowledge rather than myth. The lone remaining area where the "God hypothesis" remains dominant is that of human relations, and progress there can be expected only when scientific understanding becomes our guide. It is obvious that only a religion which is understood as a part of the evolving natural universe ("Religion Without Revelation") is compatible with science.

<u>Science</u> <u>and</u> <u>God</u>

Julian Huxley

In biological evolution, we find many different types characterised by a rapid increase in numbers and in variety of sub-types. During its evolution, it shows gradual trends towards improvement sometimes improvement in general organisation, sometimes in this or that specialised efficiency. In the great majority of cases, these trends eventually become stabilised. In plain language, they come to an end, and the type (if it does not die out) continues indefinitely on the same level of organisation or specialisation: it has exhausted its inherent possibilities of major improvement.

Further, every type of course finds itself in competition with

---

From RELIGION WITHOUT REVELATION, by Julian Huxley, published by Harper & Row, 1957. Reprinted by permission of A. D. Peters & Co., Ltd.

other evolving types; and such competition may modify the course of its evolution, restrict its improvement, reduce its numbers and variety, and sometimes even lead to its virtual or total extinction. And large-scale biological progress occurs through the replacement of one successful or dominant type by another, as in the classical example of the replacement of the cold-blooded reptiles by the warm-blooded mammals and birds as the dominant type of land animals at the close of the Mesozoic about sixty million years ago.

Gods are not organisms, but they are organised cultural entities; like other cultural entities, they can and do evolve, in a way which shows many points of resemblance (though also of difference) to the biological evolution of organisms. Substantially, they are organisations of human thought which seek to represent, canalise, and give a comprehensible interpretation of the forces affecting human destiny: formally, they are organised in the guise of personal beings.

The forces affecting human destiny that underlie the construction of gods are immensely various. They include the elemental force of nature and its catastrophes, from earthquake to pestilence; the phenomena of growth and reproduction, plant, animal and human; the emotional forces aroused by the terrifying and mysterious, and by the sense of sacredness experienced at the crises of human life, like birth and death, puberty and marriage; authority, of father and family, of priest and king, of law and church, of city, tribe and society of large; the power of all conscience, of ideas, of the forces of light struggling with the forces of darkness; the power of all compulsions, whether external or internal.

In his religions, man starts with variety and gradually organises it into some sort of a unity. In certain stages, every society has multiform gods, often of different degrees of importance, representing different special bits of destiny and its forces. Particular objects or places may be deified; or separate aspects of nature like sea, sun, or storm; or different aspects of human natures as in ancient Mesopotamia, or the tribe as in early Judaism, or the household as in ancient Rome; human individuals may be deified or divinised, whether for their mythical exploits like hero-gods, or by traditional virtue of their office like the Egyptian Pharaohs, or deliberately like Roman Emperors, or in their role as saviours like Jesus or the Buddha. There is, in fact, as in biological evolution, a proliferation of specialised variety.

Improvement of the type also takes place. In the first place, gods are transferred from the natural to the supernatural world, from the material to the non-material or spiritual. It is no longer the tree or the rock, the animal or the image which is worshipped, but the spiritual being behind the object or above the phenomena. At the same time, gods are spiritualised; in their make-up, less emphasis is laid on the crude forces of physical nature and life, more on the human ideals of justice and truth, benevolence and wise but firm authority, compassion and love. The conflict between the unimproved and the improved type of god is familiarly exemplified by the struggle of the Hebrew prophets against "idolatry."

This also illustrates another kind of improvement--the trend from variety towards unity or at least some degree of unification. At first approach may be made by erecting one god in a pantheon to the position of chief ruler, as occurred with Zeus in Greek religion: or by divinising a human ruler as symbolising the unity of a vast empire over and above the variety of gods and cults which it contains, as with the Roman Emperors.

A further radical step may take place by the conversion of a tribal god into a universal deity, as in Judaism. Or the universality and singularity of the deity may be proclaimed from the outset, as with Islam. Or finally the difficulty of embodying all attributes of divinity in a single person may be met by that brilliant device of Christian theology, triunity--the tripartite unity of the Trinity.

During cultural as during biological evolution, there is a struggle for existence between ideas and beliefs. There is not only a struggle between gods, but gods in general come into competition with other cultural entities which are seeking to interpret a similar range of phenomena, and so compete for the same area of ideological territory. The most important of these competitors

27

are scientific concepts concerning various aspects of man's destiny, beginning with the world of physical nature in which that destiny is cast, and gradually invading the field of human nature.

The so-called "conflict between religion and science" results from, or indeed is constituted by, this competition. In broadest terms, the competition is between two dominant types of cultural entity--the god hypothesis organised on the basis of mythical thinking, and the naturalistic hypothesis, organised on the basis of scientific method.

As a matter of historical fact, the results of this competition have been to expel gods from positions of effective control, from direct operative contact with more and more aspects of nature, to push them into an ever further remoteness behind or beyond phenomena. Newton showed that gods did not control the movements of the planets: La Place in a famous aphorism affirmed that astronomy had no need of the god hypothesis; Darwin and Pasteur between them did the same for biology: and in our own century the rise of scientific psychology and the extension of historical knowledge have removed gods to a position where they are no longer of value in interpreting human behavior and cannot be supposed to control human history or interfere with human affairs. To-day, God can no longer be considered as the controller of the universe in any but a Pickwickian sense. The god hypothesis is no longer of any pragmatic value for the interpretation or comprehension of nature, and indeed often stands in the way of better and truer interpretation. Operationally, God is beginning to resemble not a ruler, but the last fading smile of a cosmic Cheshire Cat . . . .

The time is ripe for the dethronement of gods from their dominant position in our interpretation of destiny, in favour of a naturalistic type of belief-system. The supernatural is being swept out of the universe in the flood of new knowledge of what is natural. It will soon be as impossible for an intelligent, educated man or woman to believe in a god as it is now to believe that the earth is flat, that flies can be spontaneously generated, that disease is a divine punishment, or that death is always due to witchcraft. Gods will doubtless survive, sometimes under the protection of vested interests, or in the shelter of lazy minds, or as

28

puppets used by politicians, or as refugees for unhappy and ignorant souls: but the god type will have ceased to be dominant in man's ideological evolution.

However, this will not happen unless the emerging naturalistic type of belief is fully adequate to its task: and that task is the formidable one of interpreting and canalising human destiny. Thus the short-lived Goddess of Reason of the French Revolution was a non-viable hybrid between the naturalistic and god type of belief.

Already some non-theistic belief-systems have emerged to dominate large sections of humanity. The two most obvious are Nazism in Germany and Marxist Communism in Russia. Nazism was inherently self-destructive because of its claim to world domination by a small group. It was also grotesquely incorrect and limited as an interpretation of destiny, analogous to some of the primitive products of the theistic types, such as deified beasts, bloodthirsty tribal deities or revengeful divine tyrants.

Marxist Communism is much better organised and more competent, but its purely materialist basis has limited its efficacy. It has tried to deny the reality of spiritual values. But they exist, and the Communists have had to accept the consequences of their ideological error, and grudgingly throw the churches open to the multitudes seeking the spiritual values which had been excluded from the system.

Before an adequate naturalistic belief-system can develop, scientific method must have been applied in all the fields contributing to human destiny: otherwise the system will be incomplete and will merely provide one of the premature syntheses that Gardner Murphy rightly stigmatises as standing in the way of fuller comprehension. To be adequate, it must include scientific knowledge about cultural as well as cosmic and biological evolution; about human nature and social nature as well as about physical and organic nature about values and gods, rituals and techniques, practical moralities and religious ideals as well as about atoms and cells, moons and suns, weather and disease-germs.

Only when scientific knowledge is organized in a way relevant

29

to our ideas about destiny can we speak of a naturalistic belief-system; and only when the scientific knowledge concerns all aspects of destiny will the belief-system begin to be adequate.

5. THE RELATION OF RELIGION AND MORALITY

Humanists believe that human beings are naturally endowed with moral possibilities. Morality does not depend upon a special gift from God nor belief in divine guidance. Max Otto assumes this point of view by arguing that many people have the moral courage to face death and to overcome misery without belief in God and without the detection of any divine purpose in the evolution of life. Morality is dependent upon the human ideals created by intelligence and the faith that human beings have in themselves and each other. The humanist can understand that kind of morality as being synonymous with religion.

The Existence of God and Morality

Max Otto

Not believing in God has worked well. It has worked better than believing did. It is responsible for a realistic acquaintance with our world and a better understanding of human nature. This would seem to furnish evidence, of a kind usually considered good, that there is no superhuman being who cares what becomes of mankind. And the vast majority of people have apparently been convinced. They show it by the way they live day in and day out. They go about their business from morning to night taking no counsel of God. True enough, they would not dream of admitting it and they are offended if anyone else does, but such paradoxical behavior is not unusual. Their refusal to be called unbelievers, like their continued attendance upon church services, though they

From THE HUMAN ENTERPRISE, Copyright 1940, Renewed 1968, pp. 324-332, 340, 342-343. Reprinted by permission of Prentice-Hall, Inc., Englewood Cliffs, New Jersey.

do not subscribe to the church creed, merely shows that something holds them back from openly admitting what they take for granted six days of the week and most of the seventh. What is it that holds them back?

One thing that holds them back is human mortality. Much of the persisting theism is crisis theism. Many people, even of those who ordinarily give no thought to God, and who never lift a finger on behalf of the values of life most intimately associated with his name, are transformed into theists when confronted by the fact or thought of death. They cannot admit that death is the ruin of life, and since the existence of God is required to save it from being just that, a sufficient belief to meet the emergency longers, though inert, in the background of their minds. I admit that it is a shallow belief, one that does not pervade their lives but comes forward only to attend funerals, weddings, and like occasions, yet it may be singularly genuine while it lasts. It lifts the believer for the moment, however temporary his belief, above the struggle for material advantage. He is made tender toward failure. A mood of reverence is awakened and a sense of the mystery of life. In a word, he lives for the time being in his better impulses. And when the theistic mood has retired again to the outermost fringe of interest, which it often does with shocking suddenness, the good words that were spoken for God in the interim echo and re-echo in memory. It is these echoes which hold many people back from accepting an explanation of the world which leaves out God, and makes them feel that anyone who faces death in the same nontheistic spirit as he faces life must be exceptionally hardhearted, if not downright vicious.

No one would claim, I trust, that belief in God is a necessity for creatures who know that they must die. For one thing, few people are called upon to undergo the ordeal of their own death. As a rule they are planning to be alive when unconsciousness overtakes them, and when they die they know nothing about it. Since men have foresight and imagination, however, it is not enough for them to know that they will not experience dying, if they also know that the time will come when they will be dead. It is usually taken for granted that unless they are supported by the hope of immortality it is a kindness not to allude to their last

32

hours.

Statistical evidence is not available one way or the other. If it were, we could show, I believe, that a certain personal quality, more than any belief a man holds for or against theism, determines his behavior in the expectation of death. I wonder whether the commander of a regiment could tell by the behavior of soldiers under fire, who was a believer and who was not. I wonder whether a sea captain whose ship is sinking could divide his sailors into the two classes. I wonder whether the confirmed criminal who walks with a firm step to his execution is sustained by theistic faith or by the same psychic hardness, reckless nerce, and need for display which made a life of crime attractive. And as for bravely bearing the death of others, I have never witnessed greater fortitude than that of devestated hearts for whom there was no balm in Gilead.

The crucial test of how a man will meet his own end is reserved for one who is snatched by the powerful arm of the law, and as he believes unjustly, out of active, sincere preoccupation with social reform and is condemned to die at a stated hour. By that test Bartolomeo Vanzetti, who was not upheld by faith in God, but by the vision of a social ideal for which he felt he was giving his life, and by the loyalty of friends, will bear comparison with Socrates. Since we are considering the possibility of meeting death without divine aid, it is well to recall the statement of Vanzetti when he was sentenced to die:

> If it had not been for these things, I might have died
> unmarked, unknown, a failure. Now we are not a failure.
> This is our career and our triumph. Never in our full life
> could we hope to do such work for tolerance, for justice,
> for man's understanding of man as we do by accident! Our
> words--our lives--our pains--nothing! The taking of our
> lives--lives of a good shoemaker and a poor fish-peddler--
> all! That last moment belongs to us--that agony is our
> triumph.

Another reason for the retention of theism is man's low opinion of himself as a moral being. Thousands who leave God out when engaged in practical pursuits, or in following the promptings of desire, are careful to keep him on hand for the sake of ideals. They feel that God is needed to validate and enforce the moral life. This they believe is especially true of the "masses." Without God, man is a purely natural creature and must act, so they think, like any other animal, though he may express his animality with superior shrewdness. A naturalistic attitude may suffice, indeed must suffice, when the need is one of feeding and housing men, keeping their bodies clean and healthy, increasing their efficiency as producers of material wealth; it can do nothing to make men decent human beings and it is worse than useless in the attainment of moral character. Generosity, ethical idealism, civic-mindedness, interest in moral growth can be expected from none but those who are inspired by God.

To say it in another way, the higher life, however conceived, does not pay in its own terms, so that unless men believe in a God who makes good the losses incurred in living it, no one will find it attractive. A general acceptance of a nontheistic philosophy, so the argument runs, would "eat all nobility out of our conception of conduct and all worth out of our conception of life."

Here we have one of those persistent half-truths that manage to outlive repeated refutation. "But men are better," said Emerson, "than their theology. Their daily life gives it the lie. Every ingenuous and aspiring soul leaves the doctrine behind him in his own experience, and all men feel sometimes the falsehood which they cannot demonstrate." Aspiration is much older than man's acquaintance with the gods, and it does not die when faith in them is lost. A natural discontent with objects less perfect than they can be imagined, and the pursuit of idealized objects that stir the feelings, are the vital forces at work in men's upward striving. The visible results at a given time may seem slight; they are not slight when estimated over years and generations and centuries.

Evidence is everywhere about us, in the community, where we live, in the street that runs by our door, in our own hearts. Men are aroused to adore supremely, to triumph over the cold hard misery of life, to serve and die without reward. I remember Justice Holmes and the Law, Jane Addams and World Peace, La Follette and the People. I think of Flaubert and his worship of

Beauty, of "The Worst Journey in the World," made by three heroes to fill a gap in the evidence for Evolution. I stand with Captain Ahab on the deck of the Pequod, scanning the horizon for Moby Dick. I follow a lantern through the darkness and the churchyard to the tomb of the Capulets with its testimony to the power of romantic love. So my mind wanders on--for there is no end to the number and variety of examples of supreme devotion-- wanders on until lost in the thicket of life. There I find devotion, heroism, self-sacrifice, loyalty to causes. What is it but this original virtue in human beings that faith in God draws upon to give itself vitality ?

Now the conclusion cannot be withstood that greatness, from every point of view, has been achieved by individuals and by whole peoples in the absence of faith in God. Men can and do develop great conceptions of conduct, can and do devote themselves to social causes with enthusiasm and self-sacrifice, without counting on help from higher powers. Co-operative faith in the intelligent use of natural and human resources has provided a sufficient incentive to high-minded conduct.

The number of those who have adopted this platform as a working hypothesis for themselves, and are solicitous that it be tried on the largest possible scale, is growing. Say against these men and women what we please, we cannot truthfully say that they are the riffraff of human nature. In my judgment theirs is the only dependable type of idealism left to man in the world today.

Perhaps the most plausible argument to be made against the foregoing considerations is that after all a study of the world in which we live discloses the slow working out of a great ethical purpose. And what can such a purpose be but the will of God? The evidence, however, does not, I think, support this interpretation.

In the first place, selection of the goal of natural events is premature. Suppose we were able to prove that a definite tendency is observable in the evolution of life on our globe, and suppose we could argue from tendency to intendency, neither of which we are in a position to do, we would still be unable to clinch the argument.

35

We have not seen the drama to the end. Once it looked as if it were designed for fishes; then for reptiles; then for lower mammals. Now it may look as if designed for man. But the play is not over. The curtain has not dropped. How can we talk about the climax of a performance of which we have witnessed only the opening scenes ?

What have we actually observed ? Has everything moved in a steadily maintained direction toward man as the culminating goal ? Evolution has been an incredible spend-thrift of life. Highly organized creatures have been developed again and again only to be pushed up blind alleys and left there to die. If there is a God whose method has been Evolution, his slogan must have been "We'll fight it out along this line if it takes a billennium!" But unlike Grant, he has always surrendered.

In this maelstrom the human species, as Thomas Huxley said--and he knew something about the subject--"splashed and floundered amid the general stream of evolution, keeping its head above water as best it might, and thinking neither of whence or whither." If the great scene we look upon, with its waxing and waning of suns, its appearance and disappearance of plant worlds, its rise and fall of animal dynasties--if all this or any part of it is the working out of a divine purpose, "friendly to man's intellectual, moral and religious education," this purpose is well hidden.

What if we disregard Evolution and examine human history ? Do we then observe the unfolding of a divine plan ? Do we find demonstrable proof of a Power not ourselves that sides with the ethical best ? Does it thwart the wrong-doer and circumvent the morally indifferent ? Do we, or do we not, see "the wicked in great power and spreading himself like a green bay tree"? What happened to Socrates ? To Jesus ? According to the best authorities, they gave their lives to God and in the hour of their need he deserted them. They are conspicuous examples, but the fact which they illustrate is a commonplace of experience.

So far as the course of human life testifies, there is no indication that anything or anyone superhuman is bent upon the triumph of humane or ethical principles. It seems to be up to us

36

and us alone . . . .

Men and women have no one to turn to but themselves and each other; but they do have themselves and each other, and if they turn to themselves and each other in good faith and with intelligence they will be surprised by the idealistic fecundity of the human mind and heart, and by the ideal possibilities of the natural environment upon which they may draw to enrich and elevate their lives . . . .

We have practical tasks to care for. We have economic, political, moral, and educational problems to solve. Our sense of human solidarity is weak. We are too quick to rise against each other. We have still to find civilized means to settle international conflicts.

These are basic obligations. The man who intentionally slights them and leaves to other people all responsibility for improving the social order he enjoys the benefits of is not playing a man's part. Yet life at its best includes not only the performance of duties but emancipation from duties. We need to keep a window open toward the uncharted. We need to follow trails leading beyond work-a-day walls to heights from which we catch glimpses of wide vistas.

6. HUMAN DESTINY

Humanists are not concerned with the question of life after death. They believe that human life is the highest development of life in nature and that its fulfillment is to be accomplished in the natural world. <u>Julian</u> <u>Huxley</u> believes that biological science has now progressed to the point where it can reveal the true destiny of human life. It is to be the agent for further evolution on this planet. Further progress can be attained only if individuals develop their full human personalities in harmonious relationship with each other. While science gives us the vision of human destiny religion adjusts us to it and aids in its fulfillment.

<u>Evolutionary</u> <u>Humanism</u>

Julian Huxley

Man is always concerned about his destiny--that is to say, his position and role in the universe, and how he is to maintain that position and fulfil that role. All societies of men develop some sort of organs for coping with this problem--organs for orientating their ideas and emotions and for constructing attitudes of mind and patterns of belief and behaviour in relation to their conception of their destiny. All these social organs concerned with destiny can, I think, properly be included under the head of religions. Then if some of them are exceedingly primitive and consist of little but magic rituals, while others are highly developed and claim to be entirely rational, they are all, from Haitian voodoo to Roman Catholicism, from neolithic fertility religions to

From RELIGION WITHOUT REVELATION, by Julian Huxley, published by Harper & Row, 1957. Reprinted by permission of A. D. Peters & Co., Ltd.

Marxist Communism, concerned with this same general function. In the same sort of way, the tube-feet of a starfish, the legs of a horse, the pseudopods of an amoeba, and the wings of a bird, though profoundly different organs from each other, are all animal organs concerned with the same general function of locomotion . . . .

With evolutionary naturalism as our basic hypothesis, we can begin exploring the new religious situations of our twentieth century, without spending more time in the unprofitable task of discussing the theoretical or practical inadequacies of earlier religious systems.

Twentieth-century man, it is clear, needs a new organ for dealing with destiny, a new system of religious beliefs and attitudes adapted to the new situation in which his societies now have to exist. The radically new feature of the present situation may perhaps be stated thus: Earlier religions and belief-systems were largely adaptations to cope with man's ignorance and fears, with the result that they come to concern themselves primarily with stability of attitude. But the need today is for a belief-system adapted to cope with his knowledge and his creative possibilities; and this implies the capacity to meet, inspire and guide change.

In other words, the primary function of earlier systems was necessity of maintaining social and spiritual morale in face of the unknown; and this they accomplished with a considerable measure of success. But the primary function of any system to-day must be to utilise all available knowledge in giving guidance and encouragement for the continuing adventure of human development.

I am here treating religious systems as social organs whose function it is to adjust man to his destiny. No previous systems could perform this function will full adequacy, for the simple reason that no previous age had sufficient knowledge to construct an adequate picture of the drama of destiny or of its protagonist, man. The present epoch is the first in which such a picture could begin to take shape.

This is due to the fact that scientific investigation has now for the first time begun to cover the entire range of phenomena involved in human destiny. Beginning with the physical phenomena and proceeding to the biological, it has now invaded the social, psychological and historical fields, and is at last being forced to deal with the phenomena of values. Immense tracts of ignorance are still to be explored, and await annexation to the growing empire of knowledge; but we can already affirm that the cosmos is unitary, that it is a process of transformation in time, and that values and other products of mental and spiritual activity play an important operative role in that sector of the process with which we are involved.

More specifically, the present is the first period in the long history of the earth in which the evolutionary progress, through the instrumentality of man, has taken the first step towards self-consciousness. In becoming aware of his own destiny, man has become aware of that of the entire evolutionary process of this planet: the two are interlocked. This is at once an inspiring and a sobering conception, to which I shall return.

The present age also differs from all earlier ages in the increased importance of science, and its universal extension. There should no longer be any talk of conflict between science and religion. Between scientific knowledge and certain religious systems, yes; but between science as increasing knowledge of nature and religion as a social organ concerned with destiny, no. On the contrary, religion must now ally itself wholeheartedly with science. Science in the broad sense is indispensable as the chief instrument for increasing our store of organised knowledge and understanding. Through evolutionary biology, it has already indicated the nature of human destiny. Scientific study is needed to give religion fuller understanding of destiny, and to help in devising better methods for its detailed realisation.

Meanwhile, science must not allow any ancient prejudices against certain aspects of previously established religions to hold it back from giving its aid when called upon.

Industry and agriculture, after a good deal of resistance on the parts of so-called practical men, have already discovered the indispensability of science, both pure and applied. It now remains for religion, together with other social activities, to make the same discovery. For without the fullest aid from science, we will assuredly not be able to bring into being a religion adequate to our needs, any more than we could have brought into being an aeroplane capable of flying or antibiotics capable of killing disease-germs.

Once it is realised that religions are the product of man's creative mind, working on the data provided by personal or collective experience, the need for enlisting science in the religious task becomes apparent. In any event, the march of knowledge and events has made it imperative to reach a new formulation of human destiny and a new attitude towards it. This is a task for the human species as a whole, to which all can bring their contribution. The co-operation of the religiously-minded and the scientifically-trained is essential for its adequate performance.

The contribution which science can make is two-fold. It can contribute an enormous body of hard-won, tested, organised knowledge; also a spirit of disinterested devotion to truth, and a willingness to apply this spirit to any problem, irrespective of prejudices or possible consequences.

An immense co-operative effort of creative discussion is needed. In what follows I submit the thesis which I am calling evolutionary humanism to that discussion, fully conscious that, though based on the accumulated results of unnumbered others, it is only the personal contribution of one biologist.

In the first place, evolutionary biology has given us a new view, impossible of attainment in any earlier age, of our human destiny. That destiny is to be the agent of the evolutionary progress of this planet, the instrument for realising new possibilities for its future.

The picture of the universe provided by modern science is of a single process of self-transformation, during which new possibilities can be realised. There has been a creation of new actualities during cosmic time. It has been progressive, and it has been a self-creation.

The entire cosmos, in all its appalling vastness, consists of the same world-stuff. Following William James, I use this awkward term deliberately in place of matter, because "matter" is commonly opposed to "mind," whereas it is now apparent that the world-stuff is not restricted to material properties. When organised in certain ways--as, for instance, in the form of human bodies and brains--it is capable of mental as well as material activities. Furthermore, the study of animals shows that there is no sharp line to be drawn between human and animal behaviour, except in the essential human capacity for the cumulative transmission of experience, knowledge, and ideas; and it is now clear that minds, in the sense of all activities with an obvious mental component, have evolved just as much as have material bodies: mental activities of every kind, from awareness and knowledge to emotion, memory and will, have become increasingly intense and efficient, and mental organization has reached ever higher levels. Through sense-organs and brains, the mind-like potentialities of the world-stuff have been progressively intensified and actualised, in the same sort of way as its electrical properties have been intensified in the electric organs of the torpedo-fish or through the agency of human constructions like dynamos.

Since natural selection is the sole or main method of biological evolution, and since it can only operate to produce results of biological utility, it is clear that the mental properties of the organisms are not mere useless by-products, but must be of value to their possessors. Furthermore, they can and do play an operative role in the evolutionary process: thus the awareness of color and pattern found in some higher animals has led to the further evolution of color-patterns of various sorts, and has assisted in the birth of that evolutionary novelty we call beauty.

If the self-creation of novelty is the basic wonder of the universe, this eliciting of mind from the potentialities of the world-stuff, and its intensification and increasing importance during evolution, is the basic wonder of life.

During evolution, the onward-flowing stream of life breaks up into a vast number of branches or trends, each resulting in improvements of one sort or another.

The great majority of these become so specialised that life in them finds itself in a blind alley, incapable of further improvement or of transformation for another way of existence. After this, they either remain essentially unchanged for tens or even hundreds of millions of years, or else wholly die out, becoming extinguished in the sands of time. We need only recall the extinction of the dinosaurs and other strange reptiles of the Mesozoic, or the lack of essential change shown by such successful groups as the birds for over twenty million years, or the ants for over fifty.

But through this radiating fan of restricted improvements and blind-alley specialisations there runs a trend towards major advance; and this current biological advance has continued through the two thousand million years of life's existence. It is marked by increase of over-all biological efficiency and by improvement in general plan of working. During its course, there has been an enormous rise in level of harmonious organisation--think of a bird or a mammal as against a flatworm or a jelly-fish; in flexibility and the capacity for self-regulation; in physiological efficiency, as shown in muscular contraction or rate of nervous conduction, or manifested in sheer strength or speed; in the range of awareness, as seen in the evolution of sense-organs--think of an eagle's eyes or an antelope's ears as against the complete blindness and deafness of a polyp or an amoeba; and in the intensity and complexity of mental processes such as knowing and perceiving, feeling and willing, learning and remembering--think of a dog or a monkey as against a sea-anemone or a snail.

When we look at the actual course of the evolutionary process, we find that general biological advance has been achieved in a series of steps, through the emergence of a series of dominant types. Each new dominant type possesses some improvement in general organisation, which enables it to spread and multiply at the expense of the previously dominant growth from among whose less specialised members it has evolved. This progressive replacement of dominant types and groups is most clearly shown in the later history of vertebrates. The reptiles replaced the moist-skinned amphibians as a dominant type of land animal, and were in turn replaced by the warm-blooded mammals and birds.

It is thus perfectly proper to use terms like higher and lower to describe different types of organism, and progress for certain types of trend. A higher organism is one which has realised more of the inherent possibilities of living substance, and biological progress denoted those trends which do not restrict the further realisation of those possibilities.

The next fact of importance is that during evolutionary time the avenues of possible progress have become progressively restricted, until today only one remains open.

Let me amplify this point. Well before the end of the Cenozoic Era, the limits of physiological efficiency seem to have been reached by life. The largest size possible to efficient land animals was attained by the dinosaurs over sixty million years ago; the temperature-regulating mechanism of higher mammals reached the profitable limit of accuracy perhaps half-way through the Cenozoic; it appears to be physically impossible to solve an acuity of vision or a speed of flight greater than that of a falcon.

The only avenue of major advance left open was through the improvement of brain and mind. This was the line taken by our own ancestors, and it was this advance which enabled man to become the latest dominant type in evolution. His rise to dominance is very recent--an affair of less than a million years--but its later course, in the short period since the waning of the last phase of glaciation, has been spectacularly rapid, and it has been accompanied by marked decline and widespread extinction of the previously dominant mammals, as well as by a radical transformation of the environment by man.

Furthermore, it is clear that man is only at the beginning of his period of evolutionary dominance, and that vast and still undreamt-of possibilities of further advance still lie before him.

Biology, I repeat, has thus revealed man's place in nature. He is the highest form of life produced by the evolutionary process on this planet, the latest dominant type, and the only organism

44

capable of further major advance or progress. Whether he knows it or not, whether he wishes it or not, he is now the main agency for the further evolution of the earth and its inhabitants. In other words, his destiny is to realise new possibilities for the whole terrestrial sector of the cosmic process, to be the instrument of further evolutionary progress of this planet . . . .

Above all, the individual should aim at fullness and wholeness of development. Every human being is confronted with the task of growing up, of building a personality, in moral and spiritual harmony with itself and with its destiny, one whose talents are not buried in a napkin, and whose wholeness transcends it conflicts, is the highest creation of which we have knowledge, and in its attainment the individual possibilities of the evolutionary process are brought to supreme fruition.

But if the individual has duties towards his own potentialities, he owes them also to those of others, singly and collectively. He has the duty to aid other individuals towards fuller development, and to contribute his mite to the maintenance and improvement of the continuing social process, and so to the march of evolution as a whole.

7. HUMANISM AND THE PROBLEMS OF HUMAN SOCIETY

Humanists, in one sense, are quite realistic in dealing with the problems of life. They believe that problems should be realistically assessed and that hopes for solutions should be based upon real possibilities. Their belief, however, in the power of human creative intelligence gives them a highly optimistic, if not utopian, view toward the solutions of the problems of human society.

For the humanist the basic problems of life arise because of the failure to use and develop those uniquely human qualities of creative intelligence and to nurture respect for those human values which enhance growing, fulfilling, harmonious human relationships. The humanists believe that traditional religion, through its emphasis upon human limitations, need for divine aid, and moral dogmas is often a cause for the development of human problems rather than a means for their solution.

Algernon D. Black recognizes that human beings need a faith by which to live. He believes that much of the loss of identity, confusion and conflict in the modern world is due to the attempt to believe in the fixed and final doctrines of the traditional religions. Life and the world are not fixed and final. He raises the question as to whether Humanism, which places its faith and hope in human possibilities is enough. He concludes that it is, in spite of the fact that it cannot guarantee a victory for the best of human values or create a perfect society. This faith gives more inner security, self-esteem, dignity and freedom and a better society than will the traditional faiths.

David E. Willcox believes that a humanistic society, though not presently in existence, is possible. While the pursuit of unending growth through production and consumption has improved the quality of life, the contemporary crises of desperate poverty, population growth, insufficient energy and uncontrolled waste, are evidences that the "dream of industrial man" is not the "path to the future." The path to a humanistic society in the future must lead to population stabilization and financial and technical aid by the

46

rich nations of the world to the poor ones. A quality life can be assured to all if, through creative intelligence and a genuine concern for the poor, we harmonize our machines with finite Earth.

Our Quest for Faith: is Humanism Enough?

Algernon D. Black

The traditional faiths are relatively recent in human history. The earth may be two billion years old. Man may have lived on this earth over a million years. In the long history of man, the polytheistic religious systems of the ancient Egyptians, Babylonians and Assyrians, of the Greeks and the Romans, go back not more than five to ten thousand years at the outside. Similarly, Hinduism, Buddhism, Shintoism and the faith of Islam, the choice of those in the Middle East and Asia, may seem ancient and venerable, but they, too, are relatively modern. In the West, the religion of Judaism is about 3,000 years old and Christianity only about 2,000 years old. In our world of emphasis on modernism and recent discovery and rapid change, these seem ancient; but the fact is that they are comparatively young in time.

Even so, many of their concepts are no longer relevant. Science and technology have changed our lives and our relationships to nature and to each other. Whereas many human communities once lived in relative isolation, now we are all close and interdependent neighbours. Whereas human beings once lived on a narrow margin, with a scarcity of the necessities of life, now we live with a productivity of abundant surplus. Whereas change in knowledge and power, in ideas and institutions was relatively slow, now we see change, rapid change, on every hand.

From THE HUMANIST ALTERNATIVE, edited by Paul Kurtz. Copyright 1973, by Prometheus Books, 1203 Kensington Ave., Buffalo, New York 14215, and used by their permission.

In the midst of the confusion and conflict of the modern world, men have lost their identity, have suffered alienation from their own feelings and from personal relationships and small communities. In many ways the individual feels alone and lonely, lost and helpless. Many have failed to find spiritual security and purpose and faith through traditional religious beliefs and affiliations. Many despair at every finding any answers to their need for faith.

In the past, men inherited their faith and were indoctrinated with the faith of a particular community and time and place. A number of human needs led men to imagine and create the beliefs, doctrines and myths of the religions of primitive peoples and of the more developed civilizations. The need for some explanation of Creation, the origin and purpose of life; the need for believing that they could tap some source of power for survival and reproduction and fertility; and the need for some belief about death--these evoked the religious life of every community.

How should we seek and find a faith to live by today? Shall we look to the faith of our fathers? Shall we be bound by what they believed? Shall we accept the idea that religious freedom means the right to believe only the way our ancestors believed? Is any departure from their faith to be taken as a lack of loyalty or lack of respect of one's elders? If we accept this, then the concept of religious freedom is severely limited.

Recently I met a group of children of junior high school age. They were from homes in the Humanist tradition. I asked the children how many believed in God. There was an almost unanimous silence. "Is there no one here who believes in God?" I asked. Finally, a child put up his hand. Then another raised her hand cautiously, saying, "I'm only a visitor. I am a Catholic."

"What do you mean by God?" I asked. "I know it's a personal question and most people don't ask it. But do you know the meaning or do you have any idea about what you mean by the God you <u>believe</u> in? And for those who don't believe, do you have any idea of what you mean by the God you <u>don't</u> <u>believe</u> in?"

The first child who put up his hand said, "Well, there must

have been somebody who made the world." He was saying the same thing as those who through the thousands of years have asked and made answers. So the priest had said many times: "Do you see this watch? Where there is a watch there must be a watchmaker." Yes, something in the human brain responds to the idea of cause and effect. There must be a cause--and a cause of the cause--and a cause of all the causes, a first cause. So also the priest or the rationalist may argue, "Here is a watch. The watch is more than mere metal and glass, a face and hands. The watch was made for a purpose. And there is a purpose to the purpose, an end beyond the end."

But beyond this dry logic and thin rational approach are other, deeper factors. These include the psychological needs for security, for protection--for a father, law-giver, judge, protector, for one who will be punishing and forgiving.

More and more human beings throughout the world have been moving away from fixed and final definitions concerning an ultimate reality or the absolute dogma of a God who created and rules the universe. More and more people are sceptical of an all-powerful, all-knowing, all-merciful, all-just and all-loving God. Many would say, "If there were such a power, such a God, how could He permit the cruelty, waste and suffering of the world?" And many are no longer satisfied with "You must take it on faith. There are things beyond human understanding. Trust! Believe! God and His ways are infinite. Man is limited and finite. You cannot grasp the larger truth. Have faith!"

Now if there is one thing that human beings want to believe, if there is one idea that most men have of God--no matter how they differ in language and theology and culture--it is this: that God is a power which will make everything come out all right in the end. He is a power that makes for righteousness. He guarantees that good will win over evil, peace over war, justice over injustice, love over hate. Most people would like to believe that the universe is weighted at least 51 per cent in favour of goodness. Most people want to believe that no matter what happens to them or their loved ones and no matter what happens to their dreams, aspirations and values, somehow there is a guarantee of victory.

49

They want to believe that there is a built-in guarantee that no matter what mistakes or evils men may do, there is a power at the heart of things which will assure that life is sustained both in life and in death. And the hunger and the longing for such assurance evokes the belief, makes it easy for man to affirm and teach and build institutions which structure and reinforce a faith.

Now we would all like to have evidence that there is such a tendency and support for what human beings value as moral and ethical. But there is no evidence. When the lightning strikes; when the earthquake swallows men, women and children; when the flood or famine or plague takes its toll, there is no evidence that nature discriminates and favours goodness. The universe appears untouched, impervious to human aspiration, dreams, values, visions.

Do the people who believe that evil will be defeated and the evildoers punished, question why there is so much crime, so much inhumanity among men--the killing, robbing, betrayal, violation of human beings ? There is no evidence that those who believe in the traditional God concepts are more law-abiding or respecting of their fellows or considerate of society than those who have turned from theism. Obviously, more and more human beings all over the world have lost their faith--if they ever really had it beyond lip-service or rather thin and vague concepts.

Thus the quest for faith must go beyond the God belief. Man has to face the fact that he does not know the beginning of the beginnings and that he does not know the purpose, and the purpose beyond all purposes, of the universe. We are all a part of some larger reality or cosmos, some process beyond our grasp. And we live in a natural world in a condition of limited knowledge and power. We sense that there are still vast areas for man's investigation. We will certainly increase our knowledge of the reality of the universe in the time before the human organism made its appearance in the evolutionary process. We may reach out into space in our solar system and even beyond it. We may penetrate further the nature of the atom and the living cell. Most important of all is the exploration of our own psychological and spiritual natures and the inter-relationships of life with life. But

50

we must not permit ourselves to stop growing or to accept the dogmas and horizons of the past as the limits of our thought. And whether we seek new symbols beyond a God or Saviour, beyond a Revelation or Salvation, or whether we remain with the old, we cannot expect to fulfill the human distinctiveness of our species unless we recognize the need for growth and development, the possibilities and potentialities of growth in the individual and in the quality of human relations and in the nature of human society.

Thus, instead of feeling confused and lost and bereft, deprived of faith, we can find that the quest for faith means a new challenge, a new sense of possibilities beyond any of the visions of the past. The Humanist does not fall into the trap of believing that man is the superpower, the highest form of life in existence. Man may be the highest form we know. But the universe does not revolve around man, nor does it necessarily exist for man. All man can do in seeking a faith is to be honest in examining his world of natural environment and his human environment and, above all, in examining himself. Out of human experience man gains a sense of life's possibilities and the choices before him in his personal life, his patterns of relationships and the kinds of community he may strive for. And with the awareness of man's potentialities and the choices before him, man faces challenge, opportunity and responsibility.

And it is at this point that we have to face up to the intelligence potentials, the aesthetic aspects and ethical elements in the human being. As far as we can see a vital drive is built into the lower forms of insect and animal life; it is part of the will to survive. Admittedly, an animal, bird or fish, may reach a point at which it can no longer fight or fend for itself or perform its natural physical functions. It is finished. Maybe there is some beyond-physical sense of impending death. But we do not know this as surely as we know the phenomenon in humans. We doubt that lower forms of life have a problem of faith.

For humans, uncertainty about whether or not to believe in particular doctrines is a part of the problem. But whether to believe in life, whether life is worth living and whether there is any meaning in some larger reality beyond the life of the individual

51

and beyond the entire human enterprise--these are the real dilemmas for human beings. True, many men may never become aware of these problems, They live their lives on certain levels and die when the time comes with seeming comfort from inherited beliefs which they have never questioned or dared to question. But more and more human beings, sensitive to suffering and waste of human potential, more and more human beings sensitive to the intellectual or aesthetic or ethical possibilities are doubting, asking, seeking.

We all feel futility and despair at certain times. "Is life worth living?" asked William James. He answered, "It depends on the liver." And so it does. But it also depends on us living together and how we live together. It depends on how we help each other feel about life. For in and through our relationships we can hurt or help. We can rob a person of the taste for life and the will to live. We can permit or create conditions in which human beings are doomed to death from illness, doomed to distrust and bitterness toward each other, doomed to self-rejection and self-destruction. And on the other hand, we can create relations and conditions which foster the taste for life, the will to live and the hunger for creativeness and love.

Humanism calls men to shed the dogmas and divisions of traditional religion. Humanism calls man to face the fact that we must live without an absolute guarantee of victory for our values. Humanism calls men to awareness of human possibilities and the choices and the responsibilities before the human individual and the human community.

Nature, with all its wonder and beauty and miraculous creative powers, is also cruel. The meadow, so beautiful with grass and flowers, with busy birds and insects, may inspire the artist and the poet with romance and dreams. But when we look more carefully, we see life feeding on life. Among the rocks and behind the flowers and under the earth, life forms are killing other life forms. What may be "natural" in the behaviour of some of the forms of insect and bird life, among the organisms in the sea and jungle, is found also among humans. But in the evolution of human life, there is a consciousness and emerging conscience.

52

The key question is whether human beings can rise to a level of awareness of the values and the choices which are within human control.

The forces of nature which are beyond man's control, the earthquakes and floods and tidal waves can be studied and offset within limits by human ingenuity. What we cannot control or do anything about should not be a source of worry or anxiety. But what is within human control, human beings had better face and deal with. Earthquakes triggered by extreme explosive forces due to nuclear explosions set off by man cannot be blamed on nature. The same applies to human carelessness in causing pollution of the earth, air or water by chemicals and radiation. Humanism does not mean that man is omnipotent. But it does mean that man must be responsible for his uses of the knowledge and the power he has won through thousands of years of intelligent study of his environment.

The important question is: "What does man make of himself?" With the resources of earth and the knowledge and power human beings now have it is not enough to survive, to exist, to be a vegetable or an animal with the capacity to breathe, eat, defecate and reproduce its kind. There is a new level of responsibility for achieving a quality of life, a quality of being and a level of consciousness and creativeness beyond anything man has thus far achieved in intellectual and aesthetic and ethical potentialities.

Many men will say they cannot live without a guarantee of victory for the best in human values, that they cannot live without a faith in another life, that they cannot live without the perfectability of man in society—that Humanism is not enough. So, too, they will say they cannot live without fixed and final doctrines. We deny this. The central problem is an ethical problem. Humanism may include the intellectual, rational, logical and scientific dimensions of man; it may include the aesthetic, sensitivity to beauty, nature and civilization; but it must also include the deep and rich emotional and spiritual elements which are part of man's relationships—the affection, compassion, the identification and the love which is a potential in human beings in all the relations of life. This is a many-dimensional Humanism. It is with this

53

perspective that we call human beings to seek out and fulfill their highest potentialities.

Men cannot live without hope. Men cannot live without faith. Hope has to do with a sense that something better is possible. Hope may include a desire and a wish in the midst of uncertainty. But faith has more strength than hope. It is a call to commitment, a readiness to strive, sacrifice, stake a life on an outcome and a fulfilment. To have faith is to have a sense of values worth living for; to try to be faithful to an ideal or a vision of possibilities.

And the quest for faith depends on the attitude that men do not give up, do not yield to the darkness, do not yield to the seemingly overwhelming tough realities. It requires that men assume that they may have the capacity to think through their difficulties and overcome their obstacles. It is a quest for clarification of purpose and meaning which will give focus to life. It is a process by which men grow through seeking and striving.

Humanism has hope and faith for man. But it makes no false promises. No one can live a perfect life. No one can fulfill his powers and gifts completely. There is not a single individual who will grow to the full use of all his intelligence. And every day millions die who have not learned to fulfill all their powers to appreciate and enjoy or create beauty. And many will never have had the experience of being loved or loving. We use only a fraction of our potentials. This is the human tragedy. And it is revealed most in our failure to achieve greater fulfilment in and through our relationships. None of us is good enough. We all fall short at some point in friendship, in understanding and loving and in being just to others.

Humanism does not hold that man is perfect or perfectable. No one who has ever lived has lived a perfect life nor will it occur in the future. All our fulfilments are partial--greater in some and less in others.

And no society is perfect or perfectable either. Will man ever achieve a truly free and just society? Will the dream of democracy ever be fulfilled perfectly? When we say to children

54

that no man is perfectable and no society will ever be perfect, we may say, "An individual may come near it. A society may come near it. There may be moments in the lives of individuals and periods in communities when they come very near fulfilment of their promise. But there are no saints and there are no Utopias." And when we say this, the child asks, "Then what's the use of trying to be a better person? What's the use of trying to work for a better world?"

How shall we answer? It may be that we have to say that the important thing is not the finished product, the perfect individual or the perfect society. The value lies in what we try to be and try to do and what happens to us in the striving. Perhaps it is in that process that we grow and mature. Perhaps it is man's fate to strive even though he knows that he will never fulfill his dream of self and his dream of society. We are not children asking for an easy and cheap gift. We are not content to live with illustrations that fulfilment is guaranteed or that our effort will bring us some sweet reward from outside of man. No. Man stands on his own feet without fear of punishment or promise of reward. Man makes his own Hell and his own Heaven, and he makes it here and now.

Is the vision of partial fulfilment enough? Is it enough to say that the important result of striving for the fulfilment of man's many dimensions is the effect on himself, the by-product is greater inner security, greater self-esteem, greater dignity and freedom and the knowledge that man shapes his own destiny?

When we say this we are aware of our failures, our fears and hates, our wars and racism, and our unreadiness to share the gifts of nature and the human gifts, the riches of man's creative achievements. Some will say that Humanism is not enough, that it cannot satisfy, that it cannot generate in man the powers he needs to deal with and overcome the difficulties of his condition and his life. Others may say, "Humanism is too much. It asks and demands too much from man." But in our quest, let us say of ourselves and of others:

> Much in each of us is unexpected and mysterious
> Each of us is more than his thoughts

In our love we seek our own perfection.
So when you criticize the world of men
Be gentle.
Love, to abide, must not demand too much,
We are trying to learn to live.

Priorities for a Humanistic Society

David E. Willcox

From the dawn of civilization there have always been a few individuals who believe the problems of the day are surmountable and dream of a perfect society in which equality ceases to be a mere slogan and all of mankind has an equal share of the Earth's bounty. Such individuals presume it is possible for there to be a time when the human animal is fulfilled and happy, future generations are assured a quality life and war is a dark memory. Believers in Utopia are perhaps hopeless dreamers, but progress in the human condition has never been achieved by those who complacently accept the status quo. The future is built by men and women who have the audacity and the courage to dream of a better world.

Since the beginning of the industrial revolution, exclusive reliance on the single value of maximization of production and consumption has appeared to be the only path toward Utopia. It is indisputable that the pursuit of quantity has accomplished immeasurable improvement in the quality of life. Prior to 1650 abject poverty was the destiny of all but the few who were wealthy, powerful or otherwise socially prominent. Infant mortality was high, life expectancy short and a continual battle against starvation the

From PHILOSOPHIC RESEARCH AND ANALYSIS (Vol. VI, No. 11, Early Winter, 1978), pp. 15-16. Reprinted by permission of the publisher and the author.

anticipated way of life. The quality of life has changed drastically for the inhabitants of those nations able to successfully develop an industrial base. The uncertainty of dependence on the land has been replaced by participation in a steady cycle of production and consumption which has built on itself and seemed to offer no bound to human prosperity.

In the twentieth century the pursuit of unending growth is the policy assumption of all nations. Whether a nation adheres to a capitalist, socialist or other doctrine each agrees that maximizing production and consumption is the only path to a better future. Nations already successful in the pursuit of material prosperity struggle to continue a steady upward curve of growth as portrayed by the hallowed calculations of gross national product. Emerging nations emulate those which have reached a higher level of prosperity. Even the very poor nations, despite their inability to succeed in the present competitive environment, envision rapid industrial growth as their only hope.

Suddenly the dream of industrial man is crumbling before our eyes. The crises of today's world are proof that endless growth in quantity is an impossible path to the future. The poor, unable to keep pace with the unrelenting competition of the international marketplace, are trapped in a debilitating cycle of desperate poverty and explosive population growth. The energy crisis is ample warning that man is consuming the natural resources of the Earth at an unsustainable rate. Wastes, a by-product of quantitative growth, are flowing uncontrolled into the atmosphere are water systems of the Earth and are approaching levels which may upset the ecological equilibrium supporting life as we know it. Modern man simply no longer has the option to follow the present pattern of unceasing quantitative growth . . . .

The first priority in building a better future is population stabilization. There are now four billion inhabitants of spaceship Earth. With present growth rates, .8 of one percent each year in the developed nations and two and one-half percent each year in the developing nations, there will be seven billion people on the Earth early in the century twenty-one and conceivably several times this number in only one hunded years. This astronomical progression in population growth is totally illogical and can only end in disaster. No agricultural innovations or restructuring of the industrial system can long support such explosive population growth. Unless growth of population is stabilized as soon as possible, the children of the future will pay the penalty. Quality of life will diminish drastically and continue downward till starvation and disease limit world population size.

Historical evidence shows that as a nation achieves a reasonable level of economic well-being for a majority of its people, population expansion tends to slow and will eventually reach equilibrium. This is substantiated by the 1.1 billion inhabitants of the developed nations who will almost certainly have attained zero growth as a group by 1985. China, Brazil, Mexico, the oil-rich nations and other rapidly emerging nations, with a population of one and one-half billion, appear to be reaching economic plateaus which should slow population growth toward a stable level by the year 2,000. The real problem sector is the 1.4 billion people of the remainder of the underdeveloped nations from India to Haiti with almost no visible hope of economic and social improvement. These nations are locked into the agonizing cycle of poverty precipitating population growth and population growth deepening poverty.

World population can be stabilized early in century twenty-one if cooperation becomes the accepted system of international relations in place of competition. By reaching and maintaining zero population growth the developed nations can be a model for stable world population. Nations currently in process of achieving economic independence must designate population control as a development goal on a par with any other. Most importantly, the developed nations and those of the emerging nations able to participate must help the desperately poor nations of the Earth to reach the moderate level of economic prosperity necessary to regulate explosive population expansion.

If world population is stabilized early in the twenty-first century, it is possible to form and maintain a worldwide agricultural and industrial system to provide for all of mankind the degree of material prosperity enjoyed by the inhabitants of the

58

wealthy nations of today. Twentiety century knowledge in science and technology has reached such an advanced stage that almost any carefully planned goal is attainable. Rather than the established pattern of linear exploitation where modern man recklessly takes from the Earth, uses to his purposes and haphazardly returns what he no longer wants to the environment; we can imitate the natural system which has created a sustainable equilibrium and bridged the boundary between waste and initial use by bringing wastes back into the system as the raw material of further processes.

Of course, the foreseeable future will not be perfect. Several centuries will elapse before the gap between the rich and the poor is completely overcome. Yet this appears to be of much less significance than the surmountable goal of progressively closing the gap. Also in century twenty-one there will be less margin for human frailty. The Earth will be even more crowded, the agricultural and industrial systems will be approaching their capacity and human knowledge will offer new paths to destruction as well as to lasting harmony. In spite of the gravity of the risks century twenty-one can be mankind's finest era. A truly humanistic society is attainable. It is possible to build a social system open in opportunity to everyone and sustainable for the generations of the future . . . .

The plight of the very poor nations of the Earth is definitely not irreversible. An adequate food supply is the immediate need and the beginnings of industrialization are a necessity for long term economic and social advancement. A high percentage of arable land in the poor nations is currently under cultivation, but yields per acre are extremely meager. Proper utilization of irrigation water, high yield crop strains and agricultural chemicals can raise yields per acre by more than enough to insure an adequate food supply, even for the almost certain doubling of population in the underdeveloped nations by the year 2,000. Concomitant with agricultural development, an industrial base must slowly be erected with careful planning toward internal self-sufficiency and maximum benefit from natural resources and other unique factors of each of the underdeveloped nations.

The strong nations have a moral responsibility to help those who cannot compete in the established system. Trade agreements between powerful nations and weaker ones must be formulated and upheld fairly. Too often manufactured products are sold by the wealthy to the poor nations in a strictly price-controlled pattern, reminiscent of the brutal efficiency of the phalanxes of ancient Rome; while in return the poor trade what they can grow or take from their land at whatever price they are allowed to receive. Financial and technical aid commitments from rich to poor will also have to rise significantly. In my opinion one percent of gross national product is required from each of the developed nations and from the more secure of the emerging nations for the next ten to fifteen years. If rigorously directed to basic development projects under the auspices of the United Nations, this is sufficient capital to allow the poor nations to proceed toward a takeoff point in economic expansion.

Responsibility is a symmetrical relation. It is imperative that the governments of the poor nations implement realistic development programs. A strifling reality in the underdeveloped world is that most of these nations have governmental structures dominated by a landed aristocracy who exploit large rural populations. No progress can occur in basic development until the rural poor are allowed to own their land and integrally participate in the reshaping of their future and the future of their nations. Education in basic agricultural technology must be available. Also irrigation water, agricultural chemicals and high yield crop strains must be accessible to the poor farmer on terms which will not force him from his land or into virtual slavery if results are slow to materialize.

If a new system of social betterment based in genuine concern for man's moral responsibility to his fellowman is effected, the chasm between the haves and have-nots will begin to narrow. The desperately poor of the Earth will then be able to attain the moderate level of economic prosperity necessary to overcome explosive population growth by early in the twenty-first century. As the struggle for day to day survival becomes less pressing, the inhabitants of the poor nations can more freely direct their creative abilities toward building a better future for themselves and their children . . . .

As poverty is overcome, a better future is within the grasp of the human animal. Early in the twenty-first century world population can be stabilized at approximately seven billion. An adequate food supply for sevel billion people is assurable for century twenty-one and beyond. With stress on labor intensive methods and the implementation of only the rudiments of modern agricultural technology the poor nations can be agriculturally self-sufficient by the turn of the century. Into the twenty-first century machinery and optimized use of chemicals promise further agricultural improvements in the underdeveloped nations. Most important for the long term stability of world agriculture, the biological revolution has arrived. Improved high yield crop strains and more efficient animal varieties are continually emerging from research laboratories as man's knowledge of molecular structure expands. These discoveries are already a significant factor in increased agricultural productivity and will be the primary factor in the future of world agriculture.

The energy needs of a population of seven billion will be substantial. By using available or easily designable technology, an abundant and essentially non-polluting solar-based worldwide energy system is feasible by century twenty-one. Sunlight can supply most in-place power needs and may even become an energy source for the synthesis of fuels for the transportation sector. Reliance on solar power will allow depletable fossil fuel energy resources--oil, gas, coal, oil shale, tar sands--to be carefully shephered. This will also allow nuclear power development to be significantly slowed and further expansion rigorously tied to proven environmental safety. For energy production the possibility of fusion by laser may be as vital as the harnessing of solar energy. If laser fusion can be commercialised and proven environmentally safe, ordinary sea water may become an energy source for the twenty-first century and beyond.

The Earth's natural resources are sufficient to sustain a worldwide industrial system. The majority of important natural resources--copper, tin, bauxite and others--can be recycled with presently available or designable technology. Where recycling is found to be virtually impossible, substitutes may be utilized. The proposed substitution of solar energy for non-recoverable fossil

61

fuel energy resources is an ideal example. In other instances, it will be necessary to fabricate a synthetic material but extensive molecular knowledge makes this a manageable goal. Modern man has a nearly open-ended theoretical capability to create synthetic materials and to assure their utilization will not be detrimental to the environment.

The wastes of a worldwide industrial system can be controlled. Available or readily buildable pollution control technology can be incorporated into factory and plant production processes to prevent all but a minute percentage of harmful wastes from escaping into the Earth's atmosphere and water systems. The transportation network can be restructured to reduce serious environmental impact. Most significantly a system of near complete recyclability is techinically possible. What cannot be recycled can be designed to be safely returnable to the environment. Pollution, a certain limit to endless quantitative growth, is not eliminable; but can be minimized to protect our finite home's natural ecological balance and lasting beauty . . . .

The course of the future greatly depends upon our present actions. If we accept and respond to present social responsibilities, the children of tomorrow will inherit a much more liveable world. With genuine concern for the very poor of the Earth, runaway population expansion can be controlled by century twenty-one. A quality life can then be assured to all if the machines of man are harmonized with the finite ecosystem. And a lasting peace is possible as the reasons for war are eliminated. Our creativity, our very human ability to reshape the world of our experience, gives us the capability to build a genuinely better future.

PART TWO

PANTHEISM

Sarvepalli Radhakrishnan
L. W. Rogers
W. T. Stace
Albert Einstein
Rabindranath Tagore
Swami Nikhilinanda
Albert Schweitzer

1. INTRODUCTION

There is some reason to believe that the term "pantheism" was first used by John Toland in the eighteenth century. The term originates from the two Greek words, "pan" meaning "all," and "theos" meaning "God." Toland identified Pantheism as being the belief of "a new Socratic society." The essential beliefs of this society were that the "force and energy of the whole . . . the creator and ruler of all, and always tending to the best end, is God, (who may be called) the mind . . . and soul of the universe . . . this force . . . being not separated from the Universe itself, except by a distinction of reason alone."[1]

Throughout the eighteenth, nineteenth and twentieth centuries there has been a controversy over the definition of Pantheism. There are those who, apparently after the example of Toland, define Pantheism as the complete identification of God and Nature, so that God is not to be conceived as separate from the sum of all the parts of the universe. Charles Hartshorne[2] refers to this view as "traditional pantheism."

On the other hand there are those who define Pantheism as the belief that all of nature is in God, and to that extent they are identical, but God is also distinct from nature. Such is the view of W. T. Stace[3] who defines Pantheism as the paradoxical middle ground between Monism, the complete identity of God and Nature, and Dualism, the complete difference between God and Nature. Hartshorne believes that this view should be termed "Panentheism"

---

[1] See Thomas McFarland, Coleridge and the Pantheist Tradition (Oxford: The Clarendon Press, 1969), pp. 266-267.

[2] The Divine Relativity (New Haven: Yale University Press, 1948), p. 90.

[3] See W. T. Stace, Mysticism and Philosophy (New York: J. B. Lippincott Company, 1960), pp. 207-250.

(all is _in_ God) rather than "Pantheism."

In spite of the reasonableness of the distinction which Hartshorne draws between the two terms, I believe it will be less confusing to use the term _Pantheism_ as the description of the religious perspective which is to be presented. There are two reasons for this: Pantheism seems to be the term most widely used, historically, to define the view to which Hartshorne subscribes;[4] and, the belief that God is nothing more than the totality, or sum, of all the parts of the world is so incomprehensible that it is difficult to believe that such a belief could be taken seriously or widely held.[5]

Three of the authors of the readings chosen for this perspective were in the Hindu tradition (Radhakrishnan, Tagore, Nikhilinanda), one a Theosophist (Rogers), two did not claim any formal or cultural religious relationships (Stace, Einstein), and one (Schweitzer) was a Christian. The general similarity of thought which is in these writings, however, is evident and altogether they present a comprehensive religious view which can properly be called Pantheistic. The basic assumptions of this Pantheistic perspective are as follows:

(1) There is no reality outside of God. All beings and things exist within the reality which is God and are therefore parts of the reality of God. Yet, God in essence is a center of conscious life which is more than the sum of all the parts.

(2) Since human conscious life exists within the consciousness of God, direct experience of God is possible. This experience, however, is not "automatic." It may be aided by logical reasoning, moral effort or aesthetic experience. In any event it is usually climaxed by the experience of mystical union with God.

---

[4] McFarland, _Ibid._, pp. 268-271.

[5] Stace and McFarland argue this point. Criticisms of such a belief are as old as Plato (See his _Parmenides_).

(3)   The mystical experience of the unity of all reality is
       essential to science in that science assumes a Uni-
       verse.

(4)   The experience of union with God does not erase all
       self-awareness but becomes the basis for unselfish
       moral life.

(5)   Since human life exists within the life of God it is not
       subject to extinction, only transformation.

The introductory article by <u>Sarvepalli Radhakrishnan</u> is
helpful because it expresses, in a general way, most of the assumptions of Pantheism which we have listed above. It also explains how he believes certain Christian teachings can be interpreted in terms of his religious ideas. This tendency to view
Pantheistic ideas as the underlying unity of all religion is characteristic of much Pantheistic thought.

<u>God and the Self</u>

Sarvepalli Radhakrishnan

While the fulness of spiritual being transcends our categories, we are certain that its nature is akin to the highest kind of
being we are aware of in ourselves. If the real were utterly transcendent to the self of man, it would be impossible for us to apprehend even dimly its presence. We would not be able to say
even that it is "wholly other." There is in the self of man, at the
very centre of his being, something deeper than the intellect,
which is akin to the Supreme. God's revelation and man's contemplation seem to be two sides of one fact. The spiritual

---

From AN IDEALIST VIEW OF LIFE, by Sarvepalli Radhakrishnan (pp. 103-110). Published by George Allen & Unwin Ltd.,
London, copyright 1937, and used by their permission.

glimpses are prophetic indications of an undeveloped power of apprehension in the human mind as well as of an underlying reality with which it is unable to establish permanent contact without an adequate development of that power. There is a real ground in man's deepest being for the experience of reality. Man as a microcosm has relations with every form of existence. While the spiritual apprehension appears in the course of our ordinary life, it is not due to it. It has its source elsewhere though it exhibits its force on the plane of the ordinary consciousness. It is due to that part of the soul which is timeless being. The consubstantiality of the spirit in man and God is the conviction fundamental to all spiritual wisdom. It is not a matter of inference only. In the spiritual experience itself, the barriers between the self and the ultimate reality drop away. In the moment of its highest insight, the self becomes aware not only of its own existence but of the existence of an omnipresent spirit of which it is, as it were, a focussing. We belong to the real and the real is mirrored in us. The great text of the Upanisad affirms it--Tat Tvam asi (That art Thou). It is a simple statement of an experienced fact. The Biblical text, "So God created man in his own image; in the image of God created he him," asserts that in the soul of man is contained the true revelation of God. "The spirit of man is the candle of the Lord." According to Plato man is potentially a participator in the eternal mode of being which he can make his own by living in detachment from the fleeting shadows of the earth. In the Theaetetus Socrates declares that we should strive to become "like unto the divine." "I and my Father are one," "All that the Father hath are mine," is the way in which Jesus expressed the same profound truth. It is not a peculiar relation between any one chosen individual and God but an ultimate one binding every self to God. It was Jesus' ambition to make all men see what he saw and know what he knew. In the Gospel according to St. Matthew, Jesus sums up the various ethical demands in the general requirement: "Be ye therefore perfect as your heavenly Father also is perfect." As Paul says, he was the first-born among many brethren. Recognizing us all as children of God and made in his image, Jesus shows us by his own example that the difference between God and man is only one of degree. St. John spoke of the spirit as "the light that lighteth every man that cometh into the world," the "spirit that guides unto all the truth." The phrase in I Peter of a birth "of the incorruptible seed by the word of God" refers to the divine in man. Plotinus' last words to his physician Eristochius are: "I was waiting for you before that which is divine in me departs to unite with itself the Divine in the Universe." The Quakers believe in the divine spark or the apex in the soul. Descartes asks: "How could I doubt or desire, how could I be conscious, that is to say, that anything is wanting in me, and that I am not altogether perfect, if I had not within me the idea of a being more perfect than myself, by comparison with whom I recognize the defects of my own nature." According to Eckhart: "There is something in the soul which is above the soul, divine, simple, an absolute nothing . . . . This light is satisfied only with the supraessential essence. It is bent on entering into the simple ground and still waste wherein is no distinction, neither Father nor Son nor Holy Ghost, into the unity where no man dwelleth." Augustine says: "And being admonished to return into myself, I entered even into my inmost self. Thou being my guide, I entered and beheld with the eye of my soul, above the same eye of my soul, above my mind, the light unchangeable." St. Catherine of Genoa says: "God is my being, my life, my strength, my Beatitude, my Goal, my Delight." "All minds partake of one original mind," says Cudworth. The individuals are the reproductions of an eternal consciousness according to Green. William James, in his Varieties of Religious Experience, writes: "The overcoming of all the usual barriers between the individual and the Absolute is the great mystic achievement. In mystic states we become one with the Absolute and we become aware of our oneness. This is the everlasting and triumphant mystic tradition, hardly altered by differences of clime and creed. In Hinduism, in Neoplatonism, in Sufism, in Christian mysticism, in Whitmanism, we have the same recurring note, so that there is about mystical utterances an eternal unanimity which ought to make a critic stop and think, and which brings it about that the mystic classics have, as has been said, neither birthday nor native land. Perpetually telling of the unity of man and God, their speech antedates language, nor do they grow old." The immanence of God, the revelation of the meaning and mystery of life in the soul of man, is the substance of the mystic testimony.

We generally identify ourselves with our narrow limited

selves and refer to spiritual experience as something given or revealed to us, as though it did not belong to us. We separate the power of spiritual apprehension from the rest of our nature and refer to it as something divine. Such a separation is unfair to humanity. The insight of the best moments reveals the deepest in us. It is wrong to regard human nature as its very self when it is least inspired and not its true self when it is most. If our self finds in these moments of vision its supreme satisfaction, and is intensely alive while they last, then that self is our true self. We cannot limit our being to the physical or the vital, the customary or the conventional. The divine in us is the source and perfection of our nature.

The Divine is both in us and out of us. God is neither completely transcendent nor completely immanent. To bring about this double aspect, contradictory accounts are given. He is divine darkness as well as "unencompassed light." The philosophers with their passion for unity emphasise the immanent aspect, that there is no barrier dividing man from the real. The unity of man and God is the fundamental thesis of the great philosophic tradition which has come down to us from the Upanisads and Plato. Aristotle, Plotinus, Samkara, Spinoza, Bradley and a host of others are witnesses to it.

Those who emphasise the transcendence of the Supreme to the human insist on the specifically religious consciousness, of communion with a higher than ourselves with whom it is impossible for the individual to get assimilated. Devotional religion is born of this haunting sense of otherness. We may know God but there is always a something still more that seems unknown and remains unspoken. A profound impression of the majesty of God always remains with the devotee who is certain that we can never reach the divine level of glory. Some of the seers of the Upanisads, the author of the Bhagavadgita, St. Theresa, John of the Cross, represent this type. For them the experiences themselves are due to the grace of God. God speaks to us, commands us, comforts us, and we speak to him in praise and prayer, reverence and worship. There are many degrees in this personal relationship, from the feeling of utter humiliation in the presence of the numinous, the other than ourselves, to the communion with a supreme Love on whose grace the worst sinner can count.

There cannot be a fundamental contradiction between the philosophical idea of God as an all-embracing spirit and the devotional idea of a personal God who arouses in us the specifically religious emotion. The personal conception develops the aspect of spiritual experience in which it may be regarded as fulfilling the human needs. Man finds his rest and strength in the spiritual experience and so he knows the spirit as that which fulfils his needs. God is represented as possessing the qualities which we lack. In a sense the Freudians are not wrong when they assert that our religion is the projection of the desires of grown-up children. Justice, love and holiness are the highest qualities we know and we imagine God as possessing them, though these qualities exist in God in a different sense from their existence in us.

To compare the Supreme with the highest kind of being we know is nearer the truth than comparing him with anything lower. Though the supreme spirit in its essential aspect is the changeless noumenal reality, its representation in the form of a personal God who is the source, guide and destiny of the world seems to be the highest open to the logical mind. The difference between the Supreme as spirit and the Supreme as person is one of the standpoint and not of essence between God as he is and God as he seems to us. When we consider the abstract and impersonal aspect of the Supreme, we call it the Absolute; when we consider the Supreme as self-aware and self-blissful being, we get God. The real is beyond all conceptions of personality and impersonality. We call it the "absolute" to show our sense of the inadequacy of all terms and definitions. We call it "God" to show that it is the basis of all that exists and the goal of all. Personality is a symbol and if we ignore its symbolic character it is likely to shut us from the truth. Even those who regard personality as the ultimate category of the universe recognise that God is vast and mysterious, mighty and ultimate.

Our myths and metaphors "do him wrong, being so majestical," and the spiritual seers know it; it is their intellectual followers who ignore it.

In the history of thought we have had different interpretations of the spiritual experience, such as Buddha's conception that it is the reality which we are to accept with reverence; Aristotle's view of the Unmoved First Mover whose supreme perfection draws the universe towards himself as the beauty of the beloved draws the lover; Spinoza's God who is that than which nothing is more real, which we are called upon to love without expecting anything in return, a personal God who is a creature of moods and passions, an ethical God who is the highest good at which men aim, and a knightly God who begs of us the favour of helping him in his great designs. The monotheists are quite certain that the gods of the polytheists are symbolic if not mythological presentations of the true God, but they are loth to admit that their own God is at bottom a symbol. All religion is symbolic, and symbolism is excluded from religion only when religion itself perishes. God is a symbol in which religion cognises the Absolute. Philosophers may quarrel about the Absolute and God, and contend that God, the holy one who is worshipped, is different from the Absolute which is the reality demonstrated by reason. But the religious consciousness has felt that the two are one . . . .

Besides the affirmation of a spiritual reality which is variously interpreted and its consubstantiality with the deepest self of man, we have also the conviction of the unity of the universe. We see the one spirit overarching us. The earth and the sky, the world and the animals--all become suddenly strange and wonderful. For our eyes are opened and they all declare the presence of the one Supreme. The universe seems to be alive with spirit, aglow with fire, burning with light. All that there is comes out of life and vibrates in it. The Upanisad says: "When all this is turned into the self, who is to be known by whom?" The supreme spirit is inescapable. It is "above, below, behind, before, to the right and to the left." "The reborn soul is as the eye which, having gazed into the sun, thenceforward sees the sun in everything," says Eckhart. George Fox asks us to "learn to see all things in the universal spirit." God is everywhere, even in the troubled sea of human history, in the tragedy and injustice of the world, in its suffering and sorrow. When we experience the harmony, the discord with which we are familiar seems unreal.

If the universe is essentially spirit, how do we account for its appearance as non-spirit? If the experience gives us the joyful awareness of the universe as a harmony, why do we have the tension, the discord and the cleavage in the universe? The world of science and common sense seems so different from the freedom of the self. Is it an illusion or is it a reality? Those who are pragmatically inclined take the practical life as the reality and treat spiritual experience as a mere dream, so deep seems to be the division between them. Some of the more careful trace the appearance of the multiple universe to the limitations of human intelligence, avidya, nescience. The human mind, being what it is, tries to reconstruct the universe from the intellectual point of view into an organic whole. For the intellect, the unity is only a postulate, an act of faith. For the spirit, the harmony is the experienced reality. It belongs to the nature of things and we have had partial and momentary premonitions of it, and we can work up the harmony if we remember that the world of ordinary experience is a feeble representation of the perfect world, a combination of light and darkness, a reflection of the pure idea in an incomplete material form. The hasty logic which declares because the one is the real, the many are an illusion, is corrected in the view that the one reveals itself in the many.

2. THE EXISTENCE OF GOD

L. W. Rogers uses logical reasoning and scientific evidence in support of his belief that matter is but a form of energy, and that all energy is an expression of life which differs only in degree from all other life, including intelligent human life. God has not created the world, it emanates from Him who is its eternal conscious center. There is, therefore, only one Life of which all else is an expression. Human souls are individualized fragments of God who only dimly perceive Him, but who, nevertheless, are not only a part of God but are "god in the making." The idea of the immanence of God gives not only a basis for human community but for the evolution of life in general.

The Immanence of God

L. W. Rogers

All of the differences of opinion about immortality run back to the various conceptions which people hold of the universe. The materialist's belief that consciousness ceases when the body dies arises from his conception of a universe in which consciousness is produced by the evolution of forms. He begins his universe with the declaration that matter and energy exist; that they have always existed; that they give rise to forms and intelligence; and that, therefore, when the forms disintegrate the intelligence they expressed ceases to be. The materialist usually makes a strong point of the scientific aspect of his philosophy and frequently reminds us that the belief in immortality is merely a hope with no substantial basis--a sort of delusion possible only to those who cannot reason soundly.

The Theosophist begins with the declaration that God exists; that He is eternal; that matter and energy are emanations from Him; that all degrees of intelligence are expressions of His life. In what way is the materialist's hypothesis more scientific or reasonable than the Theosophist's ? Both start with a first cause and postulate an eternal universe. The difference between them is that the Theosophist postulates an <u>intelligent</u> first cause. Is it not just as reasonable to say that mind has always existed as to say that matter has always existed ? Nobody will deny that consciousness is higher than matter. With one or the other, or with both, we must begin. Why begin with the lower ? In asserting that consciousness has always existed, what rule of logic do we violate that the materialist does not violate with the declaration that matter has always existed ? We know that consciousness can and does create forms from matter. Every building is visible evidence of that fact. Is it not, then, more logical to think that eternal consciousness has fashioned the forms that fill the world than to believe that eternal matter has created man ?

Those of us who believe in an intelligent first cause are sometimes reminded of the child who, when told that God had made the earth, asked his mother who made God; and thoughtless people triumphantly remind us that the question is unanswerable. But precisely the same trouble arises if you ask how matter first came to exist. It is just as hard to account for the materialist's original matter as to account for the Theosophist's original consciousness. The finite mind cannot comprehend eternity. It is difficult to see how there was never a beginning, yet it is quite impossible to think of an end; for the mind at once asks, "What after that ?" Tennyson put well that limitation of the finite mind when he wrote, "It is hard to believe in God; it is harder not to believe in Him. " In these basic declarations, then, with which each begins the universe, the Theosophist cannot be said to be either illogical or unscientific because he starts with the higher factor instead of with the lower--with eternal consciousness instead of with eternal matter and force.

Next comes the task, for each, of showing that his hypothesis

75

satisfactorily explains the universe as it now stands. Think for a moment of what the materialist must do! He must show that from a universe of original chaos, the reign of law springs up; that from unguided matter has arisen the human race with its wondrous expressions of genius and its marvelous achievements in science; that with no original intelligence nature has produced an intelligence that is steadily rising to colossal heights; that from no morality has come a morality so sublime that men sacrifice their lives for the common good; that all the exalted emotions of the race have no higher source than the mud beneath our feet; that from senseless dust has come the jester's wit, the inventor's craft, the artist's dream, the sage's mind, the martyr's zeal, the mother's love, and all the subtle lights and shades and heights and depths within the heart and brain of man! It is only necessary to state the case in order to see its absurdity. The materialist often refers to the tendency of one class of his opponents to put aside natural law and reason and rely upon faith and miracle; but if ever there was an appeal to the miraculous it is found in the belief that matter, the slave, created mind, the master!

There is more wrong with the materialist's philosophy than his acceptance of a hypothesis that is so inadequate, and the more science learns about nature the worse does his case become. Matter is the great fetish in his system of things. Deprive him of his hypothesis of eternal matter and the foundation of his philosophy is gone; yet that is precisely what modern science in recent years has done. By a single discovery it has exploded all the old theories and shown that the supposed ultimate atom is a composite thing. In other words, matter as known to the physical senses is just as much an illusion as the apparent movement of the sun through the sky. Matter is in reality one form or phase of energy, and if we put the scientific dictum in ordinary words it comes substantially to this: that matter is the lowest expression of life. Where, then, does the materialist stand? Under the search light of modern science his eternal matter is seen to be eternal life. No wonder so great a scientist as Sir Oliver Lodge wrote in one of his books that it may well be doubted if there is any longer such a thing in the world as scientific materialism. There is unquestionably widespread materialism but it is not up-to-date with science. It is merely repeating as facts theories that are exploded.

Let us amplify the hypothesis that God eternally exists, and that the material world is but an emanation from Him. If it will help those who think in materialistic terms to use language that is not intimately associated with religion, we can say that a first cause eternally exists and that its characteristics are wisdom, power and compassion. That comes to the same thing as saying that God is good, wise and powerful. The Theosophists regard that first cause as an inconceivable mighty spiritual entity, or wisdom, love and power, but he does not, by any means, hold the anthropomorphic conception of the Supreme Being so popular with millions of people. The declaration that the solar system is an emanation from God is to be taken in the most literal sense. Now that we have reached the point in scientific knowledge where matter is seen to be a form of energy, it is not so difficult to understand the old doctrine of the immanence of God. If one thinks of our solar system in its primordial condition it will be still easier to see it as the emanation of a central Being--as mighty streams of energy flowing outward from Him and gradually differentiating into various classes of matter. The theosophical view is that all forces are His forces. Consequently there is no such thing as an unintelligent force. It may, like the force we call gravity, be absolutely impersonal, but it is not unintelligent. It has its purpose in a mighty plan. All energy, all matter, all life in the system, are His life. The consciousness of an insect and that of man are but the varying expressions of the one eternal life that we call God. That is the old doctrine of immanence--that His life thrills through every form and every atom of the universe, that His consciousness embraces it all, that His will sustains it all. There is nothing in the universe that is not some kind of expression of His life. It may be at the human, at the animal, at the vegetable, or only at the mineral level of evolution, but it is none the less an expression of the life of the Supreme Being. The consciousness in man is of a high order and we call it self-consciousness. The consciousness in matter we name chemical affinity; but the two differ only in degree. There again science has rendered great service by showing that the life in a mineral responds to stimuli and can even be poisoned, as certainly as an animal can. The scientific discovery that swept away the theory of the ultimate atom, and showed that it is in fact but a center of force, is the most stupendous revelation of modern life. It is still too new to have registered its full significance in the consciousness of the race. Like all revolutions it will be followed by slow readjustment of thought; but when that readjustment is complete, there will no longer be difficulty in seeing that matter is but a form of life, and that all life is one life.

Why then, it may be asked, is that one life more intelligent at some levels than at others? Because at low levels it is being only very partially expressed through dense encasements of matter, while at higher levels it is being more fully expressed. Or, we may say that at low levels life is in the kindergarten learning response to simple vibrations, while at high levels it is at the university getting lessons that can be learned only from complex variations; but all life is some phase of God's life, for nothing in our solar system exists outside the Supreme Being.

Some devout people seem to think of God as a manufacturer and of heaven as a soul factory! To them God and the human soul are as separate as a teacher and his pupils; but if they will carefully read their Scriptures they will find there the most explicit statements to the contrary. It is not said that by His power and permission we exist. It does not say that near Him we live, but it says very pointedly that in Him we live, we move, we have our being.

How can that be? How can one being exist literally within another? It is simplicity itself when we think of the solar system as an emanation of the Supreme Being, as something generated from a central life, as an expression of that life which gives rise to the two poles within it that we know as consciousness and matter. The human soul is an individualized fragment of that divine life. Of course our limited consciousness can only imperfectly comprehend it. Imagine that central life of our universe that we call God to be like an eternal light, sending its rays out into space. Imagine those rays, as they are generated and travel outward, having the power to set up within themselves an action that results in differentiation, so that they become at least two distinct types of rays, one corresponding to that we know as life, and the other to what we know as matter. Imagine rotatory currents that imprison the rays of light within the currents of matter.

78

Imagine that the farther the rays get from their source the feebler they become until, at a vast distance, instead of being the blinding light near the central source, they are merely a feeble glow in the void. Then that fragment of a ray, enmeshed in intervening matter but still dimly glowing because it is of the very nature of the central light, of which it is an actual portion, will represent the relationship of the soul to God. It is literally a spark of the divine fire, and latent within it are the characteristics of that central light from which it originated. The theosophical conception of the soul is that it is literally an emanation of God, and since it is therefore of His own essence it becomes clear why Theosophists assert that man is God in the making . . . .

The idea of the immanence of God is as different from the popular conception as noontide is different from midnight. It is so radically different that one who accepts that ancient belief must put aside his old ideas of what man is and raise him in dignity and potential power to a level that will, at first, seem actually startling; for it means, in its uttermost significance, that God and man are but two phases of the one eternal life and consciousness that constitute our universe! The idea of the immanence of God is that He is the universe; although He is also more than it is; that the solar system is an emanation of the Supreme Being as clouds are an emanation of the sea. This conception makes a man a part of God, having potentially within him all the attributes and powers of the Supreme Being. It is the idea that nothing exists except God and that humanity is one portion of His--one phase of His being . . . .

The oneness of life was explicitly asserted by Jesus. Emerson's teaching of the immanence of God is unmistakable in both his prose and poetry. "There is no bar or wall, " he says, "in the soul where man, the effect, ceases and God, the Cause, begins. " Still more explicitly he put it:

> The realms of being to no other bow;
> Not only all are Thine, but all art Thou.

The statement is as complete as it is emphatic. "Not only all are Thine, but all art Thou. " It is an unqualified assertion that humanity is a part of God, as leaves are a part of a tree--not something a tree has created in the sense that a man creates a machine but something that is an emanation of the tree, and is a living part of it. Thus only has God made man. Humanity is a growth, a development, an emanation, an evolutionary expression of the Supreme Being.

It is upon the unity of all life that Theosophy bases its declaration of universal brotherhood, regarding it as a fact in nature. The theosophical conception is that men are separated in form but are united in the one consciousness which is the life base of the universe. Their relationship to each other is somewhat like that of the fingers to each other--they are separate individuals on the form side but they are united in the one consciousness that animates the hand. If we imagine each finger to possess a consciousness of its own, which is limited to itself and cannot pass beyond to the hand, we shall have a fair analogy of the unity and identity of interests of all living things. Under such circumstances an injury to one finger would not appear to the others as an injury to them, but if the finger consciousness could be extended to the hand the reality of the injury to all would be apparent. Likewise an injury to any human being is literally an injury to the race. The race does not recognize the truth of it because, and only because, of the limitation of consciousness. Lowell put the fact clearly when he wrote:

> He's true to God who's true to man.
> Wherever wrong is done
> To the humblest and weakest
> 'Neath the all-beholding sun,
> That wrong is also done to us;
> And they are slave most base
> Whose love of right is for themselves,
> And not for all the race.

"He's true to God who's true to man" because they are one life; because they are but different expressions of the one eternal consciousness; because they are as inseparable as the light and the warmth of the sun. It follows that being true to man is fidelity to God.

3. THE NATURE OF RELIGIOUS EXPERIENCE

The Pantheist believes that God is the eternal conscious center of Life and that human souls are but individualized fragments of that life. It is this condition which makes possible a union of God and man. W. T. Stace describes this union as mystical; it transcends all understanding and description and can only be hinted at in myth. Though only the saint can accomplish this union in depth, the hearing or reading of the mythical account of it by the common man can evoke a "far off view of the divine" which can properly be called "religious experience."

The Mystic Consciousness

W. T. Stace

There is then a "way," and an "experience," and a "destination." It is the way of the saints." Nevertheless it is "unknown." Also it is only for those who "have the courage." The destination "cannot be described." The experience likewise cannot be described, but is only "hinted at in myths and images." I shall suggest that these words, a "way" or path, followed by the "saints," which leads to an "experience" and a "destination," which "cannot be known" except through "myths and images," stand for the conception which are the essential truth of all religions.

In every religion there is a way or a path, and there is a destination or experience to which it leads. "I am the way, the

---

Abridged from Chapter 10, "The Problem of Religious Truth" (to be entitled "The Mystic Consciousness") in RELIGION AND THE MODERN MIND by W. T. Stace (J. B. Lippincott Company). Copyright 1952 by W. T. Stace. Reprinted by permission of Harper & Row Publishers, Inc.

truth and the life," says the Jesus of St. John's gospel. The Buddhist speaks of the "noble eightfold path." The destination, the experience--which is hidden--is variously described as "salvation," "heaven," "nirvana," "union with Brahman." The different religions seem to refer to different paths and different destinations. I shall maintain that always and everywhere, in all the great religions, there is in fact only one destination, one experience, even--with some qualification--one path, but that it is "hinted at" by means of different "myths and images" which constitute the differences between the religions . . . .

There are two ways of life, that which most of us follow, and which consists in making "the best of the bad job," and the "way of the saints"--the saints of any religion. What is this second way, and what is its destination? Since the way and the destination are, in Eliot's words, "unknown," since the destination "cannot be described," the present writer, who follows the first way, cannot be expected to know or describe them. No one can describe them, not even those who follow the way and have reached the destination. But I think that nevertheless something can be said. There do exist records, written by those who have followed the second way, which can be quoted. They too will be found not to express the literal and naked truth, not to "describe" the truth, because that truth is "inexpressible" in language. This is the reason why men invent myths and images which merely "hint at" it. The "experience," which is also the "destination," is "ineffable," which is the same as saying that "it cannot be described." But these direct records of the personal experience of saints and mystics are at least in some way nearer to the naked truth than are the official dogmas of the various creeds which have been, for the most part, the work of theologians, not of saints--although, of course, the theologian and the saint may in rare cases be the same person . . . .

I believe that what the saints say is true--not merely that there is some truth in it, but that it is wholly true.

It is correct that, as viewed from a certain level, there are plenty of pleasures and enjoyments available in the common way of life and that many of them are perfectly innocent. The saint is not denying this. He is not denying that you can have a good time, and that having a good time is very enjoyable. But the level at which these things are said is superficial. At a deeper level we find that all this is hollowness, vacancy, and futility. Underneath the glitter of the tinsel there is darkness. At the core there is misery. That is why we are continually absorbing ourselves in ephemeral pursuits. To be absorbed is to forget what we ourselves, in the depths, actually are. We want to forget it.

This is not true of the animals. There is something in men which is not in the animals. It is at this something which the myth of an immortal soul is hinting. What is it? The question cannot be answered, because the something "cannot be described"; it is inexpressible. If we say that it is a "hunger for the Infinite" we use the language of myth, and we also use language which is trite and hackneyed. If we say that man's true home is God, that he is estranged, and this estrangement, being his essential nature as a finite being, is the inner misery of which we speak, we are using again hackneyed language and the language of myth. But something like this is all that can be said.

It is true that man can so completely forget this inner darkness of the soul that they become unaware of it and do not know what is meant when it is spoken of. And then it may be asked: how can a man be unhappy and yet not know it? If one feels happy, then one is happy. But even at the superficial level of daily life this is not true. It is possible to believe during a period of time that one is happy and afterwards to realize that one was not. And again one may ask whether, if a man is unaware of the darkness within him and is happy on the superficial level, it would not be better for him to remain in that state and be content with it. This is the same as the old question whether it is not better to be a pig satisfied than a Socrates unsatisfied. To which the answer is: No, not unless you are a pig.

The essential truth of religion, of every religion, is that from this darkness of life there is a way out, a way into the light. The destination of your present way is futility. The destination of the other way is "bliss" or "blessedness." This is not merely a higher degree of what men call happiness. It is not merely an elevated "pleasure." Blessedness and happiness--at any rate as

83

the latter word is commonly understood--do not belong in the same order of things at all. According to all religions the way out is very long and hard. But it is possible, if you want it enough. What is the way? . . .

What then is the way, what the destination? Strickly speaking, they "cannot be described." They are ineffable. And this word "effable" must be understood in its strict sense as meaning that which cannot be said, cannot be uttered at all in any conceivable words, in any conceivable language, and never will be. But it is here that the records left by the saints themselves can be of some use. Not that even they can say that which cannot be said. But they can "hint at it" more clearly than the common dogmas of religion do. Of course the saints themselves believed in and repeated the dogmas. Christian saints Christian dogmas, Hindu saints Hindu dogmas, Muslim saints, Muslim dogmas. They were after all human beings conditioned in their intellectual beliefs by the different cultures in which they were brought up. And in so far as they repeated the doctrines of the particular religions to which they were attached, they contradicted one another. But sometimes they transcended these different cultures, and sought to utter the pure essence of religion itself. And when they did so their utterances show a surprising measure of agreement.

The essence of religion is not morality but mysticism. And the way of saints is the way of mysticism. Accordingly, I use the words "saints" and "mystic" interchangeably in this book. If this does not wholly accord with dictionary definitions, I cannot help it. My contention is that all religion is ultimately mystical, or springs from the mystical side of human nature. All religious men are therefore mystics in greater or less degree. There is no sharp line between mystic and non-mystic. Those who are commonly recognized as mystics, and who so recognize themselves, are only those whose mysticism is explicitly realized in the full light of consciousness. In the ordinary religious man that mysticism is implicit, lies below the threshold of consciousness, only faintly stirring the surface waters of the mind and not recognized as what it is either by himself or others. The "saint" is the religious man par excellence, and the substance of his life is therefore mysticism whether he, or others who watch and describe

84

him, know it or not.

I shall quote a few of the utterances of mystics taken designedly from a number of different cultures and religions. What is common to all of them is the assertion that there is a kind of experience, a way of experiencing the world, in which all distinctions between one thing and another, including the distinction between the subject and object, self and non-self, are abolished, overcome, transcended, so that all the different things in the world become one, become identical with one another. We must suppose that they are still, in a sense, different; and yet they are not different but identical. Philosophical readers will be reminded of Hegel's famous "identity in difference." But whereas Hegel only talked about this, as a theory, the saints experience it--which is quite another thing. The affirmation of the possibility, or rather the actuality, of such an experience, raises at once a host of questions. But let us, for the moment at any rate, proceed to the evidence, or rather to that minute fraction of it which space allows me to reproduce here. I merely take a few samples from a vast literature.

A notable witness is Meister Eckhart, the Catholic mystic of the thirteenth century. A few passages from his writings follow:

> There all is one, and one is all. There to her
> (the perceiving soul) all is one and one is all. Herein
> lies the soul's purity, that it is purified from a life that
> is divided and that it enters into a life that is unified.
> All that is divided in lower things will be unified so soon
> as the soul climbs into a life where there is not contrast.
> When the soul comes into a life of reasonableness (the
> true insight) it knows no contrasts. Say, Lord, when is
> a man in mere "understanding?" I say to you: "When a
> man sees one thing separated from another." And when
> is a man above mere understanding? That I can tell you:
> "When a man sees one thing separated from another."
> And when is a man above mere understanding? That I
> can tell you: "When he sees all in all, then a man

stands beyond mere understanding."[1]

In this passage our ordinary mode of experiencing the world, in which one thing is distinguished from another, is called understanding. In the true vision, which transcends it, there are no contrasts or distinctions, but "all is one." . . .

Our second witness will be a pagan writer, Plotinus. He wrote of that vision which he had himself attained:

> Our self-seeing There is a communion with the self restored to its purity. No doubt we should not speak of seeing, but instead of seen and seer boldly of a _simple unity_. For in this seeing we neither see _nor distinguish nor are there two_. The man is changed, no longer himself nor self-belonging; he is merged with the Supreme, sunken into It, one with It; only in separation is their duality. This is why the vision baffles telling; for how could a man bring back tidings of the Supreme as detached when _he has seen it as one with himself_? _It is not to be told, not to be revealed to any_ that has not himself had the happiness to see . . . . _Beholder was one with beheld_ . . . _he is become the Unity, having no diversity either in relation to himself or anything else_ . . . _reason is in abeyance and intellection and_ even the very self, caught away, God-possessed, in perfect stillness, all the beings calmed . . . .
>
> This is the life of gods and of god-like and _blessed_ men--_liberation_ from the alien that besets us here, a life taking no pleasure in the things of earth--a flight of the alone to the Alone.[2]

The italicized passages (underlined here) carry the essential

---

[1] Quoted, Rudolph Otto, _Mysticism East and West_ (New York: The Macmillan Co., 1932), p. 45.

[2] Ennead _VI. IX. II_ (eleven) in _Works_ (New York: Medici Society). Trans. Stephen Mackenna. Underline Stace.

points which are the same in all accounts whether they proceed from Christians, Muslims, pagans, Hindus, or Buddhists. These are, first, that in this experience "all in one," there is no distinction of the seer from the seen (the distinction of subject from object) nor any distinction of any one thing from any other, no division or separation or discrimination; second, that in consequence the vision transcends intellection (Eckhart's "understanding"); third, that for this reason it is ineffable--no words can speak it because all words depend on distinction of one thing from another, that is to say upon the intellect; and fourth, that this experience is liberation, blessedness, calm, peace . . . .

In Buddhism the unifying vision, that super-consciousness which is above mere "understanding" is called Nirvana. It is called "enlightenment." In northern Buddhism it is sometimes called "the Buddha-mind," or again "Mind-Essence." It is a complete mistake to suppose that Nirvana is a sort of place or condition which one reaches after death. It is a state of the soul which can be attained by men who are still in the body and walking about the earth. Buddha attained it early in life, and lived and worked in the light of it for a half a century.

Ashvaghosma, who composed a Buddhist manual called The Awakening of Faith, about the first century A.D., distinguished between the "discriminating consciousness" (Eckhart's "understanding," which distinguishes or discriminates between different things, and the "intellection" of Plotinus) and the "intuitive consciousness" or Mind-Essence in the attainment of which lies enlightenment. He says:

Mind-Essence does not belong to any individualized conception of phenomena or non-phenomena . . . It has no particularizing consciousness, it does not belong to any kind of describable nature. Individuations and the consciousness of them come into being only as sentient beings cherish false imaginations of differences.[3]

Emphasizing what we should call the relation of the moral life to the transcendent vision, the fact that the vision is the source of ethical life, he says:

> The fourth significance (of enlightenment) is an affirmation of compassionate helpfulness, for being free from all limitations of selfness, it draws all alike into its all-embracing purity and unity and peacefulness, illuminating their minds with equal brightness so that all sentient beings have an equal right to enlightenment.[4]

Why does the unifying vision lead to love and compassion, the sources of the good life? Because in it all differences are abolished, including the difference between "I" and "you" which is the source of egoism and selfishness.

From Buddhism we turn to Hinduism. The Upanishads, the work of unknown forest saints, which date back two thousand five hundred to three thousand years, have been the chief source of the best Hindu thought from their own time till now. The great theme of the Upanishads is the discovery by their authors that "atman," which means the individual soul or self of a man, is identical with Brahman, which is the name of the Universal Self, or God. I am God; or, to use the language of the Upanishads themselves, "That art thou." The difference which we make between ourselves and Brahman is maya, illusion. To overcome this illusion is salvation, for in the overcoming of it the soul passes into and becomes one with God. But the overcoming of the illusion is not an intellectual understanding of it. One may know as a matter of abstract thought that one's self is identical with God. But this does not destroy the illusion of the difference, the separation, between

---

[3] A translation of The Awakening of Faith will be found in A Buddhist Bible, edited by Dwight Goddard (2nd ed.: Thetford, Vt.: Dwight Goddard, 1938), p. 364.

[4] Ibid., p. 368.

God and the self. One may compare this situation to any common optical illusion such as seeing a mirage. You see a lake of water in the desert. You may possess the scientific knowledge that no water is there. But this does not get rid of the illusion. You still see the water there. In the same way the intellectual knowledge that one's self is identical with the divine self helps not a whit in getting rid of the illusion of difference. The identity of one's self and God has to be actually experienced. Then only, in that supreme mystical experience, is the veil of illusion rent, and the soul passes into an immediate, experienced union with Brahman. It is of this mystical experience that the Upanishads everywhere speak. And it requires no great degree of understanding to see that this experience is identical with the unifying vision of Eckhart, the ecstatic state of Plotinus, the intuitive or non-discriminating mind of Buddhism.

In the Mandukya Upanishad we are told that there are four possible states of mind. The first three are waking, dreaming, and dreamless sleep:

> The Fourth, say the wise, is not subjective experience, nor objective experience, nor experience intermediate between these two, nor is it a negative condition which is neither consciousness nor unconsciousness. It is not the knowledge of the senses, nor is it relative knowledge, nor yet inferential knowledge. Beyond the senses, beyond the understanding, beyond all expression, is the Fourth. It is the pure unitary consciousness, wherein awareness of the world and of multiplicity is completely obliterated. It is ineffable peace. It is the supreme good. It is One without a second. It is the Self. [5]

In this passage the "Self" means Brahman, the Universal Self. The "One without a second" is another expression constantly used in the Upanishads for Brahman. "Without a second"

---

[5] The quotations given from Upanishads are from the translation of Swami Prabhavananda and Frederick Manchester (Boston: Beacon Press, 1948).

means that Brahman has nothing outside it, by which it is bounded or limited. It is therefore the Infinite in that precise meaning of the religious Infinite which has already been explained.

The essential character of this supreme vision, it will be noted, is that in it all discrimination, difference, multiplicity, are transcended. As with Eckhart, it is beyond the understanding. As with all mystics, to whatever religion they belong, it is ineffable, impossible to express in language, --"cannot be described" and is "unknown" in Eliot's words. And it is peace, bliss, blessedness, the supreme good, salvation. It is the "destination" of the "way." It is that for which, in Christian thought, the myth of a heaven after death stands.

From the Mandukya Upanishad I quote the following:

> The subtle Self (Brahman) is realized in that pure consciousness <u>wherein</u> <u>there</u> <u>is</u> <u>no</u> <u>duality</u>. (Underline Stace.)

One of the commonest methods by which the <u>Upanishads</u> draw attention to the absence of all discrimination or difference in the mystic's experience of the divine is by insisting on the <u>formlessness</u> of Brahman. (It makes no difference whether we say the formlessness of Brahman or the formlessness of the mystical experience; for the two are one). Form means any kind of character which distinguishes one thing from another. Gold, for instance, is distinguished from lead by having different characters for example by the difference of yellow from gray. Since having form, having characters, is what distinguishes one thing from another, form is therefore the principle of differentiation and multiplicity, in which "all is one," will accordingly be formless, and without any characters or qualities . . . .

We must now draw together the main points of what has been said about the way, the path, the experience, the destination, of the saints in all the higher religions. Its essence is the transcendence of all multiplicity in the unifying vision of the One. In this experience not only is the distinction between this and that, for instance, between the stone and the wood, done away with, but also the distinction between the subject and the object, the experiencer and the divine which he experiences. The experience is also felt directly as being bliss, peace, blessedness. This is the source of all myths about a paradise to come. The experience also has the character of <u>eternality</u>. For since space and time are principles of division, and the experience is divisionless unity, it is therefore "above time and space." Even if the ecstatic vision lasts only a moment, which can, if we look at it from the outside, be dated, yet that moment, as seen from within itself, is timeless and eternal. For this is the meaning of eternity. It does not mean unending time, but timelessness. This eternality of the saint's experience is the source of all myths about the immortality of the soul, reincarnation, etc., in which eternity is symbolized by the notion of endless time. The experience has, finally, the character of <u>infinity</u> in the sense that there is nothing outside it to bound it, for in vision in which all is one there cannot be any other to form a boundary. This infinity of the vision is the source of all myths about the infinite wisdom, power, and knowledge of God. In these myths infinity, like eternity, is distorted to mean mere endlessness . . . .

If the solution of the religious problem here suggested is accepted, there are still a number of questions which press on us ordinary men who are not among the company of the recognized mystics. Where, it may be asked, does all this leave us? It would seem that the true religious vision is only possible to a few extraordinary men. For the great mystic is rarer even than the great poet. What then can religion mean to us? Are we not, on the account here given, wholly cut off from it? And even though we may believe that it exists, will it not be for us only a traveller's tale, something which we cannot ourselves experience or know? If so, it can mean nothing to us in our practical lives and we might as well decide to ignore it.

The answer is that it is a mistake to suppose that there is a sharp line to be drawn between the mystic and the non-mystic. We easily recognize that there is no sharp line between the poet and the non-poet. We are all poets in greater degree or less. This is proved by the fact that when the great poet speaks our spirits echo to his utterance and his vision becomes ours. We have that vision in ourselves, but he evokes it. If it were not so, if we were not ourselves inarticulate poets, his words would be nonsense syllables to us, and we should listen uncomprehendingly to them.

Something of the same sort is true of mysticism. All men, or at least all sensitive men, are mystics in some degree. There is a mystical side of human nature just as there is a rational side. I do not mean merely that we are potential mystics in the sense that we theoretically could, by living a life which is a practical impossibility for most of us, achieve the mystic consciousness. That would indeed be next to useless. I mean that we have the mystic consciousness now, although in most of us it shines only dimly. This proved by the fact that, as with poetry, the utterances of the saint or of the mystic call up a response in us, however faint it may be. Something in us answers back to his words, as also something answers back to the words of the poet. Why has the phrase of Plotinus, "a flight of the alone to the Alone," become famous and echoed down the ages? Why has it fascinated generations of men? It is not mere nonsense to men who, though they do not claim ever to have had anything which they would call a recognizable "mystical experience," yet possess spiritually sensitive minds. It must be that it stirs in them some depth of the waters of the soul which is ordinarily hidden, and which, by these words, is, if but for an instant, drawn up to, or near, the surface. Deep down in us, far below the threshold of our ordinary consciousness, there lies that same intuitive non-discriminating mentality which in the great mystic has come to the surface of his mind and exists in the full light of conscious recognition.

And it is reasonable to hold that when ordinary men have what they call "religious feelings" or "religious experiences" or any kind, whether with the conscious thought of God in their minds or without it, whether in prayer, in church, or amid scenes of nature, the wonder, the awe, the sublimity of the mountains, the sunsets, or the seas, such religious feelings, vague, unformed, unclear, hardly expressible, dim, misty, inarticulate, are a stirring of the depths of the mystic vision which, if only we could drag it up into the clear light of our surface consciousness, would be the full-fledged ecstatic vision of the great mystic. It is an ancient insight that at least some "feelings" are unformed and inchoate cognitions. And this is the justification of the religious feelings of common men. They are not sentimental and subjective emotions. They are faint mystic experiences. They are a dim vision of the eternal, appearing in the guise of feelings, or even emotions, because they are dim and vague.

It is here that the myths of the different religions have their functions and justification. No doubt, taken literally, they are false. But whether the worshipper takes them literally or recognizes them as the myths they are, they perform the function of evoking within him those religious feelings which are in fact a far-off view of the divine. A man may feel in his heart or say with his lips that God is a God of love, and may pray to that God. It does not matter whether he simple-mindedly supposes that there is, somewhere unseen all about him, listening to his words, a great benevolent ghost who regards him with the human emotion which is called love, or whether on the contrary he knows that his language and his thoughts are symbolic expressions not to be taken literally; the inward effect in him, the evocation of the eternal, may in either case be the same.

This is the justification of the myths and images, and therefore of the creeds and doctrines, of the great religions of the world. No doubt they tend to degenerate on the one side into superstitions, on the other into mere intellectual abstractions spiritually dead and powerless. No doubt they may in this way become fetters on men's minds and even sources of intellectual and spiritual disorders. They become even shams and hypocrisies. It is then that the skeptics turn on them and rend them, and in this way the skeptic too performs a function which has value in the spiritual life, a spiritual purging. But basically most men will always require myths and images to evoke in them the divine vision. And when one set of symbols has degenerated into mere abstractions or debasing superstitions, another set arises. Even the great mystics who, one might suppose, would have no need of any mere metaphorical representatives of the eternal, since they have the eternal itself, yet for the most part use the symbols of the religion in which they were born and so attach themselves to this religion or that. It is in this way that what one mystic says seems to contradict what another says. For they use different symbols for the same reality.

A man may attach himself to any church, or to none. He may be disgusted with superstitions into which institutional religions degenerate and with the shams and hypocrisies which they engender. Or he may have seen the literal falsity of their creeds, and because he has been taught to take them literally and thinks there is no other way, because he fails to see their symbolic truth and function, he rests in a mere negation. He may then call himself an agnostic or atheist. But it does not follow that he is irreligious, even though he may profess to be. His religion may subsist in the form of a sort of unclothes religious feeling, unclothed with any symbols at all, inarticulate, formless. Each man, in an institutional religion or out of it, must find his own way. And it is not justifiable for those who find it in one way to condemn those who find it in another.

And if the theory of religion which I have outlined is accepted, it should at least cause those of us who cannot find a place within any institutional religion to understand the religious side of human nature, both that of themselves and of others, and the function and justification of religious creeds for those who can still hold them, creeds to which simple-minded men have clung, and which they, the more sophisticated ones, have perhaps too hastily condemned. [6]

---

[6]The view of religion which is baldly sketched in this chapter is more fully worked out in the writer's book, _Time and Eternity_.

4. THE RELATION OF RELIGION AND SCIENCE

Albert Einstein agrees with Stace that an awareness of the impenetrable depths of life is the source of true religious feeling This awareness of the mysterious is also the source of science. The cosmic religious experience of the totality and unity of all existence is the driving force behind all scientific research. Science and religion, when so conceived, are not antagonistic to each other but supportive. Science seeks to understand natural phenomena through mathematical concepts, but the belief in a superior Mind which reveals itself in nature has its source in deep feeling which is religious.

The Meeting Place of Science and Religion

Albert Einstein

Strange is our situation here upon earth. Each of us comes for a short visit, not knowing why, yet sometimes seeking to divine a purpose.

From the standpoint of daily life, however, there is one thing we do know: that man is here for the sake of other men-- above all for those upon whose smiles and well-being our own happiness depends, and also for the countless unknown souls with whose fate we are connected by a bond of sympathy. Many times a day I realize how much my own outer and inner life is built upon the labors of my fellow-men, both living and dead, and how earn-

---

estly I must exert myself in order to give in return as much as I have received. My peace of mind is often troubled by the depressing sense that I have borrowed too heavily from the work of other men.

I do not believe we can have any freedom at all in the philosophical sense, for we act not only under external compulsion but also by inner necessity. Schopenhauer's saying--"A man can surely do what he wills to do, but he cannot determine what he wills"--impressed itself upon me in my youth, and has always consoled me when I have witnessed or suffered life's hardships. This conviction is a perpetual breeder of tolerance, for it does not allow us to take ourselves or others too seriously. It makes rather for a sense of humor.

To ponder interminably over the reason for one's own existence, or the meaning of life in general, seems to me, from an objective point of view, to be sheer folly. And yet every one holds certain ideals by which he guides his aspiration and his judgment. The ideals which have always shone before me and filled me with the joy of living are goodness, beauty, and truth. To make a goal of comfort or happiness has never appealed to me: a system of ethics built on this basis would be sufficient only for a herd of cattle.

Without the sense of collaborating with like-minded in the pursuit of the ever unattainable in art and scientific research, my life would have been empty. Ever since childhood I have scorned the commonplace limits so often set upon human ambition. Possessions, outward success, publicity, luxury--to me these have always been contemptible. I believe that a simple and unassuming manner of life is best for every one, best for the body and for the mind.

My passionate interest in social justice and social responsibility has always stood in curious contrast to a marked lack of desire for direct association with men and women. I am a horse for single harness, not cut out for tandem or team work. I have never belonged wholeheartedly to country or state, to my circle of friends, or even to my own family. These ties have always been accompanied by a vague aloofness.   And the wish to withdraw into myself increases with the years.

Such isolation is sometimes bitter; but I do not regret being cut off from the understanding and sympathy of other men. I lose something by it, to be sure, but I am compensated for it in being rendered independent of the customs, opinions, and prejudices of others; and am not tempted to rest my peace of mind upon such shifting foundations.

My political ideal is democracy. Every one should be respected as an individual, but no one idolized. It is an irony of fate that I should have been showered with so much uncalled-for and unmerited admiration and esteem. Perhaps this adulation springs from the unfulfilled wish of the multitude to comprehend the few ideas which I, with my weak powers, have advanced.

Full well do I know that in order to attain any definite goal it is imperative that one person should do the thinking and commanding and carry most of the responsibility. But those who are led should not be driven, and they should be allowed to choose their leader. It seems to me that the distinctions separating the social classes are false; in the last analysis they rest on force. I am convinced that degeneracy follows every autocratic system of violence, for violence inevitably attracts moral inferiors. Time has proved that illustrious tyrants are succeeded by scoundrels.

For this reason I have always been passionately opposed to such regimes as exist in Russia and Italy to-day. The thing which has discredited the European forms of democracy is not the basic theory of democracy itself, which some say is at fault, but the instability of our political leadership, as well as the impersonal character of party alignments.

I believe that those in the United States have hit upon the right idea. They choose a President for a reasonable length of time and give him enough power to acquit himself properly of his responsibilities. In the German Government, on the other hand, I like the state's more extensive care of the individual when he is ill or unemployed. What is truly valuable in our bustle of life is not the nation, I should say, but the creative and impressionable individuality, the personality--he who produces the noble and sublime while the common herd remains dull in thought and insensible in feeling.

This subject brings me to that vilest offspring of the herd mind--the odious militia. The man who enjoys marching in line and file to the strains of music falls below my contempt: he received his great brain by mistake--the spinal cord would have been sufficient. This heroism is commanded; this senseless violence, this accursed bombast of patriotism--how intensely I despise them! War is low and despicable, and I had rather be smitten to shreds than participate in such doings.

Such a stain on humanity should be erased without delay. I think well enough of human nature to believe that it would have been wiped out long ago had not the common sense of nations been systematically corrupted through school and press for business and political reasons.

The most beautiful thing we can express is the mysterious. It is the source of all true art and science. He to whom this emotion is a stranger, who can no longer pause to wonder and stand rapt in awe, is as good as dead: his eyes are closed. This insight into the mystery of life, coupled though it be with fear, has also given rise to religion. To know that what is impenetrable to us really exists, manifesting itself as the highest wisdom and the most radiant beauty which our dull faculties can comprehend only in their most primitive forms--this knowledge, this feeling, is at the center of true religiousness. In this sense, and in this sense only, I belong in the ranks of the devoutly religious men.

I cannot imagine a God who rewards and punishes the objects of his creation, whose purposes are modelled after our own --a God, in short, who is but a reflection of human frailty. Neither can I believe that the individual survives the death of his body, although feeble souls harbor such fear or religious egotism. It is enough for me to contemplate the mystery of conscious life perpetuating itself through all eternity, to reflect upon the marvelous structure of the universe which we can dimly perceive, and to try humbly to comprehend even an infinitesimal part of the intelligence manifested in nature.

Everything that men do or think concerns the satisfaction of the needs they feel or the escape from pain. This must be kept in mind when we seek to understand spiritual or intellectual movements and the way in which they develop. For feeling and longing are the motive forces of all human striving and productivity--however nobly these latter may display themselves to us.

What, then, are the feelings and the needs which have brought mankind to religious thought, and to faith in the widest sense? A moment's consideration shows that the most varied emotions stand at the cradle of religious thought and experience.

In primitive peoples it is, first of all, fear that awakens religious ideas--fear of hunger, of wild animals, of illness and of death. Since the understanding of causal connections is usually limited on this level of existence, the human soul forges a being, more or less like itself, on whose will and activities depend the experiences which it fears. One hopes to win the favor of this being by deeds and sacrifices, which, according to the tradition of the race, are supposed to appease the being, or to make him well disposed to man.

I call this the religion of fear.

This religion is considerably stabilized--though not caused --by the formation of a priestly caste which claims to mediate between the people and the being they fear, and so attains a position of power. Often a leader or a despot or a privileged class whose power is maintained in other ways, will combine the function of the priesthood with its own temporal rule for the sake of greater security: or an alliance may exist between the interests of the political power and the priestly caste.

A second source of religious development is found in the social feeling.

Fathers and mothers, as well as leaders of great human

communities, are fallible and mortal. The longing for guidance, for love and succor, provides the stimulus for growth of a social or moral conception of God.

This is the God of Providence, who protects, decides, rewards and punishes. This is the God who, according to man's widening horizon, loves and provides for the life of the race, or of mankind, or who even loves life itself. He is the comforter in happiness and in unsatisfied longing, the protector of the souls of the dead. This is the social or moral idea of God.

It is easy to follow in the sacred writings of the Jewish people the development of the religion of fear into the moral religion, which is carried further in the New Testament. The religions of all the civilized peoples, especially those of the Orient, are principally moral religions. An important advance in the life of a people is the transformation of the religion of fear into the moral religion. But one must avoid the prejudice that regards the religions of primitive peoples as pure fear religions and those of the civilized races as pure moral religions. All are mixed forms, though the moral element predominates in the higher levels of social life. Common to all these types is the anthropomorphic character of the idea of God.

Only exceptionally gifted individuals or especially noble communities rise essentially above this level. In these there is found a third level of religious experience, even if it is seldom found in pure form. I will call it the cosmic religious sense. This is hard to make clear to those who do not experience it, since it does not involve an anthropomorphic idea of God. The individual feels the vanity of human desires and aims, and the nobility and marvellous order which are revealed in nature and in the world of thought. He feels the individual destiny as an imprisonment and seeks to experience the totality of existence as a unity of full significance. Indications of this cosmic religious sense can be found even on earlier levels of development--for example, in the Psalms and the Prophets of the Old Testament. The cosmic element is much stronger in Buddhism, as, in particular, Schopenhauer's magnificent essays have shown us.

100

The religious geniuses of all times have been distinguished by this cosmic religious sense, which recognizes neither dogmas nor God made in man's image. Consequently there cannot be a church whose chief doctrines are based on the cosmic religious experience. It comes about, therefore, that we find precisely among the heretics of all ages men who are inspired by this highest religious experience. Often they appeared to their contemporaries as atheists, but sometimes also as saints. Viewed from this angle, men like Democritus, Francis of Assisi and Spinoza are near to one another.

How can this cosmic religious experience be communicated from man to man, if it cannot lead to a definite conception of God, or to a theology? It seems to me that the most important function of art and of science is to arouse and keep alive this feeling in those who are receptive.

Thus we reach an interpretation of the relation of science to religion which is very different from the customary view. From the study of history one is inclined to regard religion and science as irreconcilable antagonists; and this for a reason that is very easily seen. For any one who is pervaded with the sense of causal law in all that happens, who accepts in real earnest the assumption of causality, the idea of a Being who interferes with the sequence of events in the world is absolutely impossible. Neither the religion of fear, nor the social-moral religion, can have any hold on him. A god who rewards and punishes is for him unthinkable, because man acts in accordance with an inner and outer necessity, and would, in the eyes of God, be as little responsible as an inanimate object is for the movement which it makes.

Science, in consequence, has been accused of undermining morals--but wrongly. The ethical behavior of man is better based on sympathy, education and social relationships, and requires no support from religion. Man's plight would, indeed, be sad if he had to be kept in order through fear of punishment and hope of rewards after death.

It is, therefore, quite natural that the churches have always fought against science and have persecuted its supporters. But, on the other hand, I assert that the cosmic religious experience is the strongest and the noblest driving force behind scientific research. No one who does not appreciate the terrific exertions, and above all, the devotion without which pioneer creations in scientific thought cannot come into being, can judge the strength of the feeling out of which alone such work, turned away as it is from immediate practical life, can grow. What a deep faith in the rationality of the structure of the world, and what a longing to understand even a small glimpse of the reason revealed in the world there must have been in Kepler and Newton to enable them to unravel the mechanism of the heaven in long years of lonely work.

Any one who only knows scientific research in its practical applications may easily come to a wrong interpretation of the state of mind of the men who, surrounded by skeptical contemporaries, have shown the way to kindred spirits scattered over all countries in all centuries. Only those who have dedicated their lives to similar ends can have a living conception of the inspiration which gave these men the power to remain loyal to their purposes in spite of countless failures. It is the cosmic religious sense which grants this power.

A contemporary has rightly said that the only deeply religious people of our largely materialistic age are the earnest men of research.

5. THE RELATION OF RELIGION AND MORALITY

The mystic consciousness may bring one into union with God but for <u>Tagore</u> this is not yet morality. There must be a realization of the self in love which goes beyond selfish desires and brings one into harmony with that larger Self of God which is expressed in all creation. This love cannot be realized in a withdrawal from the activities of life but only in creative participation where all activities are realized as an expression of God. Such realization brings joy, peace and the kind of freedom which comes from identity with the soul of the world.

Realization in Love

Rabindranath Tagore

One day I was out in a boat on the Ganges. It was a beautiful evening in autumn. The sun had just set; the silence of the sky was full to the brim with ineffable peace and beauty. The vast expanse of water was without a ripple, mirroring all the changing shades of the sunset glow. Miles and miles of a desolate sand-bank lay like a huge amphibious reptile of some antediluvian age, with its scales glistening in shining colours. As our boat was silently sliding by the precipitous river-bank, riddled with the nest-holes of a colony of birds, suddenly a big fish leapt up to the surface of the water and then disappeared, displaying on its vanishing figure all the colours of the evening sky. It drew aside for a moment the many-coloured screen behind which there was a silent world full of the joy of life. It came up from the depths of

---

its mysterious dwelling with a beautiful dancing motion and added its own music to the silent symphony of the dying day. I felt as if I had a friendly greeting from an alien world in its own language, and it touched my heart with a flash of gladness. Then suddenly the man at the helm exclaimed with a distinct note of regret, "Ah, what a big fish!" It at once brought before his vision the picture of the fish caught and made ready for his supper. He could only look at the fish through his desire, and thus missed the whole truth of its existence. But man is not entirely an animal. He aspires to a spiritual vision, which is the vision of the whole truth. This gives him the highest delight, because it reveals to him the deepest harmony that exists between him and his surroundings. It is our desires that limit the scope of our self-realisation, hinder our extension of consciousness, and give rise to sin, which is the innermost barrier that keeps us apart from our God, setting up disunion and the arrogance of exclusiveness. For sin is not one mere action, but it is an attitude of life which takes for granted that our goal is finite, that our self is the ultimate truth, and that we are not all esentially one but exist each for his own separate individual existence.

So I repeat we never can have a true view of man unless we have a love for him. Civilisation must be judged and prized, not by the amount of power it has developed, but by how much it has evolved and given expression to, by its laws and institutions, the love of humanity. The first question and the last which it has no answer is, Whether and how far it recognises man more as a spirit than as a machine? Whenever some ancient civilisation fell into decay and died, it was owing to causes which produced callousness of heart and led to the cheapening of man's worth; when either the state or some powerful group of men began to look upon the people as a mere instrument of their power; when, by compelling weaker races to slavery and trying to keep them down by every means, man struck at the foundation of his greatness, his own love of freedom and fairplay. Civilisation can never sustain itself upon cannibalism of any form. For that by which alone man is true can only be nourished by love and justice.

As with man, so with this universe. When we look at the world through the veil of our desires we make it small and narrow, and fail to perceive its full truth. Of course it is obvious that the world serves us and fulfils our needs, but our relation to it does not end there. We are bound to it with a deeper and truer bond than that of necessity. Our soul is drawn to it; our love of life is really our wish to continue our relation with this great world. This relation is one of love. We are glad that we are in it; we are attached to it with numberless threads, which extend from this earth to the stars. Man foolishly tries to prove his superiority by imagining his radical separateness from what he calls his physical world, which, in his blind fanaticism, he sometimes goes to the extent of ignoring altogether, holding it as his direst enemy. Yet the more his knowledge progresses, the more it becomes difficult for man to establish this separateness, and all the imaginary boundaries he had set up around himself vanish one after another. Every time we lose some of our badges of absolute distinction by which we conferred upon our humanity the right to hold itself apart from its surroundings, it gives us a shock of humiliation. But we have to submit to this. If we set up our pride on the path of our self-realisation to create divisions and dis-union, then it must sooner or later come under the wheels of truth and be ground to dust. No, we are not burdened with some monstrous superiority, unmeaning in its singular abruptness. It would be utterly degrading for us to live in a world immeasurably less than ourselves in the quality of soul, just as it would be repulsive and degrading to be surrounded and served by a host of slaves, day and night, from birth to the moment of death. On the contrary, this world is our compeer, nay, we are one with it.

Through our progress in science the wholeness of the world and our oneness with it is becoming clearer to our mind. When this perception of the perfection of unity is not merely intellectual, when it opens out our whole being into a luminous consciousness of the all, then it becomes a radiant joy, an overspreading love. Our spirit finds its larger self in the whole world, and is filled with an absolute certainty that it is immortal. It dies a hundred times in its enclosures of self; for separateness is doomed to die, it cannot be made eternal. But it never can die where it is one with the all, for there is its truth, its joy. When a man feels the rhythmic throb of the soul-life of the whole world in his own soul, the is he free. Then he enters into the secret courting that goes on between this beautiful world-bride, veiled with the veil of the many-coloured finiteness, and the <u>paramatman</u>, the bridegroom, in his spotless white. Then he knows that he is the partaker of this gorgeous love festival, and he is the honoured guest at the feast of immortality. Then he understands the meaning of the seer-poet who sings, "From love the world is born, by love it is sustained, towards love it moves, and into love it enters."

In love all the contradictions of existence merge themselves and are lost. Only in love are unity and duality not at variance. Love must be one and two at the same time.

Only love is motion and rest in one. Our heart ever changes its place till it finds love, and then it has its rest. But this rest itself is an intense form of activity where utter quiescence and unceasing energy meet at the same point in love.

In love, loss and gain are harmonised. In its balance-sheet, credit and debit accounts are in the same column, and gifts are added to gains. In this wonderful festival of creation, this great ceremony of self-sacrifice of God, the lover constantly gives himself up to gain himself in love. Indeed, love is what brings together and inseparably connects both the act of abandoning and that of receiving.

In love, at one of its poles you find the personal, and at the other the impersonal. At one you have the positive assertion-- Here I am; at the other the equally strong denial--I am not. Without this ego what is love? And again, with only this ego how can love be possible?

Bondage and liberation are not antagonistic in love. For love is most free and at the same time most bound. If God were absolutely free there would be no creation. The infinite being has assumed unto himself the mystery of finitude. And in him who is love the finite and the infinite are made one . . . .

It is very characteristic of life that it is not complete within itself; it must come out. Its truth is in the commerce of the inside and the outside. In order to live, the body must maintain its various relations with the outside light and air--not only to gain life-force, but also to manifest it. Consider how fully employed the body is with its own inside activities; its heart-beat must not stop for a second, its stomach, its brain, must be ceaselessly working. Yet this is not enough; the body is outwardly restless all the while. Its life leads it to an endless dance of work and play outside; it cannot be satisfied with the circulations of its internal economy, and only finds the fulfilment of joy in its outward excursions.

The same with the soul. It cannot live on its own internal feelings and imaginings. It is ever in need of external objects; not only to feed its inner consciousness but to apply itself in action, not only to receive but also to give.

The real truth is, we cannot live if we divide him who is truth itself into two parts. We must abide in him within as well as without. In whichever aspect we deny him we deceive ourselves and incur a loss. Brahma has not left me, let me not leave Brahma . . . . If we say that we would realise him in introspection alone and leave him out of our external activity, that we would enjoy him by the love in our heart, but not worship him by outward ministrations; or if we say the opposite, and overweight ourselves on one side in the journey of our life's quest, we shall alike totter to our downfall . . . .

But true spirituality, as taught in our sacred lore, is calmly balanced in strength, in the correlation of the within and the without. The truth has its law, it has its joy. On one side of it is being chanted the Bhayadasyagnistapati, . . . on the other the Anandadhyeva khalvimani bhutani jayante . . . . Freedom is impossible of attainment without submission to law, for Brahma is in one aspect bound by his truth, in the other free in his joy.

As for ourselves, it is only when we wholly submit to the bonds of truth that we fully gain the joy of freedom. And how? As does the string that is bound to the harp. When the harp is truly strung, when there is not the slightest laxity in the strength of the bond, then only does music result; and the string transcending itself in its melody finds at every chord its true freedom. It is because it is bound by such hard and fast rules on the one side that it can find this range of freedom in music on the other. While the string was not true, it was indeed merely bound; but a loosening of its bondage would not have been the way to freedom, which it can only achieve by being bound tighter and tighter till it has attained the true pitch.

The bass and treble strings of our duty are only bonds so long as we cannot maintain them steadfastly attuned according to the law of truth; and we cannot call by the name of freedom the loosening of them into the nothingness of inaction. That is why I would say that the true striving in the quest of truth, of <u>dharma</u>, consists not in the neglect of action but in the effort to attune it closer and closer to the eternal harmony. The text of this striving should be, <u>Whatever</u> <u>works</u> <u>thou</u> <u>doest</u>, <u>consecrate</u> <u>them</u> <u>to</u> <u>Brahma</u> . . . . That is to say, the soul is to dedicate itself to Brahma through all its activities. This dedication is the song of the soul, in this is its freedom. Joy reigns when all work becomes the path to the union with Brahma; when the soul ceases to return constantly to its own desires; when in it our self-offering grows more and more intense. Then there is completion, then there is freedom, then, in this world, comes the kingdom of God.

He who thinks to reach God by running away from the world, when and where does he expect to meet him? How far can he fly --can he fly and fly, till he flies into nothingness itself? No, the coward who would fly can nowhere find him. We must be brave enough to be able to say: We are reaching him here in this very spot, now at this very moment. We must be able to assure ourselves that as in our actions we are realising ourselves, so in ourselves we are realising him who is the self of self. We must earn the right to say so unhesitatingly by clearing away with our own effort all obstruction, all disorder, all discords from our path of activity; we must be able to say, "In my work is my joy, and in that joy does the joy of my joy abide."

The Upanishad says: <u>Knowledge</u>, <u>power</u>, <u>and</u> <u>action</u> <u>are</u> <u>of</u> <u>his</u> <u>nature</u> . . . . It is because this naturalness has not yet been born in us that we tend to divide joy from work. Our day of work is not our day of joy--for that we require a holiday; for, miserable that we are, we cannot find our holiday in our work. The river finds its holiday in its onward flow, the fire in its outburst of flame, the scent of the flower in its permeation of the atmosphere; but in our everyday work there is no such holiday for us. It is because we do not let ourselves go, because we do not give ourselves joyously and entirely up to it, that our work overpowers us.

O giver of thyself! at the vision of thee as joy let our souls flame up to thee as the fire, flow on to thee as the river, permeate thy being as the fragrance of the flower. Give us strength to love, to love fully, our life in its joys and sorrows, in its gains and losses, in its rise and fall. Let us have strength enough fully to see and hear thy universe, and to work with full vigour therein. Let us fully live the life thou hast given us, let us bravely take and bravely give. This is our prayer to thee. Let us once for all dislodge from our minds the feeble fancy that would make out thy joy to be a thing apart from action, thin, formless, and unsustained. Wherever the peasant tills the hard earth, there does thy joy gush out in the green of the corn, wherever man displaces the entangled forest, smooths the stony ground, and clears for himself a homestead, there does thy joy enfold it in orderliness and peace.

O worker of the universe! We would pray to thee to let the irrestible current of thy universal energy come like the impetous south wind of spring, let it come rushing over the vast field of the life of man, let it bring the scent of many flowers, the murmurings of many woodlands, let it make sweet and vocal the lifelessness of our dried-up soul-life. Let our newly awakened powers cry out for unlimited fulfilment in leaf and flower and fruit.

6. HUMAN DESTINY

Swami Nikhilinanda believes that the human soul is immortal by nature, it cannot die. Through a process of rebirth, however, it remains embodied in the phenomenal world until all bodily desires have been fulfilled and a stage of desirelessness is reached. The free soul, having achieved desirelessness, may be embodied, but upon death of the body achieves oneness with God and is no longer reborn. The Hindu philosophy of reincarnation is not necessarily a part of Pantheistic thought, but it is compatible with the belief that the ultimate destiny of the human soul is a disembodied oneness with the divine reality from which it is always separated to some degree in the embodied state.

The Soul and its Destiny

Swami Nikhilananda

When the individual soul becomes aware of its divine nature, it no longer has to practise morality or obey religious injunctions, whose aim is to enable the aspirant still attached to the world to rid himself of lust, greed, anger, egotism, and a narrow view of life. But during the embodied state, if a person sees the distinction between good and evil, he should shun the evil and follow the good . . . .

The Upanishads speak of two souls, as it were, dwelling

From HINDUISM: ITS MEANING FOR THE LIBERATION OF THE SPIRIT, by Swami Nikhilananda, Ramakrishna-Vivekananda Center of New York, Inc. Copyright 1958, pp. 35-36, 36-37, 38-41, 46-48, 50-51, 55-56 (New York, Harper & Bros. edition, 1958). Used by permission of Ramakrishna-Vivekananda Center.

side by side in a man: the real soul and the individual or apparent soul. They are described as two birds, of similar plumage, inseparable friends, which cling to the same tree, one of them eating the fruit, and the other looking on without eating. The apparent soul experiences pain and pleasure as the result of his own actions, good and evil, and is bewildered by its impotence. But the real soul is serene and undisturbed, because it is not attached to the world. When the apparent soul realizes its oneness with the supreme soul its grief passes away. This oneness of the two souls has been stated by such Vedic statements as "That thou art," "This self is Brahman," "I am He," "Brahman is consciousness." . . .

The Vedanta philosophy describes at great length the distinction between the "seer" and the "seen," also known as the subject and the object, the ego and the non-ego. The seer is the perceiver, identical with the subject and the ego, and is conscious and intelligent by nature. The seen is what is perceived, identical with the object and the non-ego, and is insentient by nature. Thus, the seer and the seen are mutually opposed, like light and darkness. Yet it is a matter of common experience that in everyday practical life people do not distinguish between the two, but through ignorance superimpose the attributes of the one upon the other: the subject is confused with the object and vice versa. This confusion, observable in a person's daily thought and action, is expressed by such common statements as "This is I," "This is mine," whereby he identifies the "I" or the subject, which is by nature pure consciousness, with such material objects as the body, the senses, the mind, house, country, or other material objects. Furthermore, on account of the same ignorance, he associates the seer or the eternal self with such characteristics of the body as birth, growth, disease, and death; and this confusion is expressed by such statements as "I am born," "I am growing," "I am ill," or "I am dying." Discrimination between the seer and the seen is the prerequisite for knowledge of the self. The seer is the unchangeable and homogeneous consciousness or knowing principle, the subject and the real ego. The seen is what is perceived; it is matter, multiple and changeable.

It is by virtue of its non-dual nature that the seer perceives

111

an object. The eye sees the diversity of colour and shape in the outer world because it is, relatively speaking, one and unchanging. In turn, the mind--relatively speaking, one--is the perceiver of such changing characteristics of the eye as blindness, dullness, or keenness. Finally, the mind itself--endowed with such characteristics as desire, doubt, determination, fear, and fearlessness--is an object perceived by the self or consciousness, because the latter is one and without a second. This consciousness is free from all such changes as birth, growth, decay, or death. If it possessed those attributes, there would have to be someone as their perceiver. Who would that perceiver be? Another self or consciousness? And who would the perceiver of the second consciousness be? The inquiry ends in an infinite regress. The existence of the self or consciousness cannot be an object of doubt, because the doubter himself is that consciousness. The self cannot be denied, because the denier himself is that self or consciousness. The presence of an irrefragable self or consciousness is assumed in all acts of thinking. Vedanta therefore states that all entities--from the gross, tangible objects in the outer world to the body, senses, and mind--belong to the category of the "seen" or the object, and are insentient and changing. The self or consciousness, which is the true "seer" or subject, is unchanging intelligence, and can never be imagined to be non-existent. The Upanishads emphatically declare that there cannot be an absence of knowledge in the knower. Consciousness is the very stuff of the knower: atman in man and Brahman in the universe are completely identical.

The method by which a Vedantist realizes the illusory nature of the phenomenal world is called adhyaropa, and that by which he rids himself of this illusion and arrives at the knowledge of Brahman is called apavada. By adhyaropa it is explained how, on acaount of illusory superimposition which is the result of ignorance, one thing appears as another and the properties of the one are attributed to the other. Thus the idea of a snake is falsely superimposed upon a rope and the characteristics of the former are attributed to the latter. In the same manner the idea of body, senses, and mind, associated with the non-self, is falsely superimposed upon the self, and the self, which is of the nature of pure consciousness, appears as a jive, or phenomenal being, subject

112

to the various limitations of the physical world. Through the same inscrutable ignorance, the attributes of the self are superimposed upon the non-self, and the non-self appears to be conscious, intelligent, and full of bliss. Because of this ignorance, again, the universe of names and forms appears to have reality, or characteristic which actually belongs to Brahman.

Apavada is the method by which one negates, through discrimination, the attributes erroneously superimposed, and realizes the true nature of a thing. Thus, by negating the attributes of the illusory snake one discovers the true nature of the rope, by negating the attributes of the non-self one discovers the true nature of the self, and by negating the attributes of the relative world one discovers the true nature of Brahman. It should be remembered that the attributes falsely superimposed upon a thing can never affect its true nature. As the illusory snake cannot change the nature of the rope, so the superimposed attributes of birth and death, and pain and pleasure, cannot in any way change the true nature of the self. Reality cannot be affected by appearance . . . .

As Hinduism admits the reality of the jiva or the embodied individual in the relative state, it also accepts the fact of its birth and death. What happens to the soul after death? The doctrine of absolute annihilation did not appeal to the Hindu mind, since it is inconsistent with the self-love innate in every normal person, and also because, in the eyes of Hinduism, it is in conflict with the moral order of the universe. In one brief crowded life it is impossible for a man to experience the fruition of all his actions, good and evil.

On the other hand, the doctrine of eternal happiness in heaven or eternal suffering in hell did not impress the philosophers of the Upanishads. Happiness in heaven, being an effect, cannot be eternal. Anything that has a beginning must also have an end. Again, the theory of everlasting suffering is inconsistent with the belief in God's love for created beings. The soul, being an "eternal portion" of God, cannot be damned forever. Furthermore, this theory reveals a total disproportion between cause and effect: life on earth is exposed to errors and temptations over which an individual cannot always exercise control. To believe in the eternal punishment of the soul for the mistakes of a few years, without giving it a chance for correction, is to go against all the dictates of reason. Finally, the destruction of the soul at death is inconsistent with the direct and intuitive experience of enlightened seers, who perceive in deep meditation that the soul can exist independent of the body.

Hinduism holds that after death the soul assumes a new body and that this rebirth is governed by the law of karma. It makes the claim that the soul's exit from the body, and its experiences after death, can be actually witnessed by the illumined person. They cannot, however, be demonstrated by reason; furthermore, conditions being completely different on the other side of the grave, the living would not understand any report given by the dead. The doctrine of rebirth, based upon the law of cause and effect, is the most plausible of all the speculations regarding what happens to the soul after death. It is an indispensable corollary of the immortality of the soul, for without it a beginning of the soul would have to be assumed. Thus the doctrine of rebirth is more probable than improbable. One can live by it as if it were true. It explains many phenomena of life which otherwise cannot be understood. What does he know of life who only one life knows ?

The embodied soul instinctively feels itself to be limited and bound by the finite body and seeks its freedom. It is bound by desires, which create new births; but freedom comes from desirelessness. This desirelessness cannot be attained without experiencing the futility of all worldly desires. Desires are of many kinds: some can be fulfilled in a human body, some in a subhuman body, and others in a superhuman body. Thus a soul experiences the fulfillment of desires through all kinds of bodies ranging from the body of a blade of grass to that of the highest deity in the phenomenal world. When it has fulfilled every desire through repeated lives, without deriving any abiding satisfaction, and finds the relative world to be bound by the law of cause and effect, it longs for communion with Brahman, its real nature, which alone is untouched by the causal law. The phenomenal universe being by its very nature limited, a Hindu seeking liberation does not want rebirth, be it here on earth or in heaven. Liberation, in the Hindu tradition, is liberation from repeated births and deaths . . . .

A soul is born again and again, high or low, depending upon the merit or the demerit of its actions. The Upanishads speak of three courses which departed souls may follow before they are reborn on earth in a human body; it is through a human body that liberation is generally attained. Those who have led a life of extreme wickedness are born as subhuman beings. Those again who have discharged their social and moral duties, cherished desires, and sought the results of actions, repair after death to a heaven called the Plane of the Moon and reap there the fruit of their works, before they are reborn in a human body. But Brahmaloka, the highest heaven, is attained by those who have led an intense spiritual life on earth and sought the reality of God but failed in their effort. Some of the dwellers in Brahmaloka obtain liberation, and some return to earth. Such is the merry-go-round existence one leads in this phenomenal universe.

Man's eternal soul can never be permanently satisfied with non-eternal happiness. There is no real joy in the finite; real joy is only in the infinite. One who is tired of endless birth and death and heavy-laden with the experiences of the phenomenal world, which ultimately bring nothing but weariness, looks for the real freedom and bliss dwelling in every heart, but obscured by the veil of ignorance. Even the worst sinner--the vilest among men-- at some time or other gets a glimpse of his real nature and becomes eager to realize it. He then practises spiritual disciplines in order to rid his mind of its impurities. The prodigal son turns his face to his Father's house . . . .

A free soul no longer thinks in terms of bondage and liberation, which are concepts of the impure mind but never belong to atman, the spirit ever free. The embodied soul, on account of ignorance, becomes entangled in the relative life and then strives for liberation; but the enlightened soul sees neither birth nor death, neither bondage nor liberation.

A free soul, while living in the body, may experience

disease, old age, or decay; may feel hunger, thirst, grief, or fear; may be a victim of blindness, deafness, or other deformities; but having realized that these are the characteristics of the body, the mind, or the senses, he does not take them seriously and so is not overwhelmed by them. A man who sees a play on the stage does not consider it to be real, yet he enjoys it to his heart's content; likewise, a free soul living in the midst of the joys and sorrows of the world enjoys them as the unfolding of a divine play.

A free soul lives, thinks, and works under the spell of immortality. And when his days on earth are completed, he departs from the world as if he were going from one room to another.

What happens to a knower of the self after death? Where does his soul go? The unillumined go to the upper or the nether world, or return to earth for the satisfaction of unfulfilled desires; but he who is desireless is not embodied again. "Of him who is without desires, who is free from desires, the objects of whose desires have been attained, and to whom all objects of desire are but the self--the life-breath does not depart. Being Brahman, he merges in Brahman." "When all the desires that dwell in his heart are gone, then he, having been mortal, becomes immortal and attains Brahman in this very body." Where could the omnipresent soul of the knower of atman go? Just as the lifeless slough of a snake is cast off and lies on an ant-hill, so does his body lie; his soul shines as Brahman. As milk poured into milk becomes one with milk, as water poured into water becomes one with water, as oil poured into oil becomes one with oil, so the illumined soul absorbed in Brahman becomes one with Brahman. A free soul, however, out of compassion for mankind, may of his own free will again assume a human body and work for the welfare of mankind.

Once his ignorance is destroyed, a man enters into the realm of light, freedom, knowledge, and reality and never comes back to the world of darkness, bondage, ignorance, and illusion. Once the butterfly has emerged from the chrysalis, it no more crawls on the earth, but flits from flower to flower, bathes in the light of the sun.

Such is the ultimate destiny of the human soul.

7. PANTHEISM AND THE PROBLEMS OF HUMAN SOCIETY

For the Pantheist the basic problems of human life have their origin in the experience of the loss of identity with God in whom all life dwells. There are no problems which originate in those dimensions of the universe which transcend human life. Disharmony appears when individual human life loses a true sense of destiny through preoccupation with temporary fulfillment of bodily desires, or loses a sense of the oneness of all life through preoccupation with selfish goals.

W. T. Stace analyzes Western civilization in general and American civilization in particular from pantheistic assumptions. He believes that the failure to strive primarily for the spiritual values which derive from the love of God, particularly in America, is a primary cause of war, since war is a by-product of greed. This materialism also leads to unhappiness and social injustice because human wants, through advertising, are increased far beyond needs, and wealth becomes more important than justice in the distribution of goods.

Albert Schweitzer has written widely on religion and philosophical matters. It probably would be a mistake to say that all of his written thoughts fall into a pantheistic perspective, but the ideas by which he justifies a "reverance for life" clearly seem to do so. The feeling of oneness with all of life leads to acceptance of the mystery of the world, a rich and beautiful fulfillment of life for the individual and a necessity to enhance the will-to-live in all of life. Conflict can be overcome only by the establishment of a "spiritual relationship with the universe."

Why Do We Fail

W. T. Stace

Now what about our national scale of values, if one may
speak of such a thing? What sort of a scale is it? We know that
Oriental peoples and especially Indians always accuse the West in
general, but America in particular, of what they call materialism.
Mr. Vincent Sheean in his book, Lead Kindly Light, which he
wrote after a visit to India during which he was present at the
assassination of Mr. Gandhi, repeated this charge of materialism
against us. He even said that the materialism of the West is the
main cause of its constant wars, and that the only road to peace is
to alter our philosophy in this respect. These are not words
which we can afford to neglect, if we really want peace, if we
really want an end of those holocausts in which our sons are blown
to pieces. So we want to know whether this charge of materialism
against us is true or false.

First of all, what does materialism mean? It does not,
when it is made an accusation against us, have anything to do with
what is technically called materialism by writers on philosophy.
This philosophic materialism is the belief that everything in the
world is made of matter, that there are no non-material things,
that everything, including our thoughts and minds, is really composed of material atoms. What we are accused of has nothing to
do with any such scientific or metaphysical hypothesis. It has to
do with our scale of values. And I think I can give a fairly good
rough definition of it. A materialist, in this moral sense, is a
man who places money and material things generally at the top of
his scale of values. To use our old phrase from the earlier
essay, he puts the things of the body above the things of the spirit.
Or to use once again the phrase of Socrates, materialism means

"heaping up the greatest amount of money and not caring about wisdom and truth and the greatest improvement of the soul."

Now we might try to defend ourselves by saying that this charge of materialism is true of the masses of men everywhere and not especially truer of the West than of the East. This would be a poor defense, since it would consist in saying only that other people are as bad as we are. But apart from that, I am afraid we cannot say even that this defense is true. If we look at India, from whence in particular the accusation proceeds, we shall not find it to be true. The Indian scale of values has never been at all like ours. On the whole it is true to say that in India the love of God has always been put above the love of material things. India is a civilization based on religion, while ours is a civilization based on wealth. Of course I know that such generalizations as this are always suspect. And rightly. It is difficult to say even what they mean, not to mention the question of how to prove them true. Do we mean, when we make such statements, that a majority of the population in India, say more than 50 per cent, care more for religion than for material goods, and that in the United States the state of affairs is the reverse? This seems, to say the least, a very crude interpretation to give to the kind of thing we are saying. It is not so easy, so simple as that. Yet even this crude meaning is not wholly wide of the mark.

One way of judging the main values of a civilization is to look at its great men and especially at the men whom it most admires. To know what kind of man a nation most admires will give us a key to the things it thinks valuable. Another way is to look at its fruits, to ask what notable things it has contributed to the world. For instance, it seems fair to say that the Greeks placed the things of the mind and spirit, such as philosophy, science, mathematics, and art, very high in their scale of values, much higher than most other peoples have ever done, and certainly much higher than we in America do now. For art and science and philosophy are the most notable things they contributed to the world. And their great men were mostly artists, poets, philosophers, and scientists. We might still try to argue that this tells us only about their extremely few great men, the very cream of Greek society, and that we learn nothing from it about the values of those vast masses of Greek humanity who just lived and married and had children and died, leaving no record, so that we know nothing of them. That Sophocles and Aeschylus and Euripides were great poets shows only, we might say, that Sophocles and Aeschylus and Euripides were great poets. It shows nothing at all about the struggling masses of hundreds of thousands of contemporary Greeks whose names are not even known. But I do not think this is at all true. The great men of a nation on the whole are men representative of the nation. They are of one blood and stock with the masses from whom they spring, and the values cherished in the whole society, both by leaders and by the obscure, are likely to be fundamentally similar. On the whole a nation will tend to produce what it admires most, and what it does not admire will not flourish in it.

In India it is certainly true that the kind of man its vast population has always admired most is the saint, the religious man. And this fact lets us at once into the secret of its scale of values. Also any historian could easily show that most Indian institutions, including those of which we are inclined to disapprove, such as caste, have a religious basis. I cannot of course go into that. I am only trying to say what I mean, and how I would try to show, if I had time, that India is not materialist in the way they say we are, and that Indian culture does actually place spiritual values, not material values, at the top of its scale.

It may well be retorted that we certainly do not want to be like India with its grinding poverty, its oppression of the poor, its absence of all democratic values (until recently), its caste system, its gross superstitions, its diseases, its attitudes of pessimism, resignation, and stagnation. But this is really beside the point. We do not want to copy the bad things of India, but we might want to copy the good things. Even for what we in the West choose to call bad things, there might be much to be said. It is by no means certain (to me at least) that resignation and pessimism are attitudes inferior to blind energism, the itch to keep altering things, and the shallow optimism of a chimerical ideal of progress. And as regards the poverty of India, perhaps it comes as much from a religious spirit which prefers spiritual to material goods as it does from the inefficiency and ignorance to which we attribute it. But the main point is that whatever we may

121

think about these matters, the Indian scale of values which places
the love of God at the top of the scale and the love of material
things much lower down is perhaps something from which we
might learn.

All this, however, shows only that India is <u>not</u> materialistic.
It does not show that we are! Is the charge true, then, that Western civilization generally, and American civilization in particular,
are materialistic? Let us look at some of those features of our
civilization from which its basic attitudes and assumptions can be
deduced. Consider for example our attitude toward socialism.
Whether or not a socialistic organization of society would in the
end be wise, its motive at least is humanitarian. It argues that
a system of completely free enterprise actually results in an unjust distribution of wealth--in excessive wealth for a few and extreme poverty for the many. Its object is to correct this by a
system which, it believes, would insure a juster distribution.
Thus its essential aim is social justice. We cannot quarrel with
this aim; we can only doubt the wisdom of the means. I am not
arguing here either for or against socialism. It is open to doubt
whether the measures it proposes, the national ownership of the
means of production, actually tend to produce the justice which it
desires. I do not propose to discuss that issue. I want to draw
attention to another aspect of the matter. One of the great arguments against socialism, perhaps I might say the main argument,
is that it would stifle the incentive to produce, and so decrease
the total production of wealth in one community. Let us assume
that this is correct.

Under socialism the community would produce less wealth
than it does under a system of free enterprise. Whether this is
true or not I do not know. But for the purposes of argument, let
us assume that it is true. Does this show that socialism would
be a bad policy to adopt? Not unless you make another assumption which is that the sole end of the economic system is to amass
the greatest possible amount of wealth, regardless of whether it
is justly distributed or not. The socialist might quite reasonably
reply that he admits that less wealth would be produced, because
of loss of incentive, but that there would be greater justice in its
distribution. Which do you prefer, he might ask--a society

122

vastly rich but with economic injustice rampant, or a poorer society, having no more than enough for its needs, but with economic justice spread everywhere through it. You see that the question being asked is: Which do you place higher in your scale of values wealth or justice?

Now I think it would be unfair to say that those who condemn socialism on the ground that it will result in a loss of wealth do not care at all about a just distribution. No doubt they would argue that a system of free enterprise does more to insure justice than a socialistic system would. Such an argument smells rather unpleasantly of a thing that goes by the name of laissez faire. But what I want to draw attention to is not that. It is rather that this whole side of the question is commonly ignored. It tends to be taken for granted that the supreme end of the economic system is the amassing by the society of the vastest possible amount of wealth, other considerations such as those of justice being either forgotten or at best regarded as subsidiary. If I were to urge that it might be better for us if we were a relatively poor nation, say like Sweden, I should be thought hopelessly unpractical. But this emphasis on the mere amount of wealth, with very much less emphasis on its just distribution, is an indication that we in our hearts, whatever words may be on our lips, place wealth above justice in our scale of values.

There are other signs that the mere amassing of vast quantities of wealth, irrespective of the justice of its distribution, is the sole thing most of us think about in our economic reasonings. The total figures of trade, of imports and exports, the total national income--these are the things which always figure in the charts, tables, statistics that are published. And these are the figures that are quoted as being the criterion of our prosperity. Statistics tending to show how <u>much</u> we make are blazoned abroad in newspapers, books, government returns; but statistics tending to show how justly the wealth is distributed are not in evidence.

But there are countries in the world which are small and not very rich and not at all powerful, where wealth is not worshipped as the sole end--little, comparatively unimportant countries, one might perhaps say (one might give the Scandinavian countries as

123

examples); where men are content with what we should think small incomes; where very few people have refrigerators, cars, radios, televisions; where peace, quiet, home life, the thought and reading of leisure hours still form the substance of the life of the people, rather than the feverish rush after money which obtains here, and which leaves no time for the older and simpler and better patterns of living. Our scale of values, I say, without hesitation, is inferior to these, because it is more materialistic.

We see the same thing in that phrase which is so constantly on our lips--the standard of living. It is assumed by all our newspapers, by our senators and congressmen, by everyone we meet in the street, that the glory of America is its standard of living, which is higher than in any other country in the world. It is assumed that the supreme end of all policy must be to keep up or increase this standard of living at all costs. It is taken for granted that anything which would lower it is ipso facto bad. But what is the standard of living? If it meant the genuine standards of a good life, wisdom and knowledge and loving care for human happiness, we should indeed be fortunate if our country had the highest standard of living in the world. We should be right to insist that this must be the supreme end of all our efforts. But nothing of the sort is in our minds. In our national philosophy the "standard of living" means a radio, a car, a refrigerator, a television set for everybody. These material ends are what we mean by "the good life."

And where does this materialistic philosophy lead us? I think Mr. Vincent Sheean was quite right in saying that it leads us into wars. Plato said more than 2,000 years ago that wars are caused by greed and especially by the desire for luxury. And this is still true. I do not deny that there may be, and indeed frequently are, idealistic motives involved in wars. I do not deny that the late great wars were fought largely on moral issues. But the point is that these moral issues themselves would not arise if it were not for human greed . . . .

Let us now look at another remarkable phenomenon of our societies which is symptomatic of our materialism--I mean the enormous growth of advertising. Advertisement has a legitimate place and value in the social organism. Its value consists in the fact that it provides information as to what products are available on the market and where they can be got. If I wanted a razor or a can of soup and did not know who made and sold these things, I should be much at a loss. But this is the sole legitimate function of advertising. When it goes beyond this, it becomes parasitic on society, a useless, valueless, and positively harmful activity, a sign of disease, a cancer in the social body.

That the business of advertising as it actually exists in our midst is largely the art of skillful lying, I think it hardly necessary to insist. I do not deny that there is some more or less honest advertising, and it may be a fact that some of our best business firms try to keep their advertisements within the bounds of truth. But I believe that this sense of truth in advertising, though it exists, is very much the lesser portion. Most advertisers care nothing about it. You advertise a summer resort. You exaggerate its charms, and you say nothing about its disadvantages. That is, you lie. You include pictures or photographs skillfully done so as to make the gardens or the buildings look larger or more splendid than they are. You lie again. Or you advertise a toothpaste and say that it is the best on the market, that it whitens your teeth better than any other. This must be a lie, because you have not tried all other toothpastes and formed an impartial judgment as to which is the best. Possibly this does not mislead anyone very much, so that it may be said that no harm is done. But that it does not mislead only means that you are such a notorious liar that no one believes you. And as to its doing no harm, that is quite untrue. The harm of it is not only that you have become a liar, but that the sense of truthfulness and honesty in the whole community is undermined and largely destroyed. The result is a low standard of business ethics . . .

But it is not in fact this matter of the untruthfulness of most advertising that is the worst thing about it. There is a much worse evil connected with it. It is that advertising creates wants in people which did not exist before, perfectly unnecessary wants. This is, in fact, one of the main purposes of such advertising. You invent a gadget or a new food product. Sometimes, of course, you may have invented something for which there is a real need,

125

and then you are a public benefactor. But in a vast majority of cases there is no real benefit to society in your product. There may be in fact no desire for it. So you get to work to create a demand by an advertising campaign, by dinning into the ears of the public how much better it will be if it uses your product. Then when people get accustomed to using it, an artificially fostered desire for it grows up. In this way the number and variety of human wants is constantly being increased. In this way the demand for luxurious living grows. And since the demand for luxuries is a main cause of war, it follows that the art of advertisement has its own measure of responsibility for war.

And the chief evil of all this is that, whereas the best receipt for human happiness lies in keeping the number of your wants small, so that you are easily satisfied, this advertising process does the exact opposite. It constantly increases the number of your wants, makes it constantly harder for you to be satisfied, and harder for you to be happy. Happiness lies in the adjustment of what you have to what you want, the equilibrium between the two. So long as you have few wants, equilibrium is easy and men can be happy. But in our age, our civilization, the monstrous accumulation of human wants, largely caused by advertising, is a destroyer of happiness . . . .

Where then are the great philosophies or philosophers of America? Undoubtedly America's characteristic philosophy is pragmatism, and its greatest representative was John Dewey. What does this philosophy tell us about the values of life? We know what Plato thought. He ranged human values in an order-- wisdom and knowledge, honor or prestige, money or material goods, pleasure. In general it was his essential message that the things of the spirit are higher than material things, the things of the body. And this has always been the burden of the teaching of all the great prophets, saints, and sages of the world. What then is pragmatism's scale of values? I do not want to make a charge of materialism against those academic philosophers, such as John Dewey, who are the professional exponents of pragmatism. It is very difficult to say whether such an accusation would be true. But I will simply ask the question: Why is it that pragmatism makes the enormous appeal to the people of America which it undoubtedly does make? Why has it become, in some sense, the popular philosophy of America? I have myself no doubt of the answer. It is because, rightly or wrongly, the public sees in pragmatism a justification of its own materialistic values. Pragmatism, or instrumentalism, as Professor Dewey called it, teaches that all thinking--and this will include science, philosophy, and, in general, the things of the mind--is in the end only instrumental to, and justified by, its practical utility. Science and philosophy, and the things of the mind generally, are not ends in themselves, as the Greeks thought, but means to practical utility. You can see at once how this can be interpreted (I will say "twisted," if my professional philosophical friends prefer it) as justifying materialism. For practical utility means for most people the acquisition of material goods, material comforts, the things of the body. If pragmatism is interpreted in this way, it means in the end that spiritual and intellectual things are of no value in themselves, but only as they minister to material ends. This means that material ends are placed higher in the scale of values than spiritual ends. And this is the definition of materialism. Thus the vast popularity of pragmatism becomes evidence of a fundamental materialism in the minds of the American people.

We in American pride ourselves on being what we call "practical." As a philosophy of life, pragmatism is nothing but the apotheosis of the practical. But what is meant in the popular mind by being "practical"? (We will not ask what professional pragmatists mean by it.) Nothing, I think, is meant except being materialistic, valuing above everything material things and the satisfaction of purely material needs. When the ideals of the Sermon on the Mount are called unpractical, as they sometimes are, what is meant except that they exalt spiritual things and set wealth and worldly power low in the scale of values? When an artist, driven on by his vision of beauty and content to live on crusts of bread, is called an unpractical person, what is meant except that he values his vision above material comfort? I am persuaded that the word practical, as it is commonly used among us, simply means materialistic. And the mere fact that we in America regard ourselves as especially practical people simply indicates that we are materialistic people. The businessman is the practical man par excellence because it is his essential function to cater to material wants. The artist, the thinker, the philosopher, the saint, and the man of learning are not practical. They are tolerated by the practical man partly because they provide what are in his view unimportant but harmless activities to occupy men's leisure time, forms of amusement, and partly because he sees that, in various indirect ways, they can be made to minister to what he regards as the important, that is the material, things. Science, above all, he values in this way. It aids industry and provides material comforts. But for science itself simply as a form of knowledge, as ministering to the hunger of the mind, he has no use at all. Science, art, and philosophy are really so much nonsense, except in so far as they help in various ways to subserve material ends. And if he does not say that the love of God is nonsense too, that is only because he is too cowardly.

For these reasons when I see it written or hear it said that ours is the greatest civilization in the history of the world, that we are the most wonderful people, when I hear of modern progress and the progressive character of Western culture, I cannot help but wondering. I think not only of ancient Greece but even of poor benighted India, with all its poverty and bodily disease and its so-called stagnation, but with its heart set on God. And the words of the poet keep ringing in my ears:

> For frantic boast and foolish word
> Thy mercy on thy people, Lord!

All that I have been saying is, of course, very unpractical. But then I am by profession an unpractical man. It may be that these things of which I have spoken are in some sense inevitable, that we cannot now turn back along the road of materialism down which we long ago started--although I refuse to believe that it is too late. But I know that it is the road which leads to war rather than to peace, to darkness rather than to light.

Reverence for Life

Albert Schweitzer

Reverence for life means being seized by the unfathomable, forward-moving will which is inherent in all Being. It raises us above perception of the world of objects and makes us into the tree that is safe from drought because it is planted by the water.

The man who subscribes to this ethic is soon made to feel, by its demands upon him, the fire glowing within the abstract phrase, "reverence for life." Its edict is the rule of universal love. This is the ethics of Jesus reinforced by reason.

Through it man gives value to his existence, no matter what its circumstances or what paths he must tread . . . .

The idea of Reverence for Life offers itself as the realistic answer to the realistic question of how man and the world are related to each other. Of the world man knows only that everything which exists is, like himself, a manifestation of the Will-to-Live. With this world he stands in a relation of passivity and of activity. On the one hand he is subordinate to the course of events which is given in this totality of life; on the other hand he is capable of affecting the life which comes within his reach by hampering or promoting it, by destroying or maintaining it.

The one possible way of giving meaning to his existence is that of raising his natural relation to the world to a spiritual one.

As a being in a passive relation to the world he comes into a spiritual relation to it by resignation. True resignation consists in this: that man, feeling his subordination to the course of world-happenings, wins his way to inward freedom from the fortunes which shape the outward side of his existence. Inward freedom means that he finds strength to deal with everything that is hard in his lot, in such a way that it all helps to make him a deeper and more inward person, to purify him, and to keep him calm and peaceful. Resignation, therefore, is the spiritual and ethical affirmation of one's own existence. Only he who has gone through the stage of resignation is capable of world-affirmation.

As a being in an active relation to the world he comes into a spiritual relation with it by not living for himself alone but feeling himself one with all life that comes within his reach. He will feel all life's experiences as his own, he will give it all the help that he possibly can, and will feel all the saving and promotion of life that he has been able to effect as the deepest happiness that can ever fall to his lot.

Let a man once begin to think about the mystery of his life and the links which connect him with the life that fills the world, and he cannot but bring to bear upon his own life and all other life that comes within his reach the principle of Reverence for Life, and manifest this principle by ethical world- and life-affirmation expressed in action. Existence will thereby become harder for him in every respect than it would be if he lived for himself, but at the same time it will be richer, more beautiful, and happier. It will become, instead of mere living, a real experience of life.

Beginning to think about life and the world leads a man directly and almost irresistibly to Reverence for Life. Such thinking leads to no conclusions which could point in any other direction.

If the man who has once begun to think wishes to persist in his mere living he can do so only by surrendering himself, whenever this idea takes possession of him, to thoughtlessness, and stypefying himself therein. If he perseveres with thinking he can come to no other result than Reverence for Life.

Any thinking by which men assert that they are reaching scepticism or life without ethical ideas is not thinking but thoughtlessness which poses as thinking, and it proves itself to be such by the fact that it is unconcerned about the mystery of life and the world . . . .

Any profound world-view is mysticism, in that it brings men into a spiritual relation with the Infinite. The world-view of Reverence for Life is ethical mysticism. It allows union with the infinite to be realized by ethical action. This ethical mysticism originates in logical thinking. If our will-to-live begins to think about itself and the world, we come to experience the life of the world, so far as it comes within our reach, in our own life, and to devote our will-to-live to the infinite will-to-live through the deeds we do. Rational thinking, if it goes deep, ends of necessity in the non-rational of mysticism. It has, of course, to deal with life and the world, both of which are non-rational entities.

In the world the infinite will-to-live reveals itself to us as will-to-create, and this is full of dark and painful riddles for us; in ourselves it is revealed as will-to-love, which will through us remove the dilemma (Selbstentzweiung) of the will-to-live.

The world-view of Reverence for Life has, therefore, a religious character. The man who avows his belief in it, and acts upon the belief, shows a piety which is elemental . . . .

The ethics of reverence for life makes no distinction between higher and lower, more previous and less precious lives. It has good reasons for this omission. For what are we doing, when we establish hard and fast gradations in value between living organisms, but judging them in relation to ourselves, by whether they seem to stand closer to us or farther from us. This is a wholly subjective standard. How can we know what importance other living organisms have in themselves and in terms of the universe ?

In making such distinctions, we are apt to decide that there are forms of life which are worthless and may be stamped out

131

without its mattering at all. This category may include anything from insects to primitive peoples, depending on circumstances.

To the truly ethical man, all life is sacred, including forms of life that from the human point of view may seem to be lower than ours. He makes distinctions only from case to case, and under pressure of necessity, when he is forced to decide which life he will sacrifice in order to preserve other lives. In thus deciding from case to case, he is aware that he is proceeding subjectively and arbitrarily, and that he is accountable for the lives thus sacrificed.

The man who is guided by the ethics of reverence for life stamps out life only from inescapable necessity, never from thoughtlessness. He seizes every occasion to feel the happiness of helping living things and shielding them from suffering and annihilation.

Whenever we harm any form of life, we must be clear about whether it was really necessary to do so. We must not go beyond the truly unavoidable harm, not even in seemingly insignificant matters. The farmer who mows down a thousand flowers in his meadow, in order to feed his cows, should be on guard, as he turns homeward, not to decapitate some flower by the roadside, just by way of thoughtlessly passing the time. For then he sins against life without being under the compulsion of necessity.

Those who carry out scientific experiments with animals, in order to apply the knowledge gained to the alleviation of human ills, should never reassure themselves with the generality that their cruel acts serve a useful purpose. In each individual case they must ask themselves whether there is a real necessity for imposing such a sacrifice upon a living creature. They must try to reduce the suffering insofar as they are able. It is inexcusable for a scientific institution to omit anesthesis in order to save time and trouble. It is horrible to subject animals to torment merely in order to demonstrate to students phenomena that are already familiar.

The very fact that animals, by the pain they endure in experiments, contribute so much to suffering humanity, should forge a new and unique kind of solidarity between them and us. For that reason alone it is incumbent upon each and every one of us to do all possible good to nonhuman life . . . .

The elemental fact, present in our consciousness every moment of our existence, is: I am life that wills to live, in the midst of life that wills to live. The mysterious fact of my will to live is that I feel a mandate to behave with sympathetic concern toward all the wills to live which exist side by side with my own. The essence of Goodness is: Preserve life, promote life, help life to achieve its highest destiny. The essence of Evil is: Destroy life, harm life, hamper the development of life.

The fundamental principle of ethics, then, is reverence for life. All the goodness one displays toward a living organism is, at bottom, helping to preserve and further its existence.

In the main, reverence for life dictates the same sort of behavior as the ethical principle of love. But reverence for life contains within itself the rationale of the commandment to love, and it calls for compassion for all creature life.

It should also be observed that the ethics of love governs only our conduct toward others, not toward ourselves. Truthfulness, which is a fundamental element of the ethical personality, cannot be deduced from it. But the reverence we should manifest toward our own existence commands us to remain always true to ourselves, to reject all the distortions of our true selves that we might be tempted to practice in one situation or another, and never to slacken in the struggle to remain wholly truthful.

Only the ethics of reverence for life is complete. It is so in every respect. The ethics that deals only with the conduct of man toward his fellow men can be exceedingly profound and vital. But it remains incomplete. Thus it was inevitable that man's intellect should ultimately have reached the point of being offended by the heartless treatment of other living creatures, which had hitherto been considered acceptable, and should have demanded that ethics include them within its merciful purview. Ethical thought was

133

slow and hesitant about taking this demand seriously. Only in recent times has visible progress been made along these lines, and only recently has the world begun to pay some regard to the undertaking.

But already the world is beginning to recognize that the ethics of reverence for life, which requires kindness toward all living organisms, accords with the natural feelings of thinking men.

By ethical conduct toward all creatures, we enter into a spiritual relationship with the universe.

In the universe, the will to live is in conflict with itself. In us, it seeks to be at peace with itself.

In the universe, the will to live is a fact; in us, it is a revelation.

The mind commands us to be different from the universe. By reverence for life we become, in profound, elemental and vital fashion, devout.

PART THREE

NATURAL THEISM

Borden Bowne
David Elton Trueblood
Thomas Paine
Daniel L. Morris
Jacques Maritain
Arthur H. Compton
John Wild
C. S. Lewis

1. INTRODUCTION

The term "theism" seems to have had a history of interpretation since the beginning of its use in the seventeenth century.

It has been used in contrast to "atheism," a term signifying belief in <u>no</u> God. When used in contrast to the term "polytheism" it has emphasized the <u>oneness</u> of God. When used in contrast to the term "monotheism" it has emphasized a particular understanding of the one God, usually in Christian terms. When used in contrast to the term "deism" it has emphasized the <u>immanence</u> of God, and when used in contrast to the term "pantheism" it has emphasized the <u>transcendence</u> of God. It has also been used as a term synonymous to the term "deism," especially in the eighteenth century.

From this confusion it seems necessary that some clarity is needed when the term is used. This writer believes that the most sensible way in which the term "theism" can be used is to refer to a belief in a God who is transcendent to the natural world and who causes the natural world to exist through creative activity. The natural world, therefore, does not exist <u>within</u> the reality of God, as in Pantheism, but as an objective reality <u>outside</u> the transcendent God. The world, for the Pantheist, is an emanation <u>from</u> God. The world, for the Theist, is a creation <u>of</u> God. This definition of Theism, however, does not include the belief that God is completely different from the world which He has created, as has sometimes been claimed in the name of "deism" and "theism." Unless one believes that there is some affinity between the intelligence of human beings and the intelligence of God, nothing at all of God can be known. It is the theist's contention that though human being is finite and the being of God is infinite there is some affinity of being, if not identity, between them.

What we are seeking to define is not just <u>Theism</u> but a religious perspective which is called Natural Theism. "Natural" is to be understood methodologically. The knowledge which is gained about God is that which is inferred from knowledge of the beings and things in the natural world. Through an attempt to understand nature one comes to understand, through logical inference, something of a Reality beyond nature upon which nature depends. That Reality which is discovered in this way is such as to fit the definition we have drawn of Theism.

The basic assumptions of the religious perspective of Natural Theism, as we have defined it, are as follows:

1. The idea of a supernatural God is a reasonable hypothesis drawn from the evidence of nature.

2. God is experienced only through the medium of the created world, never directly through intuition or mystical vision.

3. The hypothesis that God is the cause of all natural law is supportive of science which seeks to understand that law.

4. The moral law is given to human reason in the act of creation.

5. The conditions of natural human life make immortality not only desirable but also a reasonable possibility.

The authors of the selections which follow have been identified with different organized religious groups, philosophical movements and professional interests. Trueblood is a Quaker, Lewis was an Anglican, Maritain and Wild were Roman Catholics. Paine called himself a Deist and would not identify with any kind of traditional Christianity. Bowne called himself a Theist and was instrumental in the development of Personalism. Nobel laureate Compton and Morris were physicists. In spite of these differences, however, their basic ideas and methods of understanding are similar enough to fit together into a religious perspective. It should be noted that while Roman Catholicism embraces a Natural Theism it also advocates a special knowledge of God which comes through revelation only. This revealed knowledge, however, does not contradict the knowledge gained through the natural light of

138

reason. It completes it. Thus, while Roman Catholicism advocates Natural Theism it would be wrong to say that this is completely descriptive of it.

The introductory article by <u>Bowne</u> supports the definition of Theism which has been stated above and clarifies some of the differences between Theism and Pantheism. The essential difference is to be found in the relation of God and the world. For the Pantheist the world is an emanation from God and for the Theist the world is a creation of God. The Pantheistic world is deterministic for two reasons: as a part of God it has no being of its own; and, since there is no creative power in God He must operate from necessity, not freedom. For the Theist, however, creativity is a mysterious reality which brings about new being, not out of necessity, but the free choice of purpose. Since finite human beings, who are the products of God's creative purpose, also possess freedom they may act with purpose.

<u>God and the World</u>

Borden P. Bowne

To explain the universe we need not a substance, but an agent; not substantiality, but causality. The latter expresses all the meaning of the former, and is free from misleading sense-implications. Metaphysics further shows that every agent is a unit, uncompounded and indivisible. God, then, is not the infinite stuff or substance, but the infinite cause or agent, one and indivisible. From this point all the previous views of the relation of God to the world disappear of themselves. He has no parts and is not a sum. Hence the world is no part of God, nor an emanation from him, nor a sharer in the divine substance; for all these views imply the divisibility of God and also his stuff-like nature. His

From PHILOSOPHY OF THEISM by Borden P. Bowne, pp. 173-174, 178-184, published by Harper & Brothers, 1887.

necessary unity forbids all attempts to identify him with the world, either totally or partially. If the finite be anything real, it must be viewed, not as produced from God, but as produced by God; that is, as created. Only creation can reconcile the reality of the finite with the unity of the infinite. For the finite, if real, is an agent, and as such it cannot be made out of anything, but is posited by the infinite . . . .

In any case the spirit must be viewed as created. It is not made, for making implies a pre-existent stuff. Creation means to posit something in existence which before was not. Concerning it two consistent questions are possible. (1) Who is the agent? (2) How is it possible? To the first question the answer is, God. To the second there is no rational answer.

Besides these consistent questions, various inconsistent ones are asked, as, for instance: What is the world made "out of"? The common answer is, out of nothing. Both question and answer are worthy of each other. Both are haunted by the notion of a pre-existent stuff, and, to complete the absurdity, the answer suggests nothing as that stuff; as if by some process God fashioned the nothing into something. The old saw, from nothing nothing comes, is also played off against creation, but without effect. The truth therein is merely that nothing can ever produce, or be formed into anything. But theism does not teach that nothing produces something, but rather that God, the all-powerful, has caused the world to exist. No more does theism hold that God took a mass of nothing and made something out of it, but rather that he caused a new existence to begin, and that, too, in such a way that he was no less after creation than before. God neither made the world from nothing as a raw material, nor from himself; both notions are absurd; but he caused that to be which before was not. Of course, we have no recipe for this process. Creation is a mystery; but any other view is a contradiction of thought itself. Creation is the only conception which reconciles the unity of God with the existence of the finite. Perhaps, too, we need not be especially troubled at the mystery, as mystery is omnipresent; and besides, creation is not our affair.

Some speculators have sought relief from the mystery of

creation in the claim that the world was not made from nothing, but from the potentialities of the divine nature. The only intelligible meaning of this view is that the world existed as a conception in the divine thought before it became real. This conceptual existence constituted its potentiality, but this in no way shows how that which existed as conception was posited in reality. For the rest, the claim in question is only a form of words of learned sound but without meaning.

The world depends upon a divine activity, and is not a mode of the infinite substance. But this also admits of a double interpretation. We may regard this activity as a necessary consequence of the divine nature, or as resting upon the divine will. The former view is held by all the higher forms of pantheism, and even some theists have held that God must create. This view also is double, according to our thought of being in general. In one view God exists as the all-conditioning substance, and the world, as its necessary implication, co-exists eternally with it. Spinoza's doctrine is the best expression of this view. But this conception compels us either to affirm that all things are eternal, or else to declare change to be an unaccountable illusion of the finite. This view, which might be called static pantheism, has generally been exchanged for another, which might be called dynamic pantheism. In the latter view the infinite is forever energizing according to certain laws, and producing thereby a great variety of products. But these laws are throughout expressions of its nature and admit of no change. The world-order is the divine nature, and, conversely, the divine nature is the world-order. Hence pantheists of this order have always been the stoutest opponents of miracles, for miracles imply a will apart from and above nature. If the world-order were really the divine nature, then, of course, God could not depart from that order without denying himself. This conviction is further strengthened by the natural tendency of the untaught mind to mistake the uniformities of experience for necessities of being; and thus the world-order is finally established as necessarily invariable, the mind not recognizing its own shadow. This is the view which underlies all schemes of philosophical evolution, and a large part of current scientific speculation, or rather speculation on the supposed basis of scientific facts and principles. While static pantheism says, In the beginning was

the eternal substance or the eternal reason co-existing changeless-
ly with all its implications; dynamic pantheism says, In the beginning was force, necessary and persistent, and by its inherent necessity forever generating law and system. When this view is
combined with the impersonality and unconsciousness of the world-
ground, it becomes identical with vulgar atheism. The world-
ground is simply the unitary principle and basal reality of the cosmos, and is exhausted in its cosmic manifestation. There is immanence without transcendence; and God and the world are but opposite names for the same thing.

Static pantheism is an untenable abstraction which, if allowed, would bring the universe to a standstill and load thought
with illusion. It would give us a rigid and resting being from which
all time and change would be excluded, and which could in no way
be connected with our changing experience. If we should call that
experience delusion, the delusion itself would be as unaccountable
as the fact. On this rock the Eleatic philosophy was wrecked, and
here, too, Spinoza's system went to pieces. The truth, then, in
pantheism, if there be any, lies in dynamic pantheism. But even
this view has but scanty value, and this value lies in its emphasis
of law in opposition to a blind and reckless arbitrariness. For the
rest, pantheism is unsatisfactory in all respects. First, it is
ethically objectionable, because it leads to a complete determinism, both in God and man. All things happen by necessity, and
nothing is the outcome of proper prevision and purpose. The
world and all its details are determined from everlasting. There
is no room for freedom, hence none for purpose, and hence none
for any rational distinction of good and evil.

2. THE EXISTENCE OF GOD

Elton Trueblood argues that certain scientific theories about the natural world are best supported by a theistic hypothesis. The theory of evolution presents a continuous evolvement of nature into higher forms of life of which mind is the highest. Both that evolvement and the nature of mind itself are evidence of the existence of purpose in evolution which cannot be explained solely in terms of nature itself. The second law of thermodynamics gives reason to believe in the ultimate dissipation of energy. Since this means that the natural world will have an end, it must also have had a beginning. It, therefore, could have originated only by a creative source of energy outside the natural order. Nature points beyond nature for an explanation of nature; that is, to God.

The Evidence of Nature

David Elton Trueblood

The Fact of Evolution

Though there are many minor arguments about the precise mode of evolution that has occurred and is occurring in the natural order, there is little argument in the modern world about the general principle to the effect that the forms which we see at present have come by innumerable steps, longer or shorter, from other and different forms which have preceded them. The principle of evolution, thus broadly understood, is to be distinguished, both

---

"The Fact of Evolution" (pp. 148-159) from THE LOGIC OF BELIEF by David Elton Trueblood. Copyright 1942 by Harper & Row, Publishers, Inc. Reprinted by permission of the publisher.

logically and historically, from Darwinism, the special evolutionary theory which seeks to make the notion of natural selection a sufficient means of explanation. The Darwinian is necessarily an evolutionist, but one can be an evolutionist without being a Darwinian.

The conclusion to which most biological scholars have been driven is that all living creatures are the descendants of earlier and, in many cases, less developed living creatures. Species, we now believe, have not been immutable from the beginning, but have arisen from other species. It is likely that the earliest form of life, and possibly the ancestor of all living things, was a unicellular organism, popularly known as "primordial ooze." The evidence we have is by no means adequate to demonstration, and there is truth in the contention of skeptics that evolution is a highly speculative theory, but the evidence is sufficient to satisfy most minds which have considered it fairly.

It is well known that the great intellectual struggle over evolutionary theory which took place three quarters of a century ago was occasioned largely by the inclusion of man in the evolutionary scheme. For a number of reasons it was widely supposed that this inclusion, if sustained, made religious faith difficult or even impossible. Curiously enough, it is this very inclusion which subsequent reflection has fastened upon as one of the chief features of the natural order among those which substantiate and corroborate the theistic hypothesis.

The evidence that man is akin to other living creatures by virtue of descent is abundant. Alfred Russel Wallace's summary of this evidence, though made fifty years ago, would hardly be changed by contemporary scholars.

The facts now very briefly summarized amount almost to a demonstration that man, in his bodily structure, has been derived from the lower animals, of which he is the culminating development. In his possession of rudimentary structures which are functional in some of the mammalia; in the numerous variations of his muscles and other organs agreeing with characters which are constant in some apes;

144

in his embryonic development, absolutely identical in character with that of mammalia in general, and closely resembling in its details that of the higher quadrumana; in the diseases which he has in common with other mammalia; and in the wonderful approximation of his skeleton to those of one or other of the anthropoid apes, we have an amount of evidence in this direction which it seems impossible to explain away. And this evidence will appear more forcible if we consider for a moment what the rejection of it implies. For the only alternative supposition is, that man has been specially created--that is to say, has been produced in some quite different way from other animals and altogether independently of them. But in that case the rudimentary structures, the animal-like variations, the identical course of development, and all the other animal characteristics he possesses are deceptive, and inevitably lead us, as thinking beings making use of the reason which is our noblest and most distinctive feature, into gross error.[5]

Wallace, it may be remembered, held back from the conclusion that man's higher life also came out of nature, but he seems to have been impelled by the fear that this would involve some disparagement of this higher life. But the higher life of man, found in his mental and spiritual powers, is dependent on the long series of events which Wallace helped so greatly to describe. Unique as man's mind undoubtedly is, man shares much of his mental experience with the humbler creatures. Mind is man's glory, but there are thousands of stages of mental development to be observed in the natural order. Thought and language, now so highly developed, have already been developing for a very long time in order to reach the stage illustrated in the most primitive tribes we now know. Many animals have a kind of language, even though it is qualitatively different from human language. "Thinking is grounded in the process of adjustment between organism and environment

_____

[5]Alfred Russel Wallace, "Darwinism as Applied to Man" in Representative Essays in Modern Thought, pp. 247-248.

and is indeed an extension of that process. "6

The highest point in creation, so far as we know, is the capacity to comprehend the world, but this capacity has arisen by degrees in the natural order. At one end of the evolutionary series is unconscious life and at the other is self-conscious life, but it is all one series. It is reasonable to suppose, as Aristotle taught, that the conclusion of a process gives a more adequate insight into its character than does the beginning. "Primordial ooze" and scientific accuracy belong to a single comprehensive system of historical and genealogical relations, but the science is more revealing than is the ooze.

The fact that a process is rational, does not mean that the ground of that rationality is necessarily revealed in the beginning. In fact the ground of the rationality need not appear until the end of the series of events and then it illuminates the entire process. This is well illustrated in dramatic poetry and in the lives of good men. Seen in retrospect such lives are thoroughly rationalized wholes, because of what, all along, they were becoming.

If the general evolutionary theory is true and if man's life be included in the theory, we cannot escape the conclusion, once more, that mind and nature are akin. We saw earlier that mind and nature are akin because mind truly comprehends nature. We now have an independent line of evidence in that mind arises out of nature. It is genealogically as well as cognitively akin. The convergence of two lines of evidence on one conclusion is a matter of great importance. The relation "akin to" is a symmetrical relation. If mind is akin to nature, nature likewise is akin to mind.

We are thus led to the conclusion, not that a naturalistic metaphysic is adequate, but that the explanation of nature is to be found in mind. Inasmuch as Archbishop Temple has had the honor of emphasizing the point more than most contemporary thinkers, it is appropriate to quote his conclusion, a conclusion which he rightly prints in italics. "The more completely we include Mind

---

6 Temple, Nature, Man and God, p. 128.

within Nature, the more inexplicable must Nature become except by reference to Mind. "[7] A boldly accepted naturalism leads directly to supernaturalism. How can nature include mind as an integral part unless it is grounded in mind? If mind were seen as something alien or accidental, the case would be different, but the farther we go in modern science the clearer it becomes that mental experience is no strange off-shoot. Rather it is something which is deeply rooted in the entire structure.

Science knows nothing of the wholly fortuitous. Though there are some events, especially in sub-atomic physics, to which we cannot assign causes, the general assumption is that there are causes for these events and they would be intelligible if known. This assumption has been well justified by former experience in which the apparently fortuitous or haphazard was finally seen as conforming to an intelligible rule. If, as seems likely, there are no uncaused events, then mind which comes at the apex of the world process, so far as we know it, is really an integral part of the system and a revelation of the nature of nature.

This general conclusion is greatly strengthened by modern studies which stress, in a new and striking way, the fact that the world as we know it is wonderfully adapted to the production of life and, thereby, of the consciousness which depends on life. Professor L. J. Henderson of Harvard University, approaching the subject in a mood quite unlike that of orthodox teleology, and with no theological presuppositions, has shown that a truly amazing combination of circumstances was required to make possible life on the only planet we really know. We have an environment peculiarly fitted for the emergence of life, mind, and spirit. "The fitness of the environment results," we read, "from characteristics which constitute a series of maxima--unique or nearly unique properties of water, carbonic acid, the compounds of carbon, hydrogen, and oxygen, and the ocean--so numerous, so varied, so nearly complete among all things which are concerned in the problem that together they form certainly the greatest possible

---

[7] Temple, op. cit., p. 133.

fitness."[8]

It is important to stress what Professor Henderson says about maxima. For life and consciousness to appear, it is necessary that there should be a combination of winning throws, each of which is as unlikely as a run of several hundred "heads" in tossing an honest penny. The combination is almost fantastic.

> There is, in truth, not one chance in countless millions of millions of millions that the many unique properties of carbon, hydrogen, and oxygen, and especially of their stable compounds water and carbonic acid, which chiefly make up the atmosphere of a new planet, should simultaneously occur in the three elements otherwise than through the operation of a natural law which somehow connects them together. There is no great probability that these unique properties should be without due cause uniquely favorable to the organic mechanism. These are no mere accidents; an explanation is to seek. It must be admitted, however, that no explanation is at hand.[9]

The most fruitful conclusion of such studies lies in the revelation that "cosmic and biological evolution are one." There seems to be a single orderly development with mind and matter belonging to the same inclusive system. In short, studies regarding the fitness of the environment emphasize in a new way the great lesson of evolution to which we have already pointed. "For undeniably," concludes Professor Henderson, "two things which are related together in a complex manner by reciprocal fitness can make up in a very real sense a unit--something quite different from the two alone or the sum of the two or the relationship between the two. In human affairs such a unit arises only from

---

[8] L. J. Henderson, The Fitness of the Environment, New York, 1913, p. 272.

[9] Ibid., p. 276.

effective operation of purpose."[10] Thus the evidence grows that mind is not accidental in nature, and that nature, consequently is not alien to mind.

The Second Law of Thermodynamics

Of all the conclusions reached by the last two centuries of careful scientific work, one of the most revealing, as well as disturbing, is that which points to the degradation of energy. The notion of the progressive degradation of energy, which is based on what is called the "Carnot principle" and finds its formal statement in the Second Law of Thermodynamics, has been known for a century, but we have been surprisingly slow to see its metaphysical implications.

The Second Law of Thermodynamics must be understood in connection with the First Law, that of the conservation of energy. This principle, to be distinguished from the principle of the conservation of matter, was reached independently by several scholars. Mayer, in Germany, announced his conclusions in 1842 and Joule, in England, announced his in 1843. The law holds that the amount of energy in the world is constant, though it changes in form. The fact that the amount of energy is constant does not mean that energy is always available. In so far as we can see the time will come when energy is not available for work. Because there is constant diffusion, and because there is no addition to the total energy, we must contemplate a final condition of absolute stagnation. And it is precisely this to which the Second Law points.

In all physical systems we note a leveling process. A stone thrown in a pool raises waves, but these slowly dissipate until they are no longer observable. The hot stove radiates its heat into the closed room until a uniform temperature is reached. Just as nature may be said figuratively to abhor a vacuum, so nature abhors differentiation and concentration of energy. Thus the stars radiate

---

[10]Ibid., p. 279.

their energy and this energy, so far as we know, never makes a return trip. It is a one-way process. This increase of leveling is called the "increase of entropy." There are many excellent definitions of this, but the following is one of the clearest: "As the useless energy increases, the useful decreases by the same amount. This ratio of useless to useful energy is called entropy. The law of entropy states that the ratio is constantly increasing. This means that the amount of energy available for the energizing process of the world is ever growing less."[11]

The reason why we can get work out of a heat engine is that there is a temperature differential, and the reason we can get work out of a waterfall is that there is a difference in level. The waterfall is useful because there is a low place into which the water can descend. If the leveling process were ever completed all work would be at an end. "We cannot convert the heat of a cold body into work," says Barnes, "for then, without consumption of fuel, we should get unlimited supplies of motive power. Hence we may conclude that the efficiency of a perfectly reversible engine is the maximum possible, and further that it depends solely on the temperatures between which the engine works. It is always possible to get work out of the heat of a body which is hotter than surrounding bodies. But, just as you cannot get blood out of a stone, so you cannot get work out of a body which is colder than surrounding bodies. On this simple fact the second law of thermodynamics is based."[12]

Though the law of entropy is partially a matter of speculation, inasmuch as the conclusion is large in comparison with the field of observation, the conclusion reached is far from fanciful. In fact, no less a physicist than Sir Arthur Eddington calls this law the most certain and the best grounded of all the laws of physics.

---

[11]J. A. McWilliams, Cosmology, New York, 1933, p. 42.

[12]E. W. Barnes, Scientific Theory and Religion, p. 233.

"Carnot's principle," wrote Emile Meyerson, "is a fact, and by far the most important fact, of all science."[13]

It is always possible for some new force, now unknown, to enter, but, on the basis of present observations, there seems to be no rational escape from the prospect of an ultimate dissipation of all energy. This means not only the "death" of our particular solar system, but of any physical system.

This prospect has appealed strongly to some modern minds and has been used for different purposes. The late Henry Adams accepted the concept as valid, not only for physical systems, but also social and political ones as well. Accordingly he wrote The Degradation of Democratic Dogma. To Bertrand Russell and others the concept has seemed to provide adequate ground for despair in the grand manner, a fit subject for rhetorical flourish.

A more careful and critical examination of the metaphysical implications of the Second Law came early from the philosopher, Josiah Royce. Royce was quick to see that the principle we are considering undermines what may be called a religion of progress. Many have sought a substitute for theism in the notion that this world, in spite of occasional relapses, is coming to be more and more a place which harmonizes with man's moral growth. Here is an aspect of the natural world which may be termed a power which makes for righteousness, and this power, it is supposed, is sufficient to meet man's religious needs. But, said Royce, the Carnot principle shows us that progress, as we know it, is a fact of transient significance. "Progress," wrote Royce, "is an incident of a certain thermal process, a kind of episode in the history of the dissipation of the energy of our particular mass of matter, and thus, insofar as we yet know a present occurrence just in our neighborhood, a local item in the news of the universe."[14]

Professor Royce's contention that the Second Law of Ther-

---

[13] Emile Meyerson, Identity and Reality, p. 278.

[14] Josiah Royce, The Religious Aspect of Philosophy, p. 244.

modynamics undermines a religion of progress was not based solely on considerations of time. It is true, of course, that something
can be splendid or even perfect without lasting forever. The difficulty, in Royce's mind, was the deeper one of cosmic indifference.
"It is not because progress is to endure on this planet for a short
or for a long time, but because the world in which this progress is
soon to end seems, thus regarded, wholly indifferent to progress
--this is the gloomy aspect."[15]

But while the Second Law of Thermodynamics thus limits the
rational appeal of an alternative to our grand hypothesis, it actually supports the theistic claim in a remarkable way. In the first
place it now seems clear that the physical world, which we have
come to know, is something which not only will have an end, but
also something which had a beginning. "If the universe is running
down like a clock," says Dr. Inge, "the clock must have been
wound up at a date which we could name if we knew it. The world
if it is to have an end in time, must have had a beginning in
time."[16] This follows strictly from the fact that the law of entropy
is irreversible. A clock which always runs down and is never re-
wound cannot have been running forever.

At first sight it looks as though there is a possible escape
from this conclusion in the concept of the physical world as infinite
in extent or in amount of energy. But this, in fact, is no solution
of the problem, since the notion of an infinite quantity is really
meaningless. The term "infinite sum" has no meaning. However
much there is of energy or of matter there is just that much and no
more. Energy cannot be infinite in amount because it is concerned
with actuality. Time, however, can be infinite in the sense of
possibility of events.

The chief metaphysical significance of the law of entropy consists, not of the evidence of a beginning in time, important as that
is, but rather in the evidence that the natural world is not self-

---

[15]Ibid., p. 245. The italics are Royce's.

[16]W. R. Inge, God and the Astronomers, p. 10.

explanatory. According to natural law, energy loses its efficacy. But without the operation of a totally different principle, there would be no energy to lose its efficacy. Nature points beyond nature for an explanation of nature. The Second Law of Thermodynamics thus points directly to theism as an explanation of the world and the reasoning based upon it provides a modern counterpart to the cosmological argument. [17]

Though we have, in this section, stressed the importance of time, it should be made clear that the reference to time is not strictly necessary to the validity of the argument in general. All of the changes which we know in the world of nature are dependent changes. We refer changes in plant growth to changes in soil, we refer the changes in soil to still other changes, and so on. No single step in the process would even occur apart from the other steps upon which it depends. Therefore the entire chain of causes presupposes the existence of a power which is truly originative, able to account not only for others, but also for itself. "The dependence meant in the argument," says Professor A. E. Taylor, "has nothing to do with succession in time. What is really meant is that our knowledge of any event in Nature is not complete until we know the reason for the event. So long as you only know that A is so because B is so, but cannot tell why B is so, your knowledge is incomplete. It only becomes complete when you are in a position to say that ultimately A is so because Z is so, Z being something which is its own raison d'etre, and therefore such that it

---

[17] The cosmological argument for the existence of God is the argument from the necessity of cause. The argument received its classic formulation in Book X of Plato's Laws and was greatly refined by St. Thomas Aquinas. Though criticized by Kant, it has received the assent of many modern thinkers, especially Catholic philosophers. For a good modern statement see George Hayward Joyce, Principles of Natural Theology, Longmans, Green and Co., 1934, Chapter III. The heart of the argument is the necessity of a First Cause, which arises from the impossibility that a series of secondary causes should be infinite.

would be senseless to ask <u>why</u> Z is so. "[18]

The chief strength of atheistic naturalism has lain in the notion that the material world needs no explanation, external to <u>itself</u>, that it is, indeed, a perpetual motion machine, which had no end. But when we take the Second Law of Thermodynamics seriously we can no longer hold to this doctrine. The universe as we know it, by the aid of modern science, could not have originated without the action of a creative Source of energy outside itself, and it cannot be maintained without it.[19] But a creative Source of energy outside the natural order is God.

The more we delve into the secrets of nature, the more it becomes clear that nature cannot account for itself in any of its parts or in its entirety. It is no valid answer to say with Hume's skeptical critic in the <u>Dialogues Concerning Natural Religion</u> that the necessary being which accounts for all the contingent parts may be nothing else than the <u>world as a whole</u>. It is precisely the "whole" which most demands explanation, and there is no line of evidence which makes this more clear than that which leads to the general acceptance, among scholars, of the Carnot principle.

---

[18]A. E. Taylor, "The Vindication of Religion," <u>Essays Catholic and Critical</u>, edited by E. G. Selwyn, London, 1938, p. 50.

[19]For an able discussion of this, see Joseph A. Leighton, <u>The Field of Philosophy</u>, New York, 1923, pp. 207 f.

3. THE NATURE OF RELIGIOUS EXPERIENCE

The Natural Theist does not believe that human beings can experience God directly. God is a rational inference from an empirically experienced world. <u>Thomas</u> <u>Paine</u> calls this position "deism." The natural creation is the "Word" of God which is "spoken" to all people equally. The special revelation advocated by the "Christian System" must, therefore, be rejected. When we "read" the "Word" of Creation with reason, rather than intuition or emotion, we learn of the benevolent nature of God in the gift of Creation itself. When we act in relation to each other as God has acted in relation to us, we are religious. Religious experience is guided by reason in demonstrating the benevolent acts of God in the Creation, and culminates in reverence for and appreciation of those gifts. Religious experience does not include an awareness of the mysterious depths of God, which surely exist, for that would lead us towards obscurity of religious truth and withdrawal from the world.

The <u>Age</u> <u>of</u> <u>Reason</u>

Thomas Paine

Being an Investigation of True and Fabulous Theology

It has been my intention, for several years past, to publish my thoughts upon religion; for I am well aware of the difficulties that attend the subject, and, from that consideration, had reserved

---

it to a more advanced period of life. I intended it to be the last offering I should make to my fellow-citizens of all nations, and that at a time when the purity of the motive that induced me to it, could not admit of a question, even by those who might disapprove the work.

The circumstance that has now taken place in France of the total abolition of the whole national order of priesthood, and of everything appertaining to compulsive systems of religion, and compulsive articles of faith, has not only precipitated my intention, but rendered a work of this kind exceedingly necessary, lest, in the general wreck of superstition, of false theology, we lose sight of morality, of humanity, and of the theology that is true.

As several of my colleagues, and others of my fellow-citizens of France, have given me the example of making their voluntary and individual profession of faith, I also will make mine; and I do this with all that sincerity and frankness with which the mind of man communicates with itself.

I believe in one God, and more and more; and I hope for happiness beyond this life.

I believe in the equality of man; and I believe that religious duties consist in doing justice, loving mercy, and endeavouring to make our fellow creatures happy.

But, lest it should be supposed that I believe many other things in addition to these, I shall, in the progress of this work declare the things I do not believe, and my reasons for not believing them.

I do not believe in the creed professed by the Jewish church by the Roman church, by the Greek church, by the Turkish church, by the Protestant church, nor by any church that I know of. My own mind is my own church.

All national institutions of churches, whether Jewish, Christian, or Turkish, appear to me no other than human inventions, set up to terrify and enslave mankind, and monopolize power and profit.

I do not mean by this declaration to condemn those who believe otherwise; they have the same right to their belief as I have to
mine. But it is necessary to the happiness of man, that he be men-
tally faithful to himself. Infidelity does not consist in believing, or
in disbelieving; it consists in professing to believe what he does not
believe.

It is impossible to calculate the moral mischief, if I may so
express it, that mental lying has produced in society. When a man
has so far corrupted and prostituted the chastity of his mind, as to
subscribe his professional belief to things he does not believe, he
has prepared himself for the commission of every other crime.
He takes up the trade of a priest for the sake of gain, and, in order
to qualify himself for that trade, he begins with a perjury. Can we
conceive any thing more destructive to morality than this ?

Soon after I had published the pamphlet, Common Sense, in
America, I saw the exceeding probability that a revolution in the
system of government would be followed by a revolution in the
system of religion. The adulterous connection of church and state,
wherever it had taken place, whether Jewish, Christian, or Turkish, had so effectually prohibited, by pains and penalties, every
discussion upon established creeds, and upon first principles of
religion, that until the system of government should be changed,
those subjects could not be brought fairly and openly before the
world; but that whenever this should be done, a revolution in the
system of religion would follow. Human inventions and priest-
craft would be detected; and man would return to the pure, un-
mixed, and unadulterated belief of one God, and no more.

Every national church or religion has established itself by
pretending some special mission from God, communicated to certain individuals. The Jews have their Moses; the Christians their
Jesus Christ, their apostles and saints; and the Turks their Mahomet, as if the way to God was not open to every man alike.

Each of those churches show certain books, which they call
Revelation, or the word of God. The Jews say, that their word

157

of God was given by God to Moses, face to face; the Christians say, that their word of God came by divine inspiration; and the Turks say, that their word of God (the Koran) was brought by an angel from Heaven. Each of those churches accuse the other of disbelief; and, for my own part, I disbelieve them all.

As it is necessary to affix right ideas to words, I will, before I proceed further into the subject, offer some other observations on the word revelation. Revelation when applied to religion, means something communicated immediately from God to man.

No one will deny or dispute the power of the Almighty to make such a communication, if he pleases. But admitting, for the sake of a case, that something has been revealed to a certain person, and not revealed to any other person, it is revelation to that person only. When he tells it to a second person, a second to a third, a third to a fourth, and so on, it ceases to be a revelation to all those persons. It is revelation to the first person only, and hearsay to every other, and consequently, they are not obliged to believe it.

It is a contradiction in terms and ideas, to call any thing a revelation that comes to us at second-hand, either verbally or in writing. Revelation is necessarily limited to the first communication--after this, it is only an account of something which that person says was a revelation made to him; and though he may find himself obliged to believe it, it cannot be incumbent on me to believe it in the same manner; for it was not a revelation made to me, and I have only his word for it that it was made to him.

When Moses told the children of Israel that he received the two tables of the commandments from the hands of God, they were not obliged to believe him, because they had no other authority for it than his telling them so; and I have no other authority for it than some historian telling me so. The commandments carry no internal evidence of divinity with them; they contain some good moral precepts, and such as any man qualified to be a lawgiver, or a moral legislator, could produce himself, without having recourse to supernatural intervention.

158

When I was told that the Koran was written in Heaven, and brought to Mahomet by an angel, the account comes too near the same kind of hearsay evidence and second-hand authority as the former. I did not see the angel myself, and, therefore, I have a right not to believe it.

When also I am told that a woman called the Virgin Mary said, or gave out, that this was the child without any cohabitation with a man, and that her betrothed husband, Joseph, said that an angel told him so, I have a right to believe them or not; such a circumstance required a much stronger evidence than their bare word for it; but we have not even this--for neither Joseph nor Mary wrote any such matter themselves; it is only reported by others that they said so--it is hearsay upon hearsay, and I do not choose to rest my belief upon such evidence.

It is, however, not difficult to account for the credit that was given to the story of Jesus Christ being the son of God. He was born when the heathen mythology had still some fashion and repute in the world, and mythology had prepared the people for the belief of such a story. Almost all the extraordinary men that lived under the heathen mythology were reputed to be the sons of some of the gods. It was not a new thing at that time, to believe a man to have been celestially begotten; the intercourse of god with women was then a matter of familiar opinion. Their Jupiter, according to their accounts, had cohabited with hundreds; the story therefore had nothing in it either new, wonderful or obscene; it was conformable to the opinions that then prevailed among the people called Gentiles, or Mythologists, and it was those people only that believed it. The Jews, who had kept strictly to the belief of one God, and no more, and who had always rejected the heathen mythology, never credited the story.

It is curious to observe how the theory of what is called the Christian Church, sprung out of the tail of heathen mythology. A direct incorporation took place in the first instance, by making the reputed founder to be celestially begotten. The trinity of gods, that then followed was no other than a reduction of the former plurality, which was about twenty or thirty thousand; the statue of Mary succeeded the status of Diana or Ephesus; the deification of heroes changed into the canonization of saints; the mythologists had gods for every thing; the Christian mythologists had saints for every thing; the church became as crowded with the one, as the pantheon had been with the other; and Rome was the place of both. The Christian theory is little else than the idolatry of the ancient Mythologists, accommodated to the purpose of power and revenue; and it yet remains to reason and philosophy to abolish the amphibious fraud.

Nothing that is here said can apply, even with the most distant disrespect, to the real character of Jesus Christ. He was a virtuous and an amiable man. The morality that he preached and practised was of the most benevolent kind; and though similar systems of morality had been preached by Confucius, and by some of the Greek philosophers, many years before; by the Quakers since; and by many good men in all ages, it has not been exceeded by any.

Jesus Christ wrote no account of himself, of his birth, parentage, or anything else; not a line of what is called the New Testament is of his own writing. The history of him is altogether the work of other people; and as to the account given of his resurrection and ascension, it was the necessary counterpart to the story of his birth. His historians, having brought him into the world in a supernatural manner, were obliged to take him out again in the same manner, or the first part of the story must have falled to the ground.

The wretched contrivance with which this latter part is told, exceeds every thing that went before it. The first part, that of the miraculous conception, was not a thing that admitted of publicity; and therefore the tellers of this part of the story had this advantage, that though they might not be credited, they could not be detected. They could not be expected to prove it, because it was not one of those things that admitted of proof, and it was impossible that the person of whom it was told could prove it himself.

But the resurrection of a dead person from the grave, and his ascension through the air, it is a thing very difficult as to the evidence it admits of, to the invisible conception of a child in the

160

womb. The resurrection and ascension, supposing them to have taken place, admitted of public and ocular demonstration, like that of the ascension of a balloon, or the sun at noon day, to all Jerusalem at least. The thing which every body is required to believe, requires that the proof and evidence of it should be equal to all, and universal; and as the public visibility of this last related act, was the only evidence that could give sanction to the former part, the whole of it falls to the ground, because that evidence never was given. Instead of this, a small number of persons, not more than eight or nine, are introduced as proxies for the whole world, to say they saw it, and all the rest of the world are called upon to believe it. But it appears that Thomas did not believe the resurrection; and, as they say, would not believe without having ocular and manual demonstration himself. So neither will I, and the reason is equally as good for me, and for every other person, as for Thomas.

It is in vain to attempt to palliate or disguise this matter. The story so far as relates to the supernatural part, has every mark of fraud and imposition stamped upon the face of it. Who were the authors of it is as impossible for us now to know, as it is for us to be assured that the books in which the account is related, were written by the persons whose names they bear; the best surviving evidence we now have respecting this affair is the Jews. They are regularly descended from the people who lived in the time this resurrection and ascension is said to have happened, and they said, it is not true. It has long appeared to me a strange inconsistency to cite the Jews as a proof of the truth of the story. It is just the same as if a man were to say, I will prove the truth of what I have told you, by producing the people who say it is false.

That such a person as Jesus Christ existed, and that he was crucified, which was the mode of execution of that day, are historical relations strictly within the limits of probability. He preached most excellent morality, and the equality of man; but he preached also against the corruptions and avarice of the Jewish priests, and this brought upon him the hatred and vengeance of the whole order of priesthood. The accusation which those priests brought against him was that of sedition and conspiracy against the

161

Roman government, to which the Jews were then subject and tributary; and it is not improbable that the Roman government might have some secret apprehensions of the effects of his doctrine as well as the Jewish priests; neither is it improbable that Jesus Christ had in contemplation the delivery of the Jewish nation from the bondage of the Romans. Between the two, however, this virtuous reformer and revolutionist lost his life.

It is upon this plain narrative of facts, together with another case, I am going to mention, that the Christian Mythologists, calling themselves the Christian Church, have erected their fable, which for absurdity and extravagance, is not exceeded by any thing that is to be found in the mythology of the ancients . . . .

But some perhaps will say--Are we to have no word of God --no revelation! I answer, Yes: there is a word of God; there is a revelation.

THE WORD OF GOD IS THE CREATION WE BEHOLD: And it is in this word, which no human invention can countervail or alter, that God speaketh universally to man.

Human language is local and changeable, and is therefore incapable of being used as the means of unchangeable and universal information. The idea of God sent Jesus Christ to publish, as they say, the glad tidings to all nations, from one end of the earth to the other, is consistent only with the ignorance of those who knew nothing of the extent of the world, and who believed, as those world saviors believed, and continued to believe, for several centuries (and that in contradiction to the discoveries of philosophers and the experience of navigators), that the earth was flat like a trench; and that a man might walk to the end of it.

But how was Jesus Christ to make any thing known to all nations ? He could speak but one language, which was Hebrew; and there are in the world several hundred languages. Scarcely any two nations speak the same language, or understand each other; and as to translations, every man who knows anything of languages, knows that it was impossible to translate from one language to another, not only without losing a great part of the original, but frequently of mistaking the sense; and besides all this, the art of printing was wholly unknown at the time Christ lived.

It is always necessary that the means that are to accomplish any end, be equal to the accomplishment of that end, or the end cannot be accomplished. It is in this, that the difference between finite and infinite power and wisdom discovers itself. Man frequently fails in accomplishing his ends, from a natural inability of the power to the purpose; and frequently from the want of wisdom to apply power properly. But it is impossible for infinite power and wisdom to fail as man faileth. The means it useth are always equal to the end; but human language, more especially as there is not an universal language, is incapable of being used as an universal means of unchangeable and uniform information, and therefore it is not the means that God useth in manifesting himself universally to man.

It is only in the CREATION that all our ideas and conceptions of a word of God can unite. The Creation speaketh an universal language, independently of human speech or human language, multiplied and various as they be. It is an ever-existing original, which every man can read. It cannot be forged; it cannot be counterfeited; it cannot be lost; it cannot be altered; it cannot be suppressed. It does not depend upon the will of man whether it shall be published or not; it publishes itself from one end of the earth to the other. It preaches to all nations and to all worlds; and this word of God reveals to man all that is necessary for man to know of God.

Do we want to contemplate his power? We see it in the immensity of the Creation. Do we want to contemplate his wisdom. We see it in the unchangeable order by which the incomprehensible whole is governed. Do we want to contemplate his munificence? We see it in the abundance with which he fills the earth. Do we want to contemplate his mercy? We see it in his not withholding that abundance even from the unthankful. In fine, do we want to know what God is? Search not the book called the Scripture, which any human hand might make, but the Scripture called the Creation.

163

The only idea man can affix to the name of God is that of a first cause the cause of all things. And, incomprehensible and difficult as it is for a man to conceive what a first cause is, he arrives at the belief of it, from the tenfold greater difficulty of disbelieving it. It is difficult beyond description to conceive that space can have no end; but it is more impossible to conceive a time when there shall be no time.

In like manner of reasoning, every thing we behold carries in itself the internal evidence that it did not make itself. Every man is an evidence to himself, that he did not make himself; neither could his father make himself, nor his grandfather, nor any of his race; neither could any tree, plant, or animal make itself; and it is the conviction arising from this evidence, that carries us on, as it were, by necessity, to the belief of a first cause eternally existing, of a nature totally different to any material existence we know of, and by the power of which all things exist; and this first cause man calls God.

It is only by the exercise of reason, that man can discover God. Take away that reason, and he would be incapable of understanding any thing; and, in this case it would be just as consistent to read even the book called the Bible to a horse as to a man. How then is it that those people pretend to reject reason?

Almost the only parts in the book called the Bible, that convey to us any idea of God, are some chapters in Job, and the 19th Psalm; I recollect no other. Those parts are true deistical compositions; for they treat of the Deity as through his works. They take the book of Creation as the word of God, they refer to no other book, and all the inferences they make are drawn from that volume.

I insert, in this place, the 19th Psalm, as paraphrased into English verse by Addison. I recollect not the prose, and where I write this I have not the opportunity of seeing it.

> The spacious firmament on high,
> With all the blue etherial sky,
> And spangled heavens, a shining frame,

Their great original proclaim.
The unwearied sun, from day to day,
Does his Creator's power display;
And publishes to every land,
The work of an Almighty hand.
Soon as the evening shades prevail
The moon takes up the wondrous tale,
And nightly to the listening earth,
Repeats the story of her birth;
Whilst all the stars that round her burn,
And all the planets, in their turn,
Confirm the tidings as they roll,
And spread the truth from pole to pole.
What though in solemn silence all
Move round this dark terrestrial hall;
What though no real voice, nor sound,
Amidst their radiant orbs be found,
In reason's ear they all rejoice,
And utter forth a glorious voice,
For ever singing as they shine,
The Hand That Made Us Is Divine.

What more does man want to know, than that the hand or power, that made these things is divine, is omnipotent? Let him believe this with the force it is impossible to repel, if he permits his reason to act, and his rule of moral life will follow of course.

The allusions in Job have all of them the same tendency with this Psalm; that of deducing or proving a truth that would be otherwise unknown, from truths already known.

I recollect not enough of the passages in Job, to insert them correctly; but there is one occurs to me that is applicable to the subject I am speaking upon. "Canst thou by searching find out God? Canst thou find out the Almighty to perfection?"

I know not how the printers have pointed this passage, for I keep no Bible, but it contains two distinct questions, that admit of distinct answers.

First--Canst thou by searching find out God? Yes; because in the first place, I know I did not make myself, and yet I have existence; and by <u>searching</u> into the nature of other things find that no other thing could make itself; and yet millions of other things exist; therefore it is, that I know, by positive conclusion resulting from this search, that there is a power superior to all those things, and that power is God.

Secondly--Canst thou find out the Almighty to <u>perfection</u>? No; not only because the power and wisdom He has manifested in the structure of the Creation that I behold is to me incomprehensible, but because even this manifestation, great as it is is probably but a small display of that immensity of power and wisdom, by which millions of other worlds, to me invisible by their distance, were created and continue to exist.

It is evident that both of these questions are put to the reason of the person to whom they are supposed to have been addressed; and it is only by admitting the first question to be answered affirmatively, that the second could follow. It would have been unnecessary, and even absurd, to have put a second question more difficult than the first, if the first question had been answered negatively. The two questions have different objects; the first refers to the existence of God, the second to his attributes; reason can discover the one, but it falls infinitely short in discovering the whole of the other.

I recollect not a single passage in all the writings ascribed to the men called apostles, that convey any idea of what God is. Those writings are chiefly controversial; and the subject they dwell upon, that of a man dying in agony on a cross, is better suited to the gloomy genius of a monk in a cell, by whom it is not impossible they were written, than to any man breathing the open air of the Creation. The only passage that occurs to me, that has a reference to the works of God, by which only his power and wisdom can be known, is related to have been spoken by Jesus Christ, as a remedy against distrustful care. "Behold the lilies of the field, they toil not, neither do they spin." This, however, is far inferior to the allusions in Job and in the 19th Psalm; but it is similar in idea; and the modesty of the imagery is correspondent

166

to the modesty of the man.

As to the Christian system of faith, it appears to me as a species of atheism--a sort of religious denial of God. It professes to believe in a man rather than in God. It is a compound made up of manism with but little deism, and is as near to atheism as twilight is to darkness. It introduces between man and his Maker an opaque body, which it calls a Redeemer, as the moon introduces her opaque self between the earth and sun, and it produces by this means a religious or an irreligious eclipse of light. It has put the whole orbit of reason into shade.

The effect of this obscurity has been that of turning every thing upside down, and representing it in reverse; and among the revolutions it has thus magically produced, it has made a revolution in Theology.

That which is now called natural philosophy, embracing the whole circle of science, of which Astronomy occupies the chief place, is the study of the works of God, and of the power and wisdom of God in his works, and is the true theology.

As to the theology that is now studied in its place, it is the study of human opinions, and of human fancies concerning God. It is not the study of God himself in the works that he has made, but in the works or writings that man has made; and it is not among the least of the mischiefs that the Christian system has done to the world, that it has abandoned the original and beautiful system of theology, like a beautiful innocent, to distress and reproach, to make room for the hag of superstition . . . .

From the time I was capable of conceiving an idea, and acting upon it by reflection, I either doubted the truth of the Christian system, or thought it to be a strange affair; I scarcely knew which it was: but I well remember, when about seven or eight years of age, hearing a sermon read by a relation of mine, who was a great devotee of the church, upon the subject of what is called redemption by the death of the Son of God. After the sermon ended, I went into the garden, and as I was going down the garden steps (for I perfectly recollect the spot) I revolted at the recollection of

167

what I had heard, and thought to myself that it was making God Almighty act like a passionate man, that killed his son, when he could not revenge himself any other way; and as I was sure a man would be hanged that did such a thing, I could not see for what purpose they preached such sermons. This was not one of those kind of thoughts that had any thing in it of childish levity; it was to me a serious reflection, arising from the idea I had, that God was too good to do such an action, and also too almighty to be under any necessity of doing it. I believe in the same manner at this moment; and I moreover believe, that any system of religion that has any thing in it that shocks the mind of a child, cannot be a true system.

It seems as if parents of the Christian profession were ashamed to tell their children any thing about the principles of their religion. They sometimes instruct them in morals, and talk to them of the goodness of what they call Providence; for the Christian mythology have five deities--there is God the Father, God the Son, God the Holy Ghost, The God Providence, and the Goddess Nature. But the Christian story of the God the Father putting his son to death, or employing people to do it, (for that is the plain language of the story) cannot be told by a parent to a child; and to tell him that it was done to make mankind happier and better, is making the story still worse, as if mankind could be improved by the example of murder; and to tell him that all this is a mystery, is only making an excuse for the incredibility of it.

How different is this to the pure and simple profession of Deism! The true Deist has but one Deity; and his religion consists in contemplating the power, wisdom, and benignity of the Deity in his works, and in moral, scientifical, and mechanical.

The religion that approaches the nearest of all others to true Deism, in the moral and benign part thereof, is that professed by the Quakers: but they have contracted themselves too much, by leaving the works of God out of their system. Though I reverence their philanthropy, I cannot help smiling at the conceit, that if the taste of a Quaker could have been consulted at the creation, what a silent and drab-colored creation it would have been! Not a flower would have blossomed its gaieties, nor a bird been per-

168

mitted to sing . . . .

As therefore, the Creator made nothing in vain, so also must it be believed that He organized the structure of the universe in the most advantageous manner for the benefit of man; and as we see, and from experience feel, the benefits we derive from the structure of the universe, formed as it is, which benefits we should not have had the opportunity of enjoying, if the structure, so far as relates to our system had been a solitary globe--we can discover at least one reason why a plurality of worlds has been made, and that reason calls for the devotional gratitude of man, as well as his admiration.

But it is not to us, the inhabitants of this globe, only, that the benefits arising from a plurality of worlds are limited. The inhabitants of each of the worlds of which our system is composed, enjoy the same opportunities of knowledge as we do. They behold the revolutionary motions of our earth, as we behold theirs. All the planets revolve in sight of each other; and, therefore, the same universal school of science presents itself to all.

Neither does the knowledge stop here. The system of worlds next to us exhibits, in its revolutions, the same principles and school of science, to the inhabitants of their system, as our system does to us, and in like manner throughout the immensity of space.

Our ideas, not only of the almightiness of the Creator, but of his wisdom and his beneficence, become enlarged in proportion as we contemplate the extent and the structure of the universe. The solitary idea of a solitary world, rolling or at rest in the immense ocean of space, gives place to the cheerful idea of a society of worlds, so happily contrived as to administer, even by their motion, instruction to man. We see our earth filled with abundance; but we forget to consider how much of that abundance is owing to the scientific knowledge the vast machinery of the universe has unfolded.

But, in the midst of those reflections, what are we to think of the Christian system of faith, that forms itself upon the idea of

169

only one world, and that of no greater extent, as is before shown, than twenty-five thousand miles? An extent which a man, walking at the rate of three miles an hour, for twelve hours in a day, could he keep on in a circular direction, would walk entirely round in less than two years. Alas! what is this to the mighty ocean of space, and the almighty power of the Creator!

From whence then could arise the solitary and strange conceit, that the Almighty, who had millions of worlds equally dependent on his protection, should quit the care of all the rest, and come to die in our world, because, they say, one man and one woman had eaten an apple! And, on the other hand, are we to suppose that every world in the boundless creation, had an Eve, an apple, a serpent, and a redeemer? In this case, the person who is irreverently called the Son of God, and sometimes God himself, would have nothing else to do than to travel from world to world, in an endless succession of death, with scarcely a momentary interval of life.

It has been by rejecting the evidence, that the word or works of God in the reaction affords to our senses, and the action of our reason upon that evidence, that so many wild and whimsical systems of faith, and of religion, have been fabricated and set up. There may be many systems of religion, that so far from being morally bad, are in many respects morally good; but there can be but one that is true; and that one necessarily must, as it ever will, be in all things consistent with the ever existing word of God that we behold in his works. But such is the strange construction of the Christian system of faith, that every evidence the Heavens afford to man, either directly contradicts it, or renders it absurd.

It is possible to believe, and I always feel pleasure in encouraging myself to believe it, that there have been men in the world, who persuade themselves that, what is called a pious fraud, might at least under particular circumstances, be productive of some good. But the fraud being once established could not afterwards be explained; for it is with a pious fraud as with a bad action, it begets a calamitous necessity of going on.

The persons who first preached the Christian system of

faith, and in some measure combined it with the morality preached by Jesus Christ, might persuade themselves that it was better than the heathen mythology that then prevailed. From the first preachers the fraud went on to the second, and to the third, till the idea of its being a pious fraud became lost in the belief of its being true; and that belief became again encouraged by the interests of those who made a livelihood by preaching it.

But though such a belief might, by such means, be rendered almost general among the laity, it is next to impossible to account for the continual persecution carried on by the church, for several hundred years, against the sciences, and against the professors of sciences, if the church had not some record or tradition, that it was originally no other than a pious fraud, or did not foresee, that it could not be maintained against the evidence that the structure of the universe afforded.

Having thus shown the irreconcileable inconsistencies between the real word of God existing in the universe and that which is called the word of God as shown to us in a printed book that any man might make, I proceed to speak of the three principal means that have been employed in all ages, and perhaps in all countries, to impose upon mankind.

Those three means are Mystery, Miracle, and Prophesy. The two first are incompatible with true religion, and third ought always to be suspected.

With respect to mystery, every thing we behold is, in one sense, a mystery to us. Our own existence is a mystery; the whole vegetable world is a mystery. We cannot account how it is that an acorn, when put into the ground, is made to develop itself, and become an oak. We know not how it is that the seed we sow unfolds and multiplies itself, and returns to us such an abundant interest for so small a capital.

The fact, however, as distinct from the operating cause, is not a mystery, because we see it; and we know also the means we are to use, which is no other than putting seed in the ground. We know, therefore, as much as is necessary for us to know, and that part of the operation that we do not know, and which if we did we could not perform, the Creator takes upon himself and performs it for us. We are, therefore, better off than if we had been let into the secret, and left to do it for ourselves.

But though every created thing is, in this sense, a mystery, the word mystery cannot be applied to <u>moral</u> <u>truth</u>, any more than obscurity can be applied to light. The God in whom we believe is a God of moral truth, and not a God of mystery or obscurity. Mystery is the antagonist of truth. It is a fog of human invention, that obscures truth, and represents it in distortion. Truth never envelopes itself in mystery; and the mystery in which it is at any time enveloped, is the work of its antagonist, and never of itself.

Religion, therefore, being the belief of a God, and the practice of moral truth, cannot have connection with mystery. The belief of a God, so far from having any thing of mystery in it, is of all beliefs the most easy, because it arises to us, as is before observed, out of necessity. And the practice of moral truth, or in other words, a practical imitation of the moral goodness of God, is no other than our acting towards each other as he acts benignly towards all. We <u>cannot</u> serve God in the manner we serve those who cannot do without such service; and, therefore, the only idea we can have of serving God is that of contributing to the happiness of the living creation that God has made. This cannot be done by retiring ourselves from the society of the world, and spending a recluse life in selfish devotion.

The very nature and design of religion, if I may so express it, proves, even to demonstration, that it must be free from every thing of mystery, and unincumbered with every thing that is mysterious. Religion, considered as a duty, is an incumbent upon every living soul alike, and, therefore, must be on a level to the understanding and comprehension of all. Man does not learn religion as he learns the secrets and mysteries of a trade. He learns the theory of religion, by reflection. It arises out of the action of his own mind upon the things which he sees, or upon what he may happen to hear or to read, and the practice joins itself thereto.

172

4. THE RELATION OF RELIGION AND SCIENCE

Even though <u>Daniel</u> <u>Morris</u> believes that there can be no scientific knowledge of God, he also believes that the God hypothesis is not contradictory to scientific knowledge. In this respect he disagrees with the humanist Huxley. All scientific knowledge rests upon unproven assumptions, which may, or may not, be religious in nature. In this respect he differs from the pantheist Einstein, who believes that the religious hypothesis precedes all true science. Morris claims that the assumption of a God who is infinite Spirit and who is revealed to human beings only through the physical structures and laws of the created world, is not only compatible with science, but the most reasonable assumption. In his claim that this God can be conceived of as Christian, he differs from Paine, but this is a difference within Natural Theism.

The Supernatural

Daniel L. Morris

In what I have said so far I have, I hope, laid the groundwork for what is to come. But I want to get in a word of apology and explanation at this point. From here on we are going to be concerned with theological matters. I shall probably not discuss them from the "proper" theological point of view. In fact if I did, there would be no excuse for this book; because I am not a theologian, and everything that I am going to talk about has been dealt with by theologians who know their business.

I shall speak as a scientist, with the aim of showing that

---

there is nothing in theology that is not acceptable to a genuine scientist in some fashion--as probably truth or reasonable hypothesis. I don't mean by that that I think every scientist can agree with every theologian. Scientists don't always agree with other scientists. Likewise there is always disagreement among theologians. But the propositions and methods of theology are often surprisingly similar in nature--if not in content--to those of the physical sciences.

1

Before we can talk about any of the rest of theology, we've got to consider the theo part of it. Does God exist? Philosophers down through the ages have devised a great many subtle and beautiful arguments for the existence of God. I'm not going to try to deal with them all, but will stick to one or two, and try to see what their strong and weak points are from a scientific point of view.

There is one class of arguments called "teleological." In a sense these are the most obvious ones. They deal specifically with the idea that there is a purpose or plan in the universe, and they take for their material the everyday facts that are accessible to everybody. These arguments are actually an application of the inductive method, which I have already discussed, to the particular problem of God's existence.

I have said that the inductive method contains a serious logical fallacy, yet we know that it has proved amazingly fertile in its contributions to discovery and invention. We know that always in the past, when an apple has left its branch, it has fallen toward the ground. We therefore assume that this will continue to happen. It is almost inconceivable, now, that an apple, leaving its branch, should hang unmoved in the air, or shoot off into outer space. Yet, philosophically, our only reason for assuming that it will fall is that other apples always have fallen. No matter how much we dignify the facts by speaking about the "laws" of nature, what we always come back to is a great many observations in the past. These are the only basis on which any law can be formulated.

Now, we must admit one of two things: (a) the fact that

apples continue to fall is sheer accident, subject to change without notice (and if we accept this alternative as anything but a philosophical plaything, we are not likely to be very effective scientists); or (b) there is some reality behind what we call the law of Gravitation: the law has, in a sense, a reality that transcends the reality of the fall of any individual apple. You could also express that last thought this way: it is a fact that apples fall, a fact just as real as the apples themselves.

If we accept alternative (b), then we are beginning to talk about a universe that has some sort of ruling pattern to it. As scientists we do, in fact, speak of, and deal with, the "laws of nature." Most of us realize that our knowledge of these laws is always incomplete, and will always remain so.[1] Yet we could hardly work as we do to discover the laws of nature unless we accepted their existence.

If all the talk about the objectivity of science is anything but idle chatter, these laws exist independently of me, or of you. They are there for either of us to discover. If this is so, then where did the laws come from? The theologian says that the existence of the laws is evidence for the operation of an intelligence in the universe. The more you think about it, the more convincing an argument it is. Inductively, we realize the number of laws we don't know about is much greater than the number we do. For instance, there are undoubtedly laws that govern the fact that an acorn develops into an oak tree, and a fertilized feline ovum into a kitten. We know very little about these laws. There are presumably laws that govern the eruption of novae among the stars, and we know literally nothing of these laws.

Wherever we look in the universe we find a pattern. Events

---

[1]If one apple out of ten million, or one out of 10^{20}, on the average, fails to fall to the ground, and shoots off into space instead, that fact may not happen to have been noticed as yet. If it is true, then we shall have to modify our conception of gravitation, but we shall certainly continue to assume that there is a law that governs falling bodies.

are related to other events. Sometimes the patterns are clear, sometimes rather obscure. But if in every portion that we have examined so far there is such a pattern, then, scientifically, we have the right to assume that the whole business falls into one great pattern. We have no understanding of this pattern, but we have as good a right to assert that it exists as that there is a law of gravitation, or a second law of thermodynamics. In each case we are assuming that the pattern we know from past and partial experience extends in some way to the future and the whole.

All of the parts of this great over-all pattern that are accessible to us are, in some measure, intelligible. The more we learn, the more intelligible they become. The inference is, therefore, that there is an intelligence, an infinite one, that is responsible for the whole.

In answer to this argument, it is sometimes proposed that the present state of the universe was brought about by a series of accidents. Obviously, nobody claims that each individual kitten, or star, is a separate accident. But the idea is that there was an accident which resulted, ages ago, in an accumulation of atoms (presumably produced by earlier accidents) which eventually resulted in a star. A later accident resulted in the first living cell on this star. For us, the important thing about this last accident was that the cell happened to be one that was capable of reproducing itself, without the need of another accident of the sort that first produced it. Then we have the familiar series of evolutive accidents, resulting in life, as we see it now, existing in the universe as we now know it.

The argument seems absurd to anyone who doesn't think it is true. That is usually the case with arguments. But that doesn't mean it isn't true. The people who like the Accident Theory would say that the Universal Intelligence Theory is absurd. Such an intelligence is inconceivable for us, they say. And of course they're right. Likewise, the series of accidents, considering the probabilities against, is inconceivable for us.

2

Let's leave this line of argument, and try another one. This is called the argument from the "First Cause." It is rather more strictly intellectual than teleological argument. Here again it is important that, as scientists, we start on solid ground. If we make assumptions, we must be sure we know what they are.

In this case the assumption that we start with is that anything that happens in the world has a cause. The baseball goes over the left field fence because it was hit by Joe DiMaggio's bat. The apple hit Newton on the head because apples are subject to the law of gravitation, and Newton's head happened to be underneath at the time, due to other causes. This assumption seems to be one that practically everybody is happy to accept. Nobody seriously proposes the assumption that all such events, or any such events, just happen: that it just happened that DiMaggio's bat was in the vicinity of the ball when the latter happened to reverse its direction and fly over the fence.

But if each thing that happens is caused by some earlier thing that happened, and this again was caused by something earlier still, how far back can we go? Here the theologian says that there must be some point where we stop--or rather start. There must be a first cause, otherwise nothing could be happening now. If there is such a first cause, then it is certainly justifiable to write this Cause with a capital letter, and say that it is identical with God, the creator of the universe. To me, this is one of the most convincing arguments for God's existence. I don't see how you can get around it. Notice that the argument of "accident" can't apply here, because an accident is a cause and has causes, however unpredictable the accident may have been.

There is one argument that is advanced against the first cause. There is one rational way out. This is the hypothesis that things had no beginning; the universe had been going on forever. If this is true, then obviously there never was a first cause. Mathematicians talk about infinity, and the people who hold this "no beginning" theory say simply that past time is infinite. In that case, of course, the whole universe can have been created by a series of events, each caused by earlier events, with accidents playing their part as mentioned earlier in connection with the "plan of the universe" argument.

To me, the statement that things had no beginning is sheer nonsense. Mathematicians do, it is true, talk about infinity. They have very good fun with it, and even make very good practical use of it on occasions. But they talk about it with a discretion, a circumspection, that would shame a philosopher. From a purely scientific point of view, the idea introduces complexities of a staggering sort--you have to explain, for instance, why all the matter in the universe isn't collapsed in one spot, or else spread to infinite distances apart. I grant that an idea of this sort is entertaining to contemplate, and intelligent study of it will undoubtedly produce valuable scientific results. But the study must be intelligent.

Strangely enough, in this particular philosophical disagreement, evidence is turning up from a direction where we might least expect to see it.--From science itself. One of the theories that has been increasing in respectability for the last thirty years or so is that the whole universe is expanding at a terrific rate. By rather simple mathematics (based on exceedingly complicated mathematics) it has been calculated that, if the process has been going on in the past as it is at present, then the universe did have a beginning. According to one version of this theory, the beginning was about 4×10^9 years ago. "At the age of 10^{23} second, it (the universe) had a radius of 10^{-23} centimeters, and contained a single pair of elementary particles, probably neutrons."[2] Notice that if this theory is true, then the first cause argument cannot be contradicted, at least on the basis of anything we now know.

3

There are quite a number of other arguments for the existence of God, besides the two that I have gone over. From them other things can be deduced about God, such as that he is good, as

---

H. Margenau, "Marginalia," AMERICAN SCIENTIST, Vol. 37 (3), 424 (July, 1949).

well as an intelligent creator. But they begin to get a little abstract from here on, and to require rather elaborate foundations that would take us beyond the area that I am trying to cover.

Notice, by the way, that I have been calling them arguments, rather than proofs. I don't know how philosophers feel about it, but I am very doubtful as to whether there will ever be a perfect proof for the existence of God. Proof is something alien to real life and real facts. It has its proper place in mathematics where, on the basis of certain explicit assumptions, certain conclusions can be reached. But you've got to have assumptions. You've got to start somewhere. And in real life we can never be absolutely sure of anything, so you lack this starting point. (If the theologian says, "No, you can never be sure of anything but God," that may be true, but it doesn't help at the point where we are trying to prove God's existence.) Even in mathematics, a proof is impossible unless you have all the pertinent facts among your assumptions. What human being is arrogant enough to think that we shall ever have available to us all the facts pertinent to the existence of God, since God, if he exists, is the creator of the universe and everything in it?

To sum up, I hope that I have shown that there are convincing arguments for the existence of a God who is the creator of the universe, and who is the intelligence behind the laws of that universe. These arguments are not, and can never be, absolute proofs. But we are looking at the matter from the point of view of a scientist, not of a philosopher. Scientists are not concerned with absolute truths and proofs, but with approaches to truth, and with partial truths that are valuable for further progress. Looked at in this way, the existence of God is actually a much more acceptable hypothesis than are any of the so-called laws on which we base our most precise calculations. As scientists, I think we are entirely justified in saying that we don't know that God exists. But if we do say this, then we must be careful to make the necessary next statement--that we also know nothing else, certainly not that we ourselves exist, or that there is any universe.

Contrariwise, there is nothing unscientific in saying categorically that God does exist, so long as we who say it are real people, actually do say such things as, "I saw Joe Doakes yesterday," rather than, "It seems to me that I saw someone who, if my eyes were not deceiving me resembled my idea of Joe Doakes."

4

Throughout Christian theology we are always coming across references to the human spirit. So much has been written by good philosophers about the spirit that I'm going to say just enough to show my ignorance, and then pass on.

Some scientifically trained people have insisted that the spirit doesn't exist. Some think it probably does, but are a little shamefaced about admitting it. Some think that it is as definite an entity as a one liter Pyrex Erlenmeyer flask.

A fashionable scientific point of view is that man is composed of nothing but atoms; that's all there is, there isn't any more. The idea isn't nearly as stylish now as it was twenty years ago, I think, but plenty of people still hold it. Practically everybody else in the world thinks that, in addition to whatever makes up a man's body (atoms, or flesh, bone and blood), there is something called a spirit, or sometimes a soul, which is not identical with his atoms, and is not destroyed when these revert to other combinations. According to this point of view the spirit survives in some form after the death of the body; but during life it is definitely restricted by the body.

There is some strong evidence in favor of the "atoms only" point of view. There is the fact, for instance, that when something happens to certain cells in a man's brain--when they are physically or chemically injured--the outward activity of that brain is altered. There is no question about it, certain activities that are ascribed to the spirit can be changed out of all recognition by an alteration in the physical state of the brain. One kind of injury may make me unable to move my arm. Another may set the arm to moving of itself, out of my control. This correspondence between brain areas and "spiritual" activity even extends to the realm of the emotions. If a portion of the front of my brain is cut off from the rest, there seems to be no change in my physical

180

abilities, but the indefinable quality called initiative disappears, as well as my ability to worry. This fact has been put to beneficial use in certain cases where the worry had increased to the point where it led to insanity. People who have had the operation are "cured" of the insanity, and can return to a queer kind of normal life.

Even if you don't think that this kind of evidence proves much about the existence of a spirit, or its nonexistence, it is not to be laughed off. It is of course very convincing proof for the strict limitation of the spirit, if any, by the physical makeup of the body. I might point out, though, that just because a proof makes use of the most recent discoveries in the field of neurosurgery, that doesn't mean that it is a new proof. It has been perfectly clear, as long as men have thought about the spirit at all (and that is a very long time), that the human spirit can do nothing of itself so long as it is in the human body. If I see a child falling under the wheels of an automobile two hundred feet away, it doesn't make any difference how much I want, in spirit to save that child. My spirit is limited by the fact that my arms are not two hundred feet long, or that I can't run at the speed of sound.

If I have lost my right arm, modern medicine is not required to tell me that I cannot throw both arms around my sweetheart (or maybe I should say that she certainly won't like it if I do.) We tend to lose sight, in the subtleties of the arguments of the psychologists, that they are telling us something we have never doubted. And what they are telling us has nothing to do with the case. As long as the body has any limiting effect on the spirit, it certainly doesn't matter whether this limiting effect comes into play at a microscopic or a macroscopic level.

In that case, why postulate any spirit at all?

When a baby sees a light, and grabs for it, that can perhaps be explained on the basis of certain purely physical hookups. Even more so when the baby starts sucking as soon as it finds it mother's teat. But most philosophers, and most other people whose efforts are directed toward clear thinking, draw a sharp line between the actions that we perform as the animals that we are physically, and those that we perform as men. When we eat because we are hungry, or copulate because we lust, these actions can perhaps be explained without reference to a spirit. But when we refrain from eating, even though we are dying of starvation, or refrain from copulation even though neither public opinion nor the other individual would condemn us, then it seems that some other explanation is needed.

I think I am safe in saying that you have been, or will be, faced at some time in your life with the problem of doing some specific thing that you believe is right even though in doing it you may suffer physical harm. It may be some spectacular action, life saving somebody's life at the risk of your own, or it may be something much less obvious, like resigning from a job rather than going along with unethical policies.

When you are faced with a situation of this sort, you can either do what is right, or face the physical consequences, or do what you know is wrong, and spare yourself those consequences at the expense of your own self-respect. This argument is not affected by which of these courses you choose. If you take the course that you know is right, but that is harmful to your physical makeup, then the you that takes this course can hardly be the atoms of your body. If they are capable of making a decision, it is unthinkable that they would decide against themselves. On the other hand, if you take the "easy" way out, what is the you that has lost its self-respect?

It is arguments of this sort--and whole libraries have been written on them--that have led the great majority of mankind to consider it obvious that there is in every man something beyond his physical constituents. For convenience I have called this something "spirit."

Most people have also considered that this spirit is immortal, though the conceptions of what this immortality involved have varied all the way from a sad and shadowy eternal dreariness to a glorious progression through ever greater and brighter fields of activity.

And this is what Christianity is all about. If there is in us no spirit capable of immortality, or if our spirit dies at the same time our body does, then there is no point in Christianity. The basic Christian assumption is that we have a spirit which is, or is capable of being, immortal.

The second half of this last assumption, immortality, is not susceptible to the same kind of argument as has been used to show the existence of God. But the arguments about God have themselves some bearing on the question. They show that there is nothing essentially unacceptable, from a scientific point of view, in the idea of at least one immortal spirit in the world--God himself. That does not prove, of course, that our spirits are also immortal, but it permits us to accept that hypothesis as a reasonable one, if only by analogy.

5

As we have just seen, it has been recognized for a long time that while a spirit inhabits a body, it is very limited by that body. As soon as you are willing to look that fact squarely in the face it leads to some interesting new conclusions.

The spirit, if it exists, is the entity that makes the body do many of the things it does. But at the same time, while we live on this earth the only important way in which a spirit can make contact with other spirits is through its body, and through other physical things. Experiments in extrasensory perception may indicate that there is a limited, and almost subconscious, means of direct communication from one mind to another. But in the normal course of events we exchange thoughts with other spirits only through words or gestures, both of which are in themselves purely physical occurrences. This seems obvious yet whole religions, as well as numerous philosophies, have been based on the idea that material things are in some way less real than spiritual or mental things. Most branches of Christianity have managed to steer clear of this fallacy. For Christians, spiritual matters are indeed our primary concern, but while we live on this earth it is our physical acts that determine what happens to our spirits.

Carrying the thought a little further, it is normally only through the physical world that God himself can communicate with us while we live here. In the Old Testament, you remember, God frequently talked to the prophets. We might now say that--if there was communication--it was through something like mental telepathy. Yet the only way in which these communications could be expressed understandably was by describing them as a voice from a cloud--physical vibrations in the air; or as coming through an angel who appeared in human, physical form. Even when the prophet got his instructions in a dream or vision this vision was of something that could be seen or heard, something that was conceived of in physical terms.

People sometimes wonder why God has to stay hidden from us the way he does. If he really exists, why shouldn't he show himself to us, instead of playing this silly game of hide-and-seek? This invisibility is one rather important reason why a good many people seriously doubt God's existence. The objection is partly answered by the main bulwark of Christianity. Christians say that God did once show himself here on earth. But when he did it, it was as a man that he came, so the principle that we are talking about here still applies. And the underlying question remains unanswered: why doesn't God show himself to us directly, as he really is?

The question answers itself, though. God is pure spirit, and infinite in every sense of the word. Just try to think for a moment of a very limited kind of infinity. Try to think of seeing all of an infinite plane at the same time. No eye could possibly do it. But if you see only a portion of the plane, then it is not an infinite plane for you--you have limited what you are seeing. God can't be limited. You can't see a piece of him, because he doesn't come in pieces. If you are ever to see God as he really is, you must see all of him--and if you were to do that, you'd never again see anything. The sight of infinite power, beauty, wisdom, and goodness, if it could possibly be conceived of as visible to the senses, would necessarily be such as to blast those senses.

But on the other hand, if the arguments that were taken up at the beginning of this chapter have any validity, God is visible to us in a very important way, not directly, as the spirit he is, but by means of the things he has made. He communicates with us precisely as I communicate with you--through physical things. We may not be awed by the infinite attributes of God, because they are abstract and unimaginable. But I have known very few scientists of intelligence who were not awed by the development of a baby chick in an egg, or by the sprouting of a seed. And conversely, I have known very few scientists who, if they did have any conception of what goes on in the egg or the seed, didn't believe in some kind of God.

Christ spoke of the very hairs of our heads being numbered, and said that even a sparrow couldn't fall without God knowing about it. These ideas should appeal particularly to people who are studying the comlexities of hairs, or of sparrows. To scientists, hairs and sparrows are not just broad concepts, or categories, or classes. They are real things. Each one is a definite entity, separate from, and as important as, all the others. This thought, then, has precisely the meaning to a scientist that Christ apparently meant it to have.

The things of this world are not merely something that we find here; something that happens to be under our feet, or available to our hands. First of all, these things have been created as fellows of ours--they have been made, as we have been, through the wisdom of God. And, second, they are the means by which God, the pure and infinite spirit, speaks to the spirit which is in each of us.

Christianity is often described as the most materialistic of the great religions. It does not teach that the world is bad, something to be endured or scorned, but that the world is holy, placed here at the express will of God for an express purpose. We may use or misuse it while we are in it, but that use or misuse is the interaction of the living spirit of each of us with the Spirit of God himself.

This is the basis for the idea of "sacraments" as they are used in Christian churches. A sacrament is a physical thing used with spiritual intent as a means of communication with God. For most Christians, a particular piece of bread on the altar, or water used for baptism, has a significance beyond that of other bread or other water. This is not the place to go into that. But any bread and any water may be in a very simple sense a sacrament as soon as you are willing to think about it with anything but the top of your mind.

Christians who speak of actions performed "for the glory of God" carry this sacramental principle into their everyday life. We shall see later how the principle can be applied even to pain and evil. Brother Lawrence, the seventeenth-century monk, described a life based on this principle, which he called the "practice of the presence of God." The Psalmist wrote, "The heavens declare the glory of God, and the firmament showeth his handiwork." That is good poetry, good Christianity--and good science.

5. THE RELATION OF RELIGION AND MORALITY

The Natural Theist argues that God regulates the world only through natural law which is given in creation. Maritain explains how morality is to be understood as originating in natural law rather than written law. Reason is given to human beings by God as a moral conscience. Even though the moral conscience must be developed and may be detracted by weakness or error, it always is disposed towards good rather than evil. The good towards which moral conscience aims is always the ends demanded by human nature itself. The moral person, therefore, utilizes the human quality of reason to attain the fulfillment of his nature, and also the fulfillment of God's plan for human creation. Natural law is a part of Eternal law. Belief in Eternal law, however, is not essential for morality. Maritain believes that when our belief in human nature and the freedom of the human being is grounded in a reasoned belief that we are created by God to be such, our morality will be more unshakable. The Natural Theist believes that one can be both scientific and moral without belief in the "God hypothesis," though that belief enhances and supports both efforts.

Natural Law

Jacques Maritain

The genuine idea of natural law is a heritage of Greek and Christian thought. It goes back not only to Grotius, who indeed began deforming it, but, before him to Suarez and Francisco de Vitoria; and further back to St. Thomas Aquinas . . . and still further back to St. Augustine and the Church Fathers and St. Paul

---

Reprinted from MAN AND THE STATE by Jacques Maritain, by permission of the University of Chicago Press. Copyright 1951 by the University of Chicago.

(we remember St. Paul's saying: "When the Gentiles who have not the Law, do by nature the things contained in the Law, these having not the Law, are a law unto themselves . . ."), and even further back to Cicero, to the Stoics, to the great moralists of antiquity and its great poets, particularly Sophocles. Antigone, who was aware that in transgressing the human law and being crushed by it she was obeying a better commandment, the unwritten and unchangeable laws, is the eternal heroine of natural law: for, as she puts it, they were not, those unwritten laws, born out of today's or yesterday's sweet will, "but they live always and forever, and no man knows from where they have arisen." . . .

Since I have not time here to discuss nonsense (we can always find very intelligent philosophers, not to quote Mr. Bertrand Russell, to defend it most brilliantly) I am taking it for granted that we admit that there is a human nature, and that this human nature is the same in all men. I am taking it for granted that we also admit that man is a being gifted with intelligence, and who, as such, acts with an understanding of what he is doing, and therefore with the power to determine for himself the ends which he pursues. On the other hand, possessed of a nature, or an ontologic structure which is a locus of intelligible necessities, man possesses ends which necessarily correspond to his essential constitution and which are the same for all--as all pianos, for instance, whatever their particular type and in whatever spot they may be, have as their end the production of certain attuned sounds. If they do not produce these sounds they must be tuned, or discarded as worthless. But since man is endowed with intelligence and determines his own ends, it is up to him to put himself in tune with the ends necessarily demanded by his nature. This means that there is, by the very virtue of human nature, an order or a disposition which the human will must act in order to attune itself to the essential and necessary ends of the human being. The unwritten law, or natural law, is nothing more than that . . . .

Any kind of thing existing in nature, a plant, a dog, a horse, has its own natural law, that is, the normality of its functioning, the proper way in which, by reason of its specific structure and specific ends, it "should" achieve fulness of being either in its growth or in its behaviour. Washington Carver, when he was a child and healed sick flowers in his garden, had an obscure knowledge, both by intelligence and congeniality, of that vegetative law of theirs. Horse-breeders have an experiential knowledge, both by intelligence and congeniality, of the natural law of horses, a natural law with respect to which a horse's behaviour makes him a good horse or a <u>vicious</u> <u>horse</u> in the herd. Well, horses do not enjoy free will, their natural law is but a part of the immense network of essential tendencies and regulations involved in the movement of the cosmos, and the individual horse who fails in that equine law only obeys the universal order of nature on which the deficiencies of his individual nature depend. If horses were free, there would be an ethical way of conforming to the specific natural law of horses, but that horsy morality is a dream because horses are not free . . . .

What I am emphasizing is the first basic element to be recognized in natural law, namely the <u>ontological</u> element; I mean the <u>normality of functioning</u> which is grounded on the essence of that being; man. Natural law in general, as we have just seen, is the ideal formula of development of a given being; it might be compared with an algebraical equation according to which a curve develops in space, yet with man the curve has freely to conform to the equation. Let us say, then, that in its ontological aspect, natural law is an <u>ideal</u> <u>order</u> relating to human actions, a <u>divide</u> between the suitable and the unsuitable, the proper and the improper, which depends on human nature or essence and the unchangeable necessities rooted in it. I do not mean that the proper regulation for each possible human situation is contained in the human essence, as Leibniz believed that every event in the life of Caesar was contained beforehand in the idea of Caesar. Human situations are something existential. Neither they nor their appropriate regulations are contained in the essence of man. I would say that they ask questions of that essence. Any given situation, for instance the situation of Cain with regard to Abel, implies a relation to the essence of man, and the possible murder of the one by the other is incompatible with the general ends and innermost dynamic structure of that rational essence. It is rejected by it. Hence the prohibition of murder is grounded on or required by the essence of man. The precept: thou shall do no murder, is a precept of natural law. Because a primordial and most general end of human nature is to preserve being--the being of that existent who is a person, and a universe unto himself; and because man insofar as he is man has a right to live.

Suppose a completely new case or situation, unheard of in human history; suppose, for instance, that what we now call geno-cide were as new as that very name. In the fashion that I just explained, that possible behavior will face the human essence as incompatible with its general ends and innermost dynamic structure: that is to say, as prohibited by natural law. The condemnation of genocide by the General Assembly of United Nations has sanctioned the prohibition of the crime in question by natural law--which does not mean that that prohibition was part of the essence of man as I know not what metaphysical feature eternally inscribed in it--nor that it was a notion recognized from the start by the conscience of humanity.

To sum up, let us say that natural law is something both on-tological and ideal. It is something ideal, because it is grounded on the human essence and its unchangeable structure and the intelligible necessities it involves. Natural law is something on-tological, because the human essence is an ontological reality, which moreover does not exist separately, but in every human being, so that by the same token natural law dwells as an ideal order in the very being of all existing men.

In that first consideration, or with regard to the basic onto-logical element it implies, natural law is coextensive with the whole field of natural moral regulations, the whole field of natural morality. Not only the primary and fundamental regulations but the slightest regulations of natural ethics mean comformity to natural law--say, natural obligations or rights of which we perhaps have now no idea, and of which men will become aware in a distant future . . . .

Natural law is not a written law. Men know it with greater or less difficulty, and in different degrees, running the risk of error here as elsewhere. The only practical knowledge all men have naturally and infallibly in common as a self-evident principle, intellectually perceived by virtue of the concepts involved,

190

is that we must do good and avoid evil. This is the preamble and the principle of natural law; it is not the law itself. Natural law is the ensemble of things to do and not to do which follow therefrom in <u>necessary</u> fashion. That every sort of error and deviation is possible in the determination of these things merely proves that our sight is weak, our nature coarse, and that innumerable accidents can corrupt our judgment. Montaigne maliciously remarked that among certain peoples, incest and thievery were considered virtuous acts. Pascal was scandalized by this. All this proves nothing against natural law, any more than a mistake in addition proves anything against arithmetic, or the mistakes of certain primitive peoples, for whom the stars were holes in the tent which covered the world, prove anything against astronomy.

Natural law is an unwritten law. Man's knowledge of it has increased little by little as man's moral conscience has developed. The latter was at first in a twilight state. Anthropologists have taught us within what structures of tribal life and in the midst of what half-awakened magic it was primitively formed. This proves merely that the knowledge men have had of the unwritten law has passed through more diverse forms and stages than certain philosophers or theologians have believed. The knowledge which our own moral conscience has of this law is doubtless still imperfect, and very likely it will continue to develop and to become more refined as long as humanity exists. Only when the Gospel has penetrated to the very depth of human substance will natural law appear in its flower and perfection . . . .

At this point let us stress that human reason does not discover the regulations of natural law in an abstract and theoretical manner, as a series of geometrical theorems. Nay more, it does not discover them through the conceptual exercise of the intellect, or by way of rational knowledge. I think that Thomas Aquinas' teaching, here, should be understood in a much deeper and more precise fashion than is usual. When he says that human reason discovers the regulations of natural law through the guidance of the <u>inclinations</u> of human nature, he means that the very mode or manner in which human reason knows natural law is not rational knowledge, but knowledge <u>through</u> <u>inclination</u>. That kind of knowledge is not clear knowledge through concepts and conceptual judgments; it is obscure, unsystematic, vital knowledge by connaturality or congeniality, in which the intellect, in order to bear judgment, consults and listens to the inner melody that the vibrating strings of abiding tendencies make present in the subject.

When one has clearly seen this basic fact, and when, moreover, one has realized that St. Thomas' views on the matter call for an historical approach and a philosophical enforcement of the idea of development that the Middle Ages were not equipped to carry into effect, then at last one is enabled to get a completely comprehensive concept of Natural Law. And one understands that the human knowledge of natural law has been progressively shaped and molded by the inclinations of human nature, starting from the most basic ones. Do not expect me to offer an a priori picture of those genuine inclinations which are rooted in man's being as vitally permeated with the preconscious life of the mind, and which either developed or were released as the movement of mankind went on. They are evinced by the very history of human conscience. Those inclinations <u>were</u> <u>really</u> <u>genuine</u> which in the immensity of the human past have guided reason in becoming aware, little by little, of the regulations that have been most definitely and most generally recognized by the human race, starting from the most ancient social communities. For the knowledge of the primordial aspects of natural law was first expressed in social patterns rather than in personal judgments: so that we might say that that knowledge has developed within the double protecting tissue of human inclinations and human society . . . .

I have said that natural law is unwritten law: it is unwritten law in the deepest sense of that expression, because our knowledge of it is no work of free conceptualization, but results from a conceptualization <u>bound</u> to the essential inclinations of being, of living nature, and of reason, which are at work in man, and because it develops in proportion to the degree of moral experience and self-reflection, and of social experience also, of which man is capable in the various ages of his history. Thus it is that in ancient and mediaeval times attention was paid, in natural law, to the obligations of man more than to his rights. The proper achievement--a great achievement indeed--of the XVIIIth Century has been to bring out in full light the <u>rights</u> of man as also required by natural law. That discovery was essentially due to a progress in moral and social experience, through which the root inclinations of human nature as regards the rights of the human person were set free, and consequently, knowledge through inclination with regard to them developed. But, according to a sad law of human knowledge, that great achievement was paid for by the ideological errors, in the theoretical field, that I have stressed at the beginning. Attention even shifted from the obligations of man to his rights only. A genuine and comprehensive view would pay attention both to the obligations and the rights involved in the requirements of natural law.

How could we understand human rights if we had not a sufficiently adequate notion of natural law ? The same natural law which lays down our most fundamental duties, and by virtue of which every law is binding, is the very law which assigns to us our fundamental rights. It is because we are enmeshed in the universal order, in the laws and regulations of the cosmos and of the immense family of created natures (and finally in the order of creative wisdom), and it is because we have at the same time the privilege of sharing in spiritual nature, that we possess rights vis-a-vis other men and all the assemblage of creatures. In the last analysis, as every creature acts by virtue of its Principle, which is the Pure Act; as every authority worthy of the name (that is to say, just) is binding in conscience by virtue of the Principle of beings, which is pure Wisdom: so too every right possessed by man is possessed by virtue of the right possessed by God, Who is pure Justice, to see the order of His wisdom in beings respected, obeyed, and loved by every intelligence. It is essential to law to be an order of reason; and natural law, or the normality of functioning of human nature known by knowledge through inclination, is law, binding in conscience, only because nature and the inclinations of nature manifest an order of reason, --that is of Divine Reason. Natural law is law only because it is a participation in Eternal Law.

6. HUMAN DESTINY

In his argument that there is no scientific answer to the
question of life after death physicist Arthur Compton advocates the
Natural Theist's position on the nature of science. His further
claim that the immortality of human life is a reasonable conclusion
to be drawn from certain "experimental" facts of life is also a
Natural Theistic position. If we assume that freedom of choice is
real then it is possible that consciousness may persist after physical death. If we assume that the evolutionary process is working
towards the development of human life it is possible that the preservation of that life in eternity is a part of cosmic purpose. The
acceptance of both of these possibilities is a moral and religious
matter which is a reasonable completion of scientific truth, and
does not contradict it in any way.

Death, or Life Eternal?

Arthur H. Compton

Science speaks much less clearly on the question of immortality than on the related one of the existence of an order and a
supreme Intelligence in nature. A man trained in the school of
science has a deep-seated reluctance to present evidence which
can only be considered a suggestion. Yet many who profess to
speak for science have drawn the definite conclusion that death
is the end of all. It takes but little investigation to find that this
faith in the completeness of physical death is usually based upon
an uncritical acceptance of a common sense realism, similar to
that which accepts a brick as the hard, heavy, red object that can

---

From THE FREEDOM OF MAN by Arthur H. Compton (pp.
120-153), published by Yale University Press, copyright 1935,
and used by permission of the publisher.

be held in the hands. Just as a more careful examination shows the brick to consist of a group of molecules, atoms, and electrons --a complex system of electrical fields wholly different from the common sense picture--so the "obviousness" of death is found to disappear when more closely studied. Though it is true that science presents no weighty evidence for life eternal, it is only fair to point out also that science has found no cogent reason for supposing that what is of importance in a man can be buried in a grave. The truth is that science cannot supply a definite answer to this question. Immortality relates to an aspect of life which is not physical, that is, which cannot be detected and measured by any instrument, and to which the application of the laws of science can at best be only a well-considered guess.

If one is to have either a positive faith in a future life or a conviction that death is the end, such beliefs must, it seems to me, be based upon religious, moral, or philosophical grounds rather than upon scientific reasoning. It is primarily to clear the way for such metaphysical thinking that it seems desirable to consider certain scientific aspects of death. Few of us living in the present age would accept a doctrine which is demonstrably contrary to scientific fact or to the spirit of the scientific thought. On the other hand our lives would be exceedingly narrow if we based our thoughts and actions solely upon facts that can be subjected to scientific tests. Science, that is, erects a foundation on which our emotional and religious life, if it is to be stable, must be built. The strength and form of the foundation, however, by no means determine the architectural merit of the structure that is to be erected. If a belief in immortality is found to be of value to man, it will not be because of any scientific basis on which the belief rests, but because certain important ideals toward which men are striving can be attained only by a more complete life than is possible in the flesh . . . .

Immortality is a word with such a variety of connotations that it will be desirable to consider briefly some of its aspects regarding which there will be general agreement. No one doubts the influence of a great man's life after he has gone. The ideas of the discoverer of the use of fire are of permanent value. His "spirit" thus lives forever though his name may be all but forgotten in a legend of Promethus. The thoughts and actions of Washington and Lincoln intimately affect the present course of American life. Recognizing the persistence of such influence, we sometimes refer to the "immortals" as those great men of history who have permanently affected the direction of civilization. The hope of attaining such immortality is one of the most powerful driving motives of the world's leaders. We all, in fact, share with George Eliot the longing:

> "O, may I join the choir invisible
> Of those immortal dead who live again
> In minds made better by their presence; live
> In pulses stirred to generosity
> In deeds of daring rectitude, in scorn
> For miserable aims that end with self,
> In thought sublime that pierce the night like stars,
> And with their mild persistence urge man's search
> To vaster issues. "

To a greater or less extent, for good or evil, all of us must have a certain degree of such continuous life.

Similarly, there is a very real biological sense in which life is eternal. Though each person, or to be more general each organism dies, the race or species lives on unless some world-wide catastrophe occurs which makes it extinct. In his recent book, The Universe About Us, Sir James Jeans assigns a million billion years as a reasonable life expectancy for the human race on earth. Though a million billion years may not, strictly speaking, be life eternal, it is probably as long a life as most of us want.

The biological center of life is the germ cell, and this, with divisions and subdivisions, grows and lives forever. What the fruit of the apple is to the seed, the body of man is to his germ cell. The apple may decay, but the seed, grows into a new tree, which flowers and begets new seeds. The fruit and the tree will die, but there is eternal continuity of life in the cells which develop from seed to tree to flower to seed, over and over again. It is thus because we concentrate our attention upon the tree or the fruit that we say the end of life is death. These are merely the outer wrappings, the hull which surrounds the living germ. Biologically speaking, life, whether it be of an apple seed or of the germ cells of man, is essentially continuous and eternal.

"But," you say, "that is not the kind of eternal life in which I am primarily interested. My body may be merely the hull that surrounds the living germ; but what will happen to me when the hull decays?"

Beyond this point we must cease to speak with assurance. For when you ask, "What will happen to me," you are concerned not with your body but with your consciousness, mind, or soul, what ever you choose to call it, which is not material and regarding which science offers no objective data. Direct observations can be made of the actions of the body, and for the body death is found to be the inevitable end. Our only knowledge of the state of consciousness of others is, however, that which can be inferred from their actions, as interpreted in terms of our own state of consciousness when we act in a similar manner. Since we have not experienced physical death, our idea of what happens to the consciousness associated with an organism at death can be only reasoned guess, based upon some assumption about the relation of body and mind. In order to test whether such a guess is correct, it would be necessary to receive an authentic and reliable statement from one who has experienced physical death. Lacking the assurance of the tested truths of science, at best such an affirmation is a kind of extrapolation far beyond the region of observational test. Even in such a relatively exact science as physics it is a rare theory whose predictions can thus be extrapolated with confidence.

. . .

Let us examine, however, certain of the hypotheses regarding the relationship between body and mind which have been found useful, and follow out their consequences regarding consciousness after death. First there is the materialistic hypothesis used by certain psychologists, according to which thought is a function of the brain. Every sensation, every idea that we have, even every decision we make is a consequence of some action occurring in the

197

brain. On this view it is obvious that destruction of the brain must carry with it the destruction of consciousness.

This hypothesis has been adopted primarily in order to simplify the problem of behavior by reducing it to a set of mechanical laws. If thought is a by-product of some molecular change in the brain, and if these molecular changes follow definite physical laws, there will be a straightforward sequence of molecular changes starting with the initial stimulus and ending with the final action of the organism. Thoughts may be associated with these various changes, but they cannot alter the end result, for this is determined by the physical laws which govern the molecular actions. The problem of man's behavior is thus simplified by reducing him to an automaton.

Chapter II gives in some detail my reasons for believing that this simplified behavior fails as a complete description of our actions. In some reflect actions and habitual acts we may behave as automatons; but where deliberation occurs we feel that we choose our own counsel. In fact, a certain freedom of choice may, it seems to me, be considered as an experimental fact with which we must reconcile our theories. Because the mechanist's basic hypothesis leaves no room for such freedom, I see no alternative other than to reject the hypothesis as inadequate.

On the other hand, if freedom of choice is admitted, it follows by the same line of reasoning that one's thoughts are not wholly the result of molecular reactions determined by physical laws. For if they were, one's thoughts would be fixed by the physical conditions, and his choice would be made for him. Thus, if there is freedom, there must be at least some thinking possible independent of any corresponding physical change in the brain. On such a view it is no longer impossible that consciousness may persist after the brain is destroyed.

That there is a close correlation between the brain's activity and mental processes is, however, evident. Such phenomena as intoxication, anaesthesia, delirium, and so on, show an intimate connection between the condition of a man's brain and his state of mind. It is tempting likewise to interpolate the declining

mental powers with advancing disease or old age to mean blank unconsciousness in death.

The problem of the connection between mind and matter is
one regarding which all our efforts at solution have been baffled.
Modern psychology dislikes the idea of a soul or spirit separable
from the body. Certainly in a living organism body and life cannot be separated. Similarly, if I understand my psychology right,
it is commonly supposed that consciousness is not a separable element, but an essential part of the organism. All throughout its
evolution, increased complexity of function has been accompanied
in some mysterious way by the development of consciousness.
Following this view, Bishop Barnes contends "That concurrent
physical and physical phenomena are two aspects of a single process of change . . . . Man's whole mental and spiritual nature is
conditioned by his physical nature and pathological states, no mental or spiritual movement taking place without a concomitant physical movement." On the other hand, perhaps all psychologists
would admit with William James that "it has not been proved, and
it seems unprovable, that the actual body is the adequate cause and
not a purely contingent condition of our spiritual life."

An examination of the evidence in fact shows that the correspondence between brain activity and consciousness is not as close
as is frequently supposed. Thus my colleague Professor Lashley
has pointed out that both in animals and man a large portion of the
brain may be damaged, or even removed, without destroying consciousness or seriously disturbing the mental processes. On the
other hand, such a relatively minor disturbance as a tap on the
skull may, so far as we can tell, completely destroy consciousness for a considerable period of time. Moreover, Bergson has
given what seems to be convincing evidence for his statement that
"there is infinitely more in a human consciousness than in a corresponding brain," and that "the mind overflows the brain on all
sides, and cerebral activity corresponds only to a very small part
of mental activity."

It was in part from such considerations that William James
was led to reject the view that thought is produced by the brain in
favor of the hypothesis that the brain transmits the thought to the

body, where the appropriate action occurs. On this view the brain would correspond to the detecting tube of a radio receiver, without which no music can be received. Stopping of the sound by destroying the tube does not imply the destruction of the musician whose song is being carried by the ether waves. Such a view of the relation between thought and brain accounts satisfactorily for the observed parallelism between the two, and yet leaves room for the thought processes of great diversity. James recognizes that during life thought needs grain for its organ of expression; but this does not exclude the possibility of a condition in which thought is independent of brain.

. . .

In view of this failure to get conclusive evidence of a direct character, let us consider some of the more important deductions that have been drawn from the theory of evolution. An argument against immortality which carries considerable weight is based upon the value of consciousness to the organism . . . From the biological point of view the appearance of consciousness in animals enables them to compete more successfully in the struggle of life. This suggests that consciousness is the servant of the biological organism. In the evolutionary process we should on this view expect consciousness to appear only where it can be of some value to the organism with which it is associated. For a babe at birth consciousness is of little value, and it seems to be only feebly developed. In youth and maturity, however, it is of vital importance that the organism be aware of what is going on, and consciousness is accordingly most highly developed. Clearly, consciousness can be of no value to a dead organism. From the biological point of view, therefore, we should expect an efficient evolutionary process to bring about the cessation of consciousness with death.

There is, however, an alternative position which is at least equally tenable, and which points toward the opposite conclusion. This is that the evolutionary process is working toward the development of conscious persons rather than toward the development of a physical organism. In the previous chapters we have indicated how evidence from both the physical and biological sciences makes it difficult to escape the conclusion that our world is controlled by a supreme Intelligence, which directs evolution according to some great plan. We could, in fact, see the whole great drama of evolution moving toward the making of persons with free intelligence capable of glimpsing God's purpose in nature and of sharing that purpose. In such a case we should not look upon consciousness as the mere servant of the biological organism, but as an end in itself. A intelligent mind would be its own reason for existence.

Our survey of the physical universe indicated that mankind is very possibly nature's best achievement in this direction. If in the world scheme conscious life is the thing if primary importance, what is happening on our earth is thus of great cosmic significance. The thoughts of man, which have come to control to so great an extent the development of life upon this planet, are conceivably to the Lord of Creation among the most important things in the world. From this point of view we might expect nature to preserve at all costs the living souls which it has evolved at such labor. This would mean the immortality of the individual consciousness.

Thus science finds itself incapable of giving a definite answer, at present at least, to the problem of immortality. While according to the mechanistic view the mind could not survive the brain, the evidence seems definitely against this view, and no cogent reason remains for supposing that the soul dies with the body. The evidence of revived persons brought back from Hades, though inconclusive, must be considered strongly against persistence of consciousness. If consciousness is merely the servant of the living organism, we should expect the two to die together; but if, as seems perhaps more plausible, intelligent consciousness is the objective of the evolutionary process, we might expect it to be preserved . . . .

. . .

If we desire to reach a more definite result, we must go beyond science into ethics and religion. Such an excursion is outside of the proper scope of this book, and its author can serve only as an amateur guide. Yet for the sake of completeness the nature of these arguments should be indicated. It is recognized that they will not have the general appeal of well-tested scientific evidence;

but for many of those who are prepared to accept the postulates on which they are based, these lines of thought carry such weight as to make a belief in immortality the basis for the planning of life.

One of the most effective of these arguments is that based on the belief that God is good. It is summarized by Barnes as follows:

"We are forced to assume that the Universe is rational. The assumption is largely confirmed by our experience and, unless it were true, the Universe would be unknowable. In that case God's works and ways would be unintelligible and experience would not lead to any understanding of Him. Now if, on the contrary, the character of the ordering of all that happens is for our thought rational, we are forced to conclude that God would not have allowed the majority of human beings to have lives, so wretched and incomplete as we observe them to be, were it not that earthly existence is but the first part, a mere beginning of the complete life of the human spirit . . . .

In brief, our plea for personal survival can be set out as follows. We have been led by the processes of reason to postulate that the world is the realm of Creative Spirit, of Mind which is purposive. Argument from the existence of the Moral Law, or, in other words, of man's feeling that he is compelled to believe that goodness is objectively valid--such argument leads us to the conclusion that the Creative Spirit, in and for whom the Universe exists, is good. But our arguments must be pronounced unsatisfactory, and the conclusions derived from them must be rejected, unless personal immortality be a fact."

We have found strong reasons for believing that, in spite of this physical insignificance, man as an intelligent person is of extraordinary importance in the cosmic scheme. If we were to use our own best judgment, what would we say if the most important thing about a noble man? Would it be the strength of his body, or the brilliance of his intellect? Would we not place first the beauty of his character? A man's body is at its prime before middle life, and his intellect probably somewhat after middle life. But it takes a whole lifetime to build the character of a noble man. The exercise and discipline of youth, the struggles and failures and successes, the pains and pleasures of maturity, the lineliness and tranquillity of age--these make up the fire through which he must pass to bring out the pure gold of his soul. Having been thus perfected, what shall nature do with him? Annihilate him? What infinite waste!

> "Thous wilt not leave us in the dust:
> Thou madest man, he knows not why,
> He thinks he was not made to die;
> And thou thast made him: thou art just."

Thus the poet cries, as he considers the impossibility that a God of justice and love should forget the men whom he has made to be his own companions.

7. NATURAL THEISM AND THE PROBLEMS
OF HUMAN SOCIETY

The Natural Theist believes that the fundamental problems of human society originate in the failure of human beings to follow Natural Law. Natural Law is the light of reason, given by God for the natural fulfillment of human nature. When this reason operates in the awareness of its origin and in conformity to the Law of Nature, which it is able to discern, it is a sufficient guide to the good life.

John Wild believes that there is a natural order of human culture wherein religion is the "master art." In the natural order those arts dealing with material needs are subordinated to the governing arts, which are in turn subordinated to those arts which develop the intellect as the highest part of human nature. It is this human reason which finds its source in religion and nurtures and sustains the natural order as a means to an eternal end. When this natural order is inverted rational guidance is undermined resulting in cultural barbarism, wherein the means to the ends of human nature are treated as the ends.

C. S. Lewis examines the "right to sexual happiness" in the light of the Law of Nature. The Law of Nature declares a mutuality of rights under which people are made good. Sexual happiness must be judged by this moral law and if not it turns into an unbridled selfish passion which ignores the rights and feelings of other people. It also may contribute to the undermining of a moral society, whose guiding light must be reason rather than passion.

Religion and the Natural Order of Human Culture

John Wild

Religion and Culture

There is a widespread tendency at the present time to separate religion from the rest of human culture on the ground that it is
concerned with another world, divorced from the natural world
which we inhabit. But this is a great mistake. As was clearly
recognized by the great pagan philosophers, Plato and Aristotle,
religion is deeply rooted in human nature. The best way of gaining
an understanding of this essential fact is to think of the goods which
are provided by the other cultural activities of man. No one of
these alone is capable, nor are all of them together capable, of
ultimately satisfying the aspiration of the human will.

Material artifacts provided by the constructive activities of
poietic groups are good things. But we are not purely material
entities. Hence without something more we remain restless and
unsatisfied. Man cannot live on bread alone. The realization of
the natural rights to nurture, education, and freedom of expression, provided by the political activities of politic groups are good
things. They give to each individual the opportunity of living.
They do not give him life itself. Man cannot live on government
alone . . . . So far as they go, they are very good, but they do not
go far enough . . . . Even after it has assimilated the deepest
truths which are naturally accessible to it, the human mind is
still unsatisfied and endorses the famous words of Socrates in the
"Apology" that human knowledge alone is of little worth. More is
needed.

Perhaps this more is to be achieved in the integral life of

sustaining groups, where all these instrumental goods are to be found merged together in the concrete life of the family, the community, and the temporal world. But temporal happiness alone still fails to quiet the restless urge of the human will. This is because human reason is able to apprehend the existence of a perfect and eternal good. It is this apprehension which elicits in the human will a natural appetite for an unchanging good and frees it from any necessary, animal obsession with the particular, finite goods of temporal life. This does not mean that we are not necessarily attached to such finite goods as are naturally required. It does mean that we are not necessarily attached to any one of them or to all of them together, as to our ultimate end. The ultimate end lies beyond these goods . . . .

Human aspiration is naturally directed to an eternal end. An eternal first cause brought this aspiration into existence and still sustains it. Why, then, should it not grant further aid in enabling it to reach its end? Philosophy can go this far and even further.

From what it knows of the nature of man it can infer something about the general nature of such aid, if it be granted. Such knowledge may be of use in distinguishing between genuine Grace and spurious imitations, for if any supposed revelation fails to meet these specifications it cannot really aid us in attaining the natural end, and we may therefore safely conclude that it is spurious. What we know of human nature may be summarized under three heads.

First, man is a natural or material being, emerging by a continuous process of evolution from the subhuman things of the changing world, and dependent upon them in myriad ways for his existence . . . . Second, the highest and most distinctive part of human nature is the immaterial intellect and the voluntary aspiration it elicits . . . . Third, man is by nature a social creature who can be perfected only by cooperative action with his fellow creatures in attaining a common good . . . . Grace must perfect nature, not destroy it. Hence authentic religion always befriends nature, enlightens reason, and aims at the final perfection of man in a unique form of social order . . . .

The Problem of Evil . . .

The Origin of Evil. Individual weakness and corruption,
social disorder and chaos, are at present ubiquitous and evident
facts of life. All through the ages men have sought from human
philosophy alone an explanation of these hard facts. But they have
looked in vain. It is not too difficult to understand the reason why.
By nature man is either good or he is evil. But whichever we assume we cannot give an intelligent account of the evil which is now
so clearly a fact. Once evil has come into existence we can see
how it tends to increase and leads to further evil. This is not the
question. How did the very first evil originally come into existence? This is the problem of original evil, or sin, which defies a
purely philosophical solution.

Let us start with the pessimistic alternative. Why not suppose that human nature was simply evil from the very beginning?
Then we shall not have to explain any "origin" of evil. We simply
accept it as a primordial fact. But what was responsible for this
fact? Man did not bring himself into existence. He cannot sustain
himself. He owes his existence to manifold causes outside himself, which work together to sustain what we call the order of nature. Hence if human nature as such is evil, then the whole order
of nature which produced it is evil, together with its first cause.
We have then committed ourselves to the assertion that everything
whatsoever, being itself, is evil. But what meaning can be given
to this assertion?

Evil means privation--the lack of some being in a thing required for its perfection, as blindness (privation of sight) is an
evil in man. To say that being itself is evil, therefore, is to say
that being is deprived (of being)--what is, is not. But this is contradictory and unintelligible. Unless something were good in the
first place, nothing could be frustrated or deprived, and evil would
be impossible. Being itself cannot be evil. The alternative of a
radical pessimism is inconceivable. We must assume that human
nature is good to begin with . . . .

We seem to have fallen into an inescapable dilemma. On the
one hand, if human nature as such is radically evil, we cannot

explain good, or evil, which requires something to frustrate, as a parasite requires a host. On the other hand, if human nature is good, we seem to be unable to explain the origin of evil. Is there any way out of this dilemma? There is one way, which involves a recognition of the religious fact that human beings are linked with a higher being who transcends their nature and all their human faculties. How does this explain the difficulty? The explanation briefly is this.

Human nature is good, but it is also finite, or limited. Finiteness is not evil. A mouse is not in an evil state because it lacks the proper perfections of a lion. A lion is not in an evil state because it lacks the proper perfections of a man. Human nature lacks many perfections, but it does not become evil unless it is deprived of some proper perfection required by its nature. These proper perfections, however, fall into two groups, not merely one, as we mistakenly tend to suppose. First, there are certain perfections which human nature can provide for itself, once it has been brought into existence. The first, or original, evil could not have involved any such perfection as this, for human nature, being good, would certainly have supplied it. We cannot explain the original evil unless we recognize the existence of a second class of proper perfections . . . .

There must be certain perfections required by our nature which it cannot provide of itself alone, but only with the aid of some higher being beyond it, to whose commands it must first freely and humbly submit. A human being could act in accordance with his uncorrupted but finite nature and still disobey such a command whose nature he could not fully understand. This offers us an intelligible explanation of original evil, the only one which has as yet been offered--perhaps the only one which can be offered.

The fact of moral evil is to some degree evident to all men. This fact cannot be intelligibly explained without recourse to some being higher than man. Such reflections as these on the mysterious and unnatural fact of evil, add further weight to the other natural motives which have led men throughout the ages to cultivate religion. Most men are at least vaguely aware of the fact that the cosmos is no work of theirs, that it is the work of some cause, and that this cause transcends their faculties. Their recognition of the moral law . . . reveals a link between themselves and this being. This leads naturally to religious worship. Their sense of guilt shows them that the link has been broken--that it needs to be restored. In any right-minded man this must strengthen his natural urge to religious devotion.

Weighed down by the evil he finds in himself and in the cultural life around him, such an individual will rightly join with his fellows in trying to link himself with something higher and better that is capable, not only of directing his own scattered interests and impulses, but of guiding the whole vast array of confused social activities toward their natural end. Without such a link the people perish, and human culture sinks into mass pride and barbarism.

Social Disorder or Cultural Inversion . . . . Social evil is not a positive entity, as we are so apt to think of it, but rather a lack of conformity with natural law which deprives our individual acts of rational order . . . . Such a diseased culture is commonly referred to as barbaric . . . .

We are apt to use the term barbarism in referring both to primitive people who have an undeveloped culture and little scientific knowledge, and to "civilized" states possessing science and technique, but in a disordered form. This leads us to slur over the importance of the latter phenomenon and to be less critical of ourselves, for we tend to take the easy view that if the arts and sciences are cultivated in a given community, we have no right to call it uncultured or barbaric . . . . A nation like modern Germany, for example, may possess all the arts and crafts developed to a high degree of efficiency, and yet be a highly inverted or barbaric state.

Such disorder does not necessarily express itself in chaos; in fact, when most acute, it expresses itself in a rigid kind of order that is very difficult to distinguish in its incipient stages from the incipient states of culture. It must be remembered that related things can be mutually subordinated in two ways: the higher to the lower or the lower to the higher. The miser's

209

actions are not chaotic or disorderly in any apparent sense; he would be better off if they were. He has subordinated the end to the means in a perfectly orderly way, but in the wrong way.

This sort of anatropism, or inversion, is far more possible in a great human culture (sustaining group), where the different arts and techniques are not held together within the nature of a single, substantial being, and have a certain natural autonomy of their own. In such a community it is possible for all the arts to be cultivated, as well as to be ordered with respect to one another, but in an order which is partially, even completely, upside down . . . .

Art is the rational guidance of power. Art becomes anatropic, or barbaric, to the extent that this guidance is undermined, even though subordinate technique and power remain. A single art or function becomes inverted when, instead of forming and controlling its natural subject matter, it merely pretends to exercise this function, but really allows the subject matter to go its own way. Such a false or inverted technician in medecine we call a "quack." With a great display of technical virtuosity, especially in vocabulary, the quack pretends to direct and to treat the patient decisively. In reality he fawns over his charge, feeling for what the patient thinks is wrong rather than giving an objective diagnosis. Finally, for a fee he administers something temporarily soothing.

In the lower arts, which deal with visible material things or situations, such deception is relatively rare. It is difficult for a shoemaker to sell us shoes that are not shoes at all or for a navigator merely to pretend to get us across the sea. Here the lack of any material result is easily detected. But inversion may easily occur between the different arts. Thus, instead of really ordering and regulating the agencies and interests of the community, the politician may merely evade difficult decisions, yield to strong interests, and let things take their course. Instead of eliminating wasteful and unnecessary demands, and regulating distribution in such a way that legitimate and necessary demands are satisfied, the hygienic arts may treat all demands as though they were equally legitimate, and without attempting actual control, passively accept any chance mode of distribution.

210

As disorder increases, the instrumental arts become discon-
nected from their natural sustaining groups, but continue to be
elaborated with no clear reference to the natural needs they fulfill,
as though they lived a life of their own in competition with the life
they now serve only haphazardly. A remedy for overproduction is
sought in the scramble for more markets in underdeveloped countries rather than in the imposition of order and discipline. A
remedy for underproduction is sought in a feverish expansion of
productive apparatus and in a restless search for the raw materials
of unexploited countries to feed them.

The result of both is the gradual surge of imperialism, from
which, as Plato long ago pointed out (Republic, Book II, 372A-374
E), arise war and the chief evils of mankind. This inversion a-
mong the material arts and government is the first degree of cultural barbarism. As Plato also points out in his Gorgias, such an
inversion occurred in the progressive era of fifty-century Athens,
so similar to our own 19th century. Both periods ended in a great
"world war. "

Such a general inversion of the arts could not occur, of
course, if the higher, rational phases of culture were adequately
maintained. It is here that cultural disease takes its inception,
since it is here that culture as a whole is first conceived and
directed . . . .

When the higher arts are inverted by what the ancients
called sophistry, culture rots. True religion is confused with
a comfortable sham. True philosophy is confused with quacker-
ies, which pander to the ingrained habits and instincts of those
whom it is their duty to instruct. Not only is each art individually inverted, but the whole order of the higher arts is turned
topsy-turvy. Religion, instead of providing needed guidance to
philosophy, mixes itself with the subordinate discipline, achieving a bastard product which is neither religion nor philosophy.

Philosophy, in turn, unable to order or interpret the sciences, passively accepts their results, piecing them together in
a mere encyclopedia, or yields to the dictates of some fashionable science, which thinks its special methodology is capable of

211

unlocking all the secrets of being. Left without firm guidance from philosophy and science, the educational arts fall into a chaos of separate disciplines, and finally, without any broad and stable pattern of knowledge, gradually fall under the dominion of politics or of some group which has usurped political power . . . .

The Natural Order of Human Culture . . .

Man is a rational or philosophical animal, and the governing of man therefore is a philosophical art. Being is understood, so far as possible, by the pure theoretical sciences and philosophy. This understanding is intuitively enjoyed by an appreciation of the fine arts and their artifacts. Have we not then reached the highest arts?

If man's reason were without limitation and if man himself were the highest being in the universe, this would certainly be true. But whereas the light of human reason extends to the whole range of being, the light itself is certainly flickering and faint; and altogether aside from the weighty evidence which points to the contrary, it would seem a bit provincial for man to hold that there is no higher being anywhere than he. Unless his reason is aided by further light, it leaves many crucial questions unanswered, and his aspiration weakens and falters. The record of history has shown that without the support of religion the finest achievements of sacrificial endeavor are hardly possible and that human culture drifts into confusion and barbarism.

Since religion, so far as it really exists, apart from human pretence, is derived from a more-than-human source, it cannot be called an art or technique except in an analogous sense. Overarching the whole of culture and the whole of life, it sharpens the individual's intellect, sustains and guards his highest aspirations. Certainly no other science, technique, or discipline can justifiably claim to be the master art.

Can these higher arts be revived from confusion and lethargy? Can they be infused with new life? Will a natural order of culture be established? In view of the anarchy now prevailing in the higher arts and the many inversions and disorders now con-

212

fronting us, it is not easy to answer these questions with a confident affirmation. The correction of these disorders will surely require sacrificial endeavor and arduous struggle on the part of individuals from whom the impetus must come. If human powers alone were the only ground for hope, it would be difficult to face this situation in the light of history without falling into despair. But possibly there are other grounds for hope. The higher arts, though exerting little cultural influence, are still alive. In spite of many inversions of order, all the arts are being practiced. What is needed is to bring them into a sound, natural order of subordination. The main prerequisite for this is rational insight and understanding. There never was a time when it was more important for us to clarify our concepts of life and civilization, and to think them through to their ultimate foundations.

We Have No 'Right to Happiness'

C. S. Lewis

'AFTER ALL,' SAID CLARE, 'THEY HAD A RIGHT TO HAPPINESS.'

We were discussing something that once happened in our own neighbourhood. Mr. A. had deserted Mrs. A. and got his divorce in order to marry Mrs. B., who had likewise got her divorce in order to marry Mr. A. And there was certainly no doubt that Mr. A. and Mrs. B. were very much in love, and if nothing went wrong with their health or their income, they might reasonably expect to be very happy.

From GOD IN THE DOCK (pp. 317-322) by C. S. Lewis, published by William B. Erdmans Publishing Company, Copyright 1970, and used by permission of the publisher.

It was equally clear that they were not happy with their old partners. Mrs. B. had adored her husband at the outset. But then he got smashed up in the war. It was thought he had lost his virility, and it was known that he had lost his job. Life with him was no longer what Mrs. B. had bargained for. Poor Mrs. A., too. She had lost her looks--and all her liveliness. It might be true, as some said, that she consumed herself by bearing his children and nursing him through the long illness that overshadowed their earlier married life.

You mustn't, by the way, imagine that A. was the sort of man who nonchalantly threw a wife away like the peel of an orange he'd sucked dry. Her suicide was a terrible shock to him. We all knew this, for he told us so himself. 'But what could I do?' he said. 'A man has a right to happiness. I had to take my one chance when it came.'

I went away thinking about the concept of a 'right to happiness.'

At first this sounds to me as odd as a right to good luck. For I believe--whatever one school of moralists may say--that we depend for a very great deal of our happiness or misery on circumstances outside all human control. A right to happiness doesn't, for me, make much more sense than a right to be six feet tall, or to have a millionaire for your father, or to get good weather whenever you want to have a picnic.

I can understand a right as a freedom guaranteed me by the laws of the society I live in. Thus, I have a right to travel along the public roads because society gives me that freedom; that's what we mean by calling the roads 'public.' I can also understand a right as a claim guaranteed me by the laws and correlative to an obligation on someone else's part. If I have a right to receive L.100 from you, this is another way of saying that you have a duty to pay me L.100. If the laws allow Mr. A. to desert his wife and seduce his neighbour's wife, then, by definition, Mr. A. has a legal right to do so, and we need bring in no talk about 'happiness.'

But of course that was not what Clare meant. She meant that he had not only a legal but a moral right to act as he did. In other words, Clare is--or would be if she thought it out--a classical moralist after the style of Thomas Aquinas, Grotius, Hooker and Locke. She believes that behind the laws of the state there is a Natural Law.

I agree with her. I hold this conception to be basic to all civilization. Without it, the actual laws of the state become an absolute, as in Hegel. They cannot be criticized because there is no norm against which they should be judged.

The ancestry of Clare's maxim, 'They have a right to happiness,' is august. In words that are cherished by all civilized men, but especially by Americans, it has been laid down that one of the rights of man is a right to 'the pursuit of happiness.' And now we get to the real point.

What did the writers of that august declaration mean?

It is quite certain what they did not mean. They did not mean that man was entitled to pursue happiness by any and every means --including, say, murder, rape, robbery, treason and fraud. No society could be built on such a basis.

They meant 'to pursue happiness by all lawful means'; that is, by all means which the Law of Nature eternally sanctions and which the laws of the nation shall sanction.

Admittedly this seems at first to reduce their maximum to the tautology that men (in pursuit of happiness) have a right to do whatever they have a right to do. But tautologies, seem against their proper historical context, are not always barren tautologies. The declaration is primarily a denial of the political principles which long governed Europe: a challenge flung down to the Austrian and Russian empires, to England before the Reform Bills, to Bourbon France. It demands that whatever means of pursuing happiness are lawful for any should be lawful for all; that 'man,' not men of some particular caste, class, status or religion, should be free to use them. In a century when this is being unsaid

215

by nation after nation and party after party, let us not call it a barren tautology.

But the question as to what means are 'lawful'--what methods of pursuing happiness are either morally permissible by the Law of Nature or should be declared legally permissible by the legislature of a particular nation--remains exactly where it did. And on that question I disagree with Clare. I don't think it is obvious that people have the unlimited 'right to happiness' which she suggests.

For one thing, I believe that Clare, when she says 'happiness,' means simply and solely 'sexual happiness.' Partly because women like Clare never use the word 'happiness' in any other sense. But also because I never heard Clare talk about the 'right' to any other kind. She was rather leftist in her politics, and would have been scandalised if anyone had defended the actions of a ruthless man-eating tycoon on the ground that his happiness consisted in making money and he was pursuing his happiness. She was also a rabid teetotaller; I never heard her excuse an alcoholic because he was happy when he was drunk.

A good many of Clare's friends, and especially her female friends, often felt--I've heard them say so--that their own happiness would be perceptibly increased by boxing her ears. I very much doubt if this would have brought her theory of a right to happiness into play.

Clare, in fact, is doing what the whole western world seems to me to have been doing for the last 40-odd years. When I was a youngster, all the progressive people were saying, 'Why all this prudery? Let us treat sex just as we treat all our other impulses.' I was simple-minded enough to believe they meant what they said. I have since discovered that they meant exactly the opposite. They meant that sex was to be treated as no other impulse in our nature has ever been treated by civilized people. All the others, we admit, have to be bridled. Absolute obedience to your instinct for self-preservation is what we call cowardice; to your acquisitive impulse, avarice. Even sleep must be resisted if you're a sentry. But every unkindness and breach of faith seems to be condoned provided that the object aimed at is 'four bare legs in a bed.'

216

It is like having a morality in which stealing fruit is considered wrong—unless you steal nectarines.

And if you protest against this view you are usually met with chatter about the legitimacy and beauty and sanctity of 'sex' and accused of harbouring some Puritan prejudice against it as something disreputable or shameful. I deny the charge. Foam-born Venus . . . golden Aphrodite . . . Our Lady of Cyprus . . . I never breathed a word against you. If I object to boys who steal my nectarines, must I be supposed to disapprove of nectarines in general? Or even of boys in general? It might, you know, be stealing that I disapproved of.

The real situation is skillfully concealed by saying that the question of Mr. A.'s 'right' to desert his wife is one of 'sexual morality.' Robbing an orchard is not an offense against some special morality called 'fruit morality.' It is an offense against honesty. Mr. A's action is an offense against good faith (to solemn promises), against gratitude (toward one to whom he was deeply indebted) and against common humanity.

Our sexual impulses are thus being put in a position of preposterous privilege. The sexual motive is taken to condone all sorts of behaviour which, if it had any other end in view, would be condemned as merciless, treacherous and unjust.

Now though I see no good reason for giving sex this privilege, I think I see a strong cause. It is this.

It is part of the nature of a strong erotic passion—as distinct from a transient fit of appetite—that it makes more towering promises than any other emotion. No doubt all our desires make promises, but not so impressively. To be in love involves the almost irrestibly conviction that one will go on being in love until one dies, and that possession of the beloved will confer, not merely frequent ecstasies, but settled, fruitful, deep-rooted, lifelong happiness. Hence all seems to be at stake. If we miss this chance we shall have lived in vain. At the very thought of such a doom we sink into fathomless depths of self-pity.

217

Unfortunately these promises are found often to be quite untrue. Every experienced adult knows this to be so as regards all
erotic passions (except the one he himself is feeling at the moment).
We discount the world-without-end pretensions of our friends'
amours easily enough. We know that such things sometimes last--
and sometimes don't. And when they do last, this is not because
they promised at the outset to do so. When two people achieve lasting happiness, this is not solely because they are great lovers but
because they are also--I must put it crudely--good people; controlled, loyal, fairminded, mutually adaptable people.

If we establish a 'right to (sexual) happiness' which super-
sedes all the ordinary rules of behaviour, we do so not because of
what our passion shows itself to be in experience but because of
what it professes to be while we are in the grip of it. Hence,
while the bad behaviour is real and works miseries and degrada-
tions, the happiness which was the object of the behaviour turns
out again and again to be illusory. Everyone (except Mr. A. and
Mrs. B.) knows that Mr. A. in a year or so may have the same
reason for deserting his new wife as for deserting his old. He will
feel again that all is at stake. He will see himself again as the
great lover, and his pity for himself will exclude all pity for the
woman.

Two further points remain.

One is this. A society in which conjugal infidelity is tolerated must always be in the long run a society adverse to women.
Women, whatever a few male songs and satires may say to the
contrary, are more naturally monogamous than men; it is a biological necessity. Where promiscuity prevails, they will therefore always be more often the victims than the culprits. Also,
domestic happiness is more necessary to them than to us. And
the quality by which they most easily hold a man, their beauty,
decreases every year after they have come to maturity, but this
does not happen to those qualities of personality--women don't
really care twopence about our looks--by which we hold women.
Thus in the ruthless war of promiscuity women are at a double
disadvantage. They play for higher stakes and are also more
likely to lose. I have no sympathy with moralists who frown at

218

the increasing crudity of female provocativeness. These signs of desperate competition fill me with pity.

Secondly, though the 'right to happiness' is chiefly claimed for the sexual impulse, it seems to me impossible that the matter should stay there. The fatal principle, once allowed in that department, must sooner or later seep through our whole lives. We thus advance toward a state of society in which not only each man but every impulse in each man claims <u>carte</u> <u>blanche</u>. And then, though our technological skill may help us survive a little longer, our civilization will have died at heart, and will--one dare not even add 'unfortunately'--be swept away.

PART FOUR

EXISTENTIAL THEISM

S. Kierkegaard
Rudolf Bultmann
Paul Tillich
Henry Margenau
Martin Buber
Miguel de Unamuno
Gabriel Marcel
Ralph Harper

1. INTRODUCTION

Existentialism has been largely a contemporary "movement," though many interpreters see the roots of it, or similarities to it, in much earlier thought.

Existentialism has always been very difficult to define. The reasons for this difficulty are several. There are those who have been so classified, like Unamuno, who reject all such classification. Not to do so, they think, would destroy the highly personal and individual emphasis which they are seeking. Those who have not rejected the classification of existentialist have sometimes taken pains to interpret the term differently from others who accept the classification.

Within the group of those who are usually interpreted as being existentialists there is a clear distinction made between those who are <u>atheistic</u> and those who are <u>theistic</u>. Perhaps these differences cause the most confusion in the attempt to define the term.

There are similarities of belief between the atheistic and theistic existentialists. They both believe that self-understanding is primary and basic to the interpretation of life. This understanding is not to be sought in concepts about the self but in concrete human existence itself. We exist before we seek to interpret ourselves or, as Sartre puts it, "Existence precedes essence." The fundamental fact is human existence and all understanding begins with self-understanding.

The atheistic and theistic Existentialists also agree, essentially, as to the condition of human existence. Anxiety and despair about death, meaninglessness of life and the unreliability of human reason arise out of a longing for being from which human being is estranged.

In this condition of estrangement existentialists assume different possibilities for overcoming it. Some who have been called

223

existentialists, such as Franz Kafka, see no hope at all for over-coming the estrangement. Life, to the end, remains tragic and meaningless. In this case Existentialism becomes a kind of Nihil-ism, a philosophy of nothingness. Others, such as Sartre, believe that though human efforts to overcome the estrangement are always doomed, it is possible to be moral. In the midst of tragic and ab-surd existence we can choose to be ourselves against compulsions which seek to turn us into objects. Sartre insists that though this atheistic Existentialism does not lead to complete fulfillment of the longing for being ("being-in-itself-for-itself") it does allow us to remain human and demands a strong humanistic ethic.

The clear methodology which distinguishes Existential The-ism from these other types of Existentialism, is that human beings in the condition of human existence can be opened to the ground of being. Unlike Natural Theism it is not reason which opens the "door" of being, but a total act of personal faith arising out of the human condition. The being which is opened up remains mysteri-ous, but an existential fulfillment is gained which allows us to ac-cept the anxieties and mysteries of life.

We assume the following definitions of Existential Theism:

1. Knowledge of a transcendent God cannot be gained through logical reasoning or scientific evidence. Be-lief in God grows out of the anxiety experienced in the longing for the infinite by a finite being.

2. Faith does not bring knowledge of God which can be put into doctrines and concepts, but an awareness of the Presence of God as mysterious being. Faith does not elevate the human being into the consciousness of God, but creates the condition in which God can break through into human consciousness.

3. Existential faith opens up a depth of subjective reli-gious truth which completes and compliments object-ive scientific truth.

4. Moral relations which foster and preserve the sanctity

224

of persons are rooted in the relation to God made possible through existential faith.

5.   Belief in immortality is not based upon rational arguments but existential need.

Kierkegaard has been significantly influential in the development of Existential Theism. His penetrating analysis of the paradoxical nature of reason, in the introductory article which follows, lays the foundation for existential faith. Reason, in discovering its own limits, contains a passion for the Unknown. Reason, thus, collides with the Unknown, but it cannot be known. Since we always reason from existence, rather than toward existence, all attempts of the natural theist to "prove" the existence of God fail. The distinction from Humanism is to be found in the passionate engagement of the "absolutely different" which cannot be known.

The Absolute Paradox

Soren Kierkegaard

The supreme paradox of all thought is the attempt to discover something that thought cannot think. This passion is at bottom present in all thinking, even in the thinking of the individual, in so far as in thinking he participates in something transcending himself. But habit dulls our sensibilities, and prevents us from perceiving it . . . .

From "The Absolute Paradox: A Metaphysical Crotchet," in S. Kierkegaard's PHILOSOPHICAL FRAGMENTS OR A FRAGMENT OF PHILOSOPHY, 2nd edition (copyright (c) 1936, 1962 by Princeton University Press). Originally Translated and Introduced by David Swenson. New Introduction and Commentary by Niels Thulstrup. Translation revised and Commentary Translated by Howard V. Long, pp. 46-57. Omission of footnotes. Reprinted by permission of Princeton University Press.

But what is this unknown something with which the Reason collides when inspired by its paradoxical passion, with the result of unsettling even man's knowledge of himself? It is the Unknown. It is not a human being, in so far as we know what man is; nor is it any other known thing. So let us call this unknown something: <u>God</u>. It is nothing more than a name we assign to it. The idea of demonstrating that this unknown something (God) exists, could scarcely suggest itself to the Reason. For if God does not exist it would of course be impossible to prove it; and if he does exist it would be folly to attempt it. For at the very outset, in beginning my proof, I will have presupposed it, not as doubtful but as certain (a presupposition is never doubtful, for the very reason that it is a presupposition), since otherwise I would not begin, readily understanding that the whole would be impossible if he did not exist. But if when I speak of proving God's existence I mean that I propose to prove that the Unknown, which exists, is God, then I express myself unfortunately. For in that case I do not prove anything, least of all an existence, but merely develop the content of a conception. Generally speaking, it is a difficult matter to prove that anything exists; and what is still worse for the intrepid souls who undertake the venture, the difficulty is such that fame scarcely awaits those who concern themselves with it. The entire demonstration always turns into something very different from what it assumes to be, and becomes an additional development of the consequences that flow from my having assumed that the object in question exists. Thus I always reason from existence, not toward existence, whether I move in the sphere of palpable sensible fact or in the realm of thought. I do not for example prove that a stone exists, but that some existing thing is a stone. The procedure in a court of justice does not prove that a criminal exists, but what the accused, whose existence is given, is a criminal. Whether we call existence an "accessorium" or the eternal "prius," it is never subject to demonstration. Let us take ample time for consideration. We have no such reason for haste as have those who from concern for themselves or for God or for some other thing, must make haste to get its existence demonstrated. Under such circumstances there may indeed be need for haste, especially if the prover sincerely seeks to appreciate the danger that he himself, or the thing in question, may be non-existent unless the proof is finished; and does not surreptitiously entertain the thought that it exists whether

226

he succeeds in proving it or not.

If it were proposed to prove Napoleon's existence from Napoleon's deeds, would it not be a most curious proceeding? His existence does indeed explain his deeds, but the deeds do not prove <u>his</u> existence, unless I have already understood the word "his" so as thereby to have assumed his existence. But Napoleon is only an individual, and in so far there exists no absolute relationship between him and his deeds; some other person might have performed the same deeds. Perhaps this is the reason why I cannot pass from the deeds to existence. If I call these deeds the deeds of Napoleon the proof becomes superfluous, since I have already named him; if I ignore this, I can never prove from the deeds that they are Napoleon's, but only in a purely ideal manner that such deeds are the deeds of a great general, and so forth. But between God and his works there exists an absolute relationship; God is not a name but a concept . . . . The works of God are such that only God can perform them. Just so, but where then are the works of God? The works from which I would deduce his existence are not immediately given. The wisdom of God in nature, his goodness, his wisdom in the governance of the world--are all these manifest, perhaps, upon the very face of things? Are we not here confronted with the most terrible temptations to doubt, and is it now impossible finally to dispose of all these doubts? But from such an order of things I will surely not attempt to prove God's existence; and even if I began I would never finish, and would in addition have to live constantly in suspense, lest something so terrible should suddenly happen that my bit of proof would be demolished. From what works then do I propose to derive the proof? From the works as apprehended through an ideal interpretation, i.e., such as they do not immediately reveal themselves. But in that case it is not from the works that I prove God's existence. I merely develop the ideality I have presupposed, and because of my confidence in <u>this</u> I make so bold as to defy all objections, even those that I have not yet been made. In the beginning of my proof I presuppose the ideal interpretation, and also that I will be successful in carrying it through; but what else is this but to presuppose that God exists, so that I really begin by virtue of confidence in him?

And how does God's existence emerge from the proof? Does

it follow straightway, without any breach of continuity? Or have we not here an analogy to the behaviour of these toys, the little Cartesian dolls? As soon as I let go of the doll it stands on its head. As soon as I let it go--I must therefore let it go. So also with the proof for God's existence. As long as I keep my hold on the proof, i.e., continue to demonstrate, the existence does not come out, if for no other reason than I am engaged in proving it; but when I let the proof go, the existence is there. But this act of letting go is surely also something; it is indeed a contribution of mine. Must not this also be taken into the account, this little moment, brief as it may be--it need not be long, for it is a leap. However brief this moment, if only an instantaneous now, this "now" must be included in the reckoning. If anyone wishes to have it ignored, I will use it to tell a little anecdote, in order to show that it really does exist. Chrysippus was experimenting with a sorites to see if he could not bring about a break in its quality, either progressively or retrogressively. But Carneades could not get it in his head when the new quality actually emerged. Then Chrysippus told him to try making a little pause in the reckoning, and so--so it would be easier to understand. Carneades replied: With the greatest pleasure, please do not hesitate on my account; you may not only pause, but even lie down to sleep, and it will help you just as little; for when you awake we will begin again where you left off. Just so; it boots as little to try to get rid of something by sleeping as to try to come into the possession of something in the same manner.

Whoever therefore attempts to demonstrate the existence of God (except in the sense of clarifying the concept, and without the "reservatio finalis" noted above, that the existence emerges from the demonstration by a leap) proves in lieu thereof something else, something which at times perhaps does not need a proof, and in any case needs none better; for the fool says in his heart that there is no God, but whoever says in his heart or to men: Wait just a little and I will prove it--what a rare man of wisdom is he! If in the moment of beginning he will never come to begin, partly from fear of failure, since God perhaps does not exist, and partly because he has nothing with which to begin. --A project of this kind would scarcely have been undertaken by the ancients. Socrates at least, who is credited with having put forth the physicoteleological proof for God's existence, did not go about it in any such manner.

228

He always presupposes God's existence, and under this presupposition seeks to interpenetrate nature with the idea of purpose. Had he been asked why he pursued this method, he would doubtless have explained that he lacked the courage to venture out upon so perilous a voyage of discovery without having made sure of God's existence behind him. At the word of God he casts his net as if to catch the idea or purpose; for nature herself finds many means of frightening the inquirer, and distracts him by many a digression.

The paradoxical passion of the Reason thus comes repeatedly into collision with the Unknown, which does indeed exist, but is unknown, and in so far does not exist. The Reason cannot advance beyond this point, and yet it cannot refrain in its paradoxicalness from arriving at this limit and occupying itself therewith. It will not serve to dismiss its relation to it simply by asserting that the Unknown does not exist, since this itself involves a relationship. But what then is the Unknown, since the designation of it as God merely signifies for us that it is unknown? To say that it is the Unknown because it cannot be known, and even if it were capable of being known, it could not be expressed, does not satisfy the demands of passion, though it correctly interprets the Unknown as a limit; but a limit is precisely a torment for passion, though it also serves as an incitement. And yet the Reason can come no further, whether it risks an issue "via negationis" or "via eminentia."

What then is the Unknown? It is the limit to which the Reason repeatedly comes, and in so far, substituting a static form of conception for the dynamic, it is the different, the absolutely different. But because it is absolutely different, there is no mark by which it could be distinguished. When qualified as absolutely different it seems on the verge of disclosure, but this is not the case; for the Reason cannot even conceive an absolute unlikeness. The Reason cannot negate itself absolutely, but uses itself for the purpose, and thus conceives only such an unlikeness within itself as it can conceive by means of itself; it cannot absolutely transcend itself, and hence conceives only such a superiority over itself as it can conceive by means of itself. Unless the Unknown (God) remains a mere limiting conception, the single idea of difference will be thrown into a state of confusion, and become many ideas of many differences. The Unknown is then in a condition of dispension . . . and the Reason may choose at pleasure from what is at hand and the imagination may suggest (the monstrous, the ludicrous, etc.).

But it is impossible to hold fast to a difference of this nature. Every time this is done it is essentially an arbitrary act, and deepest down in the heart of piety lurks the mad caprice which knows that it has itself produced its God. If no specific determination of difference can be held fast, because there is no distinguishing mark, like and unlike finally become identified with one another, thus sharing the fate of all such dialetical opposites. The unlikeness clings to the Reason and confounds it, so that the Reason no longer knows itself and quite consistently confuses itself with the unlikeness. On this point paganism has been sufficiently prolific in fantastic inventions. As for the last named supposition, the self-irony of the Reason, I shall attempt to delineate it merely by a stroke or two, without raising any question of its being historical. There lives an individual whose appearance is precisely like that of other men; he grows up to manhood like others, he marries, he has an occupation by which he earns his livelihood, and he makes provision for the future as befits a man. For though it may be beautiful to live like the birds of the air, it is not lawful, and may lead to the sorriest of consequences: either starvation if one has enough persistence, or dependence on the bounty of others. This man is also God. How do I know? I cannot know it, for in order to know it I would have to know God, and the nature of the difference between God and man; and this I cannot know, because the Reason has reduced it to likeness with that from which it was unlike. Thus God becomes the most terrible of deceivers, because the Reason has deceived itself. The Reason has brought God as near as possible, and yet he is as far away as ever.

2. THE EXISTENCE OF GOD

Concepts of God, according to Rudolf Bultmann, originate in our experience of finitude. Our experience of powerlessness, moral unfulfillment and transciency prompt us to conceptualize God as omnipotent, holy, eternal and transcendent. While these concepts are formulated out of our inquiry about God they do not give us knowledge of God, only the knowledge of what we are and what we long for. God remains that "mysterious life-stream" which is wholly other and cannot be known. The current of that mysterious stream, however, can break through our finitude, immerse us momentarily and raise us up to our real nature as an "eternal" entity.

The Concept of God

Rudolf Bultmann

We will find the answer to this question if we simply inquire into what men generally mean when they speak of God. Luther, in explaining the first commandment in the Larger Catechism, defines the meaning of God thus: 'what you set and trust your heart to is really your God!'

Thus naturally 'money and means' can be a 'God,' and 'art, cleverness, power, favour, friendship and honour' too, that is in so far as anyone 'sets all his heart on them.' And thus Germany is God, when somebody today professes 'I believe in Germany.'

In going on to say that a God of such a kind is not the one

Reprinted with permission of Macmillan Publishing Co., Inc., from ESSAYS, PHILOSOPHICAL AND THEOLOGICAL by Rudolf Bultmann. Copyright SCM Press Ltd. 1955.

true God, Luther is not as yet saying anything specifically Christian. For no one else in the world calls money and means, art and honour and so on 'God': and even those whose faith is in Germany would not say directly 'Germany is God,' but at most would express it in this way; that God confronts them in Germany—reveals himself in Germany.

(a)   In the first place, that is, this belongs to the concept of God: God is the person or the power <u>one</u> <u>sets</u> <u>one's</u> <u>heart</u> <u>on</u>, and relies on, expecting everything good for him and taking refuge in him in all distresses. But while everywhere in the world such a power is actually called God, that is, with a special name, it becomes at the same time clear that God is not, for everyone, an <u>individual</u> power or great being within the world and alongside others, but that he is the power which has power over <u>every</u> single thing within the world. Only in this way indeed can one take refuge in this power in all one's distresses. To the idea of God as such belongs the <u>idea</u> <u>of</u> <u>omnipotence</u>.

(b)   But everywhere people speak of God, the idea of God also has a polemical or critical significance. For everywhere the proclamation of God stands in contrast to the attitude of men in so far as they are, in fact, willing only to make sure of a power from which they may expect everything that is good and to which they can take refuge in all their distresses; yet in so far as in the general run of life they do not inquire about this power above everything else, but from time to time allow the individual thing that is of service to them or impresses them to gain the mastery over them. Everywhere God is spoken of, people know that his power is <u>one</u> <u>which</u> <u>makes</u> <u>demands</u>, and that his omnipotence goes together with his <u>claims</u>: that he does not only demand veneration as a 'jealous' God, but is also the guardian of law and morality.

His omnipotence becomes an annihilating power to the man who does not let it become his master, in any form whatsoever. <u>The</u> <u>Almighty</u> <u>is</u> <u>at</u> <u>the</u> <u>same</u> <u>time</u> <u>the</u> <u>Holy</u> <u>One</u> <u>who</u> <u>demands</u> <u>sacrifices</u>, <u>the</u> <u>judge</u> <u>who</u> <u>demands</u> <u>and</u> <u>who</u> <u>judges</u>. Thus Luther says that we learn from the first commandment 'how God will not suffer any presumption or reliance on anything else, and demands nothing higher from us than confidence from the heart in all that is good.'

And so to the idea of God as such belonged the idea of holiness.

(c)   Expressed in this also is the idea that God stands in detachment from the world. Naturally this thought is not made to emerge clearly everywhere that God is spoken of: but is contained in the idea of God as such, and that appears when—as happens everywhere—God's eternity is spoken of. Even those who speak of a God immanent in the world ascribe to him the attribute of eternity: for to them, too, God's being, in the world, is not simply identical with the mere existence of the phenomena of the world. God only is to be seen beyond it, not with the eyes of the body but with those of the spirit. He is not simply there in the individual thing which confronts me, but must be seen by me—felt and experienced by me, beyond that. And even where he is put on the same level as the world as a whole, he is not simply there in what the world presents to our view. On the contrary, he is then spoken of as the universal law, the effective 'life force,' and so on. But, above all, the world never confronts man as a whole, but in its individual parts with its individual powers. And where God is preached as the power of the world as a whole, it is always expected of the individual that he should free himself from the aspects of the individual case and see himself in the whole, as a part of it—as what in his subjectivity as an individual he is not in the least, but what he is doubtless "sub specie aeterni, " but in his actual existence must still become. The eternal God is beyond the world that confronts me at any given time, and beyond myself. And even the man who proudly speaks of the "deus in nobis" admits that; for he, too, actually seeks to say not that he is divine merely in himself, but that his real ego, which he has always still to lay hold of, and which is always to provide him with the criterion for his activity, is divine. In relation to his existing subjectivity the divine ego is just as transcendent as the command of the moral law, even when it counts as a law of his own will—it is transcendent, as opposed to the subjective desires of the individual.

To the idea of God belongs both the idea of eternity and transcendence and that of omnipotence, demand and holiness.

The Knowledge Comprised in the Concept of God

But what does man know of God in knowing that? Is he acquainted with God because he has a concept of God? Not in the least. In it he has only reached the stage of an inquiry about God; and the knowledge contained in this inquiry is fundamentally none other than man's knowledge of himself; a knowledge about what he has not and is not, and yet of what he would like to have and to be; a knowledge of the limitations and insignificance of man.

(a) The man who speaks of God's omnipotence knows about his own powerlessness; and so he knows that in his life he is constantly subject to forces, to the propitious and to the detrimental forces of nature and history, which play with him--forces of destiny and of death. His life remains mysterious and uncanny, if he is unable to speak of a highest power that is master of all powers, as of one from which he can expect everything that is good, and in which he can take refuge in all his distresses--one in face of which even death is brought to nothing, or becomes nothing worth. Such a power is represented either by one of these powers whose rule he thinks he can comprehend, to which he can feel himself related, and which he now enthrones alongside which all others seem as nothing; to him--whether it is that of the spirit or the reason, or that of blood. Or else it is a power standing behind and above all these powers, working through them unseen and unperceived, the law of life for the entire world, or again a Lord beyond the entirety of the world.

However it may be with regard to that, the knowledge contained in such an utterance is that of the uncanniness and the enigmatic nature of life--of the mystery and finitude of man. From it arises the inquiry concerning the power which could bring light into the darkness, order into the confusion, and life into death. It is a knowledge of dread, and it is no wonder, if the question arising from it persuades itself, or lets itself be persuaded of an answer which will still the dread; if what is incomprehensible is objectivized, and the uncanny is banished in that it is hypostasized and worshipped as an omnipotent deity.

(b) Man knows about demands being made upon him when he speaks of a demanding God, of God as judge. He knows that he is not what he ought to be. That still does not mean that he knows

234

himself to be a sinner, and to be on the wrong track; first of all it means he knows just that he is on the way, that he is always other than the man he ought to be, and that even when he thinks he has acted rightly his life has no fulfilment, but remains continually subject to fresh demands. He knows about his real nature, and he knows that in everything which belongs to the 'now,' or the 'moment,' he is never really himself. He is, as it were, always searching for himself.

If he is honest, however, he can know something still more, that is, that he can continually and often does go astray in this transitional stage. He knows that he can become and often does become guilty and that he has constantly to conquer and educate himself--that he has to bring sacrifices and free himself from his past.

In short, he knows that he stands between good and evil--that 'two souls, alas, are dwelling in his heart' (Faust, Part I, I.III2, Vor dem Tor) and that his way is therefore a struggle in which alone he is to become what he really is--but that, however, as he is, he is never in his real being, but at best is on the right track, though always inhibited by the things that try to seduce him, and by what his own past has made of him, from which he has to free himself.

And from this knowledge of continually having demands made on him and of being unfulfilled comes his talking of God as the Holy One, and the Demanding One: whether he makes himself conscious of the power and dignity of the demand, or inquires about God as the idea which brings light into the insecurity and darkness of his way, gathering into a unity all the different claims which he knows to be directed at him; or whether it is a question of his speaking of God as the norm by which he measures his own and other peoples' behaviour, and by which he judges history. The knowledge contained in such talk about God is man's knowledge about himself, about his having demands made upon him, and his being in a transitional stage, and about his real nature, which is continually present to him. From this knowledge arises the inquiry about God as the authority pointing out the right way, or as the guarantor of man's dignity, and of the unity and significance of history. And the question is plausibly answered to the effect that knowledge about my having demands made upon me is knowledge about God, and that the dignity of man is to be found in having such demands made upon him --that the deity comes down from his throne as ruler of the universe when man embodies in his will the demand to do good; and that the dispeace that belongs to his transitional stage, and his knowledge about his real nature, is already a proof of the "deus in nobis."

(c) Man knows about his transient nature when he speaks of God's eternity and transcendence. What he says about God is his idea of the finitude of the world and of himself. No individual thing in the world has a final value for him. No action is a perfect one:

> 'Alas, for even our deeds, just like our sorrows,
> Block up for us the course of life.'

No individual situation brings fulfilment to what he wishes and what he strives for. That which ought to be attained always remains to be achieved. The dread lest fortune, when it seems to be there, will be destroyed, always lurks in the background; so too does the knowledge that the blissful hour hurries past in haste, and that he himself is not yet ready for the end. The fleeting nature of time takes everything away with it--indeed, he cannot even wish that it were otherwise; for neither does time bring any 'moment' to which he could say:

> 'But stay a while, thou art so fair!'

Man always knows:

> 'Fortune is there, where thou art not!'

And so he is counselled by resignation:

> 'Advancing let him find both pain and joy,
> He who, each moment, nought can satisfy.'

Out of this situation arises talk about something transcendent and eternal, a sphere in which all that we are not in this world, here

236

in the realm of development and decay, is reality: where there is no subjection to time and space, where life is, without death, and light without darkness. And there arises the inquiry about God as the power which lifts man out of his state of subjection, and gives him life capable of despising death; it gives eternity in the 'moment,' and lifts one out of the transitory nature of what is commonplace making the world a translucent symbol of the transcendent and nothing more.

And it is indeed understandable that such inquiries easily answer themselves or lead to an answer being given; for without an answer man just could not live. If, then, the answer takes the form of saying that it is a question of running away from what belongs to this world, in the vision which belongs to the spirit, through which man gains a share in the eternal realm of ideas, or in an ascetic attitude to life and a mystical experience, God being therefore described as what is wholly other as opposed to everything that belongs to the here and now--as the numinous, in face of which all his thoughts are silenced, and with which man only becomes one in feeling, being swallowed up into the divine in blissful moments, and consumed by divine fire: if the answer is given in these terms--that the mysterious life-stream is itself divine, the life-stream which flows powerfully on as the only one in all the vicissitudes of life--then each individual form, every 'here' and 'now' must certainly be immersed like the wave in the flowing current; but the current itself is what is transcendent and eternal. Man cannot, of course, cling on to the individual phenomenon of the moment; but he is free for eternity when he traces in himself the rushing of this current within him, and surrenders himself to it: if it is the current of the cosmic life force, or that of blood, which binds together the individuals of a people and pulsates through all generations of the people conceived as an 'eternal' entity.

Knowledge about God is in the first instance a knowledge which man has about himself and his finitude, and God is reckoned to be the power which breaks through this finitude of man and thereby raises him up to his real nature.

3. THE NATURE OF RELIGIOUS EXPERIENCE

For <u>Paul</u> <u>Tillich</u> religious experience is identified with the self-acceptance of being in spite of the experience of the anxiety of meaninglessness or doubt, which is inevitably a part of finitude. The acceptance of anxiety without an affirmation of our being leads to hopeless despair, and the acceptance of our own being without anxiety leads to an escapism which is a distortion of life. Tillich believes that the power to accept the condition of despair rests in the power of being which, along with non-being, is present in us. The faith which accepts this <u>power</u> of being gives us the courage to accept this power of acceptance, which is absolute faith. While this absolute faith does not lead us to any specific content which can be called God, it does open us up to the power of being as it is manifested in the non-being of finitude. Unlike the humanist Fromm, Tillich believes that the act of self-negation which, paradoxically, is present in the self-acceptance of our anxieties, is essential to genuine self-affirmation, and both the negation and affirmation are grounded in the power of being itself which participates in our being. Tillich believes that while both the pantheistic idea of union with God and the natural theistic idea of the objective awareness of God affirm the power of being, they deny non-being or human finitude. He also recognizes that while atheistic existentialists affirm non-being they are, tragically, unable to affirm the power of being.

The Power of Being

Paul Tillich

Courage is the self-affirmation of being in spite of the fact of nonbeing. It is the act of the individual self in taking the anxiety of nonbeing upon itself by affirming itself either as part of an embracing whole or in its individual selfhood. Courage always includes risk, it is always threatened by nonbeing, whether the risk of losing oneself and becoming a thing within the whole of things or of losing one's world in an empty self-relatedness. Courage needs the power of being, a power transcending the nonbeing which is experienced in the anxiety of fate and death, which is present in the anxiety of emptiness and meaninglessness, which is effective in the anxiety of guilt and condemnation. The courage which takes this threefold anxiety into itself must be rooted in a power of being that is greater than the power of oneself and the power of one's world . . . . This means that every courage to be has an open or hidden religious root. For religion is the state of being grasped by the power of being-itself. In some cases the religious root is carefully covered, in others it is passionately denied; in some it is deeply hidden and in others superficially. But it is never completely absent. For everything that is participates in being-itself, and everybody has some awareness of this participation, especially in the moments in which he experiences the threat of nonbeing . . . .

Since the relation of man to the ground of his being must be expressed in symbols taken from the structure of being, the polarity of participation and individualization determines the special character of this relation as it determines the special character of the courage to be. If participation is dominant, the relation to being-itself has a mystical character, if individualization prevails the relation to being-itself has a personal character, if both poles are accepted and transcended the relation to being-itself has the character of faith.

In mysticism the individual self strives for a participation in the ground of being which approaches identification. Our question is not whether this goal can ever be reached by a finite being but whether and how mysticism can be the source of the courage to be. We have referred to the mystical background of Spinoza's system, to his way of deriving the self-affirmation of man from the self-affirmation of the divine substance in which he participates. In a

239

similar way all mystics draw their power of self-affirmation from the experience of the power of being-itself with which they are united. But one may ask, can courage be united with mysticism in any way ? It seems that in India, for example, courage is considered the virtue of the "kshatriya" (knight), to be found below the levels of the Brahman or the ascetic saint. Mystical identification transcends the aristocratic virtue of courageous self-sacrifice. It is self-surrender in a higher, more complete, and more radical form. It is the perfect form of self-affirmation. But if this is so, it is courage in the larger though not in the narrower sense of the word. The ascetic and ecstatic mystic affirms his own essential being over against the elements of nonbeing which are present in the finite world, the realm of Maya. It takes tremendous courage to resist the lure of appearances. The power of being which is manifest in such courage is so great that the gods tremble in fear of it. The mystic seeks to penetrate the ground of being, the all-present and all-pervasive power of the Brahman. In doing so he affirms his essential self which is identical with the power of the Brahman, while all those who affirm themselves in the bondage of Maya affirm what is not their true self, be they animals, men, or gods. This elevates the mystic's self-affirmation above the courage as a special virtue possessed by the aristocratic-soldiery. But he is not above courage altogether. That which from the point of view of the finite world appears as self-negation is from the point of view of ultimate being the most perfect self-affirmation, the most radical form of courage.

In the strength of this courage the mystic conquers the anxiety of fate and death. Since being in time and space and under the categories of finitude is ultimately unreal, the vicissitudes arising from it and the final nonbeing ending it are equally unreal . . . .

The pole of individualization expresses itself in the religious experience as a personal encounter with God. And the courage derived from it is the courage of confidence in the personal reality which is manifest in the religious experience. In contradistinction to the mystical union one can call this relation a personal communion with the source of courage. Although the two types are in contrast they do not exclude each other. For they are united by the polar interdependence of individualization and participation.

The courage of confidence has often, especially in Protestantism, been identified with the courage of faith. But this is not adequate, because confidence is only one element in faith. Faith embraces both mystical participation and personal confidence . . . . Luther directed his attack against the objective, quantitative, and impersonal elements in the Roman system. He fought for an immediate person-to-person relationship between God and man . . . . Luther's courage of confidence is personal confidence, derived from a person-to-person encounter with God . . . . Luther, and in fact the whole period, experienced the anxiety of guilt and condemnation as the main form of their anxiety. The courage to affirm oneself in spite of this anxiety is the courage which we have called the courage of confidence. It is rooted in the personal, total, and immediate certainty of divine forgiveness . . . .

The encounter with God in Luther is not merely the basis for the courage to take upon oneself sin and condemnation, it is also the basis for taking upon oneself fate and death. For encountering God means encountering transcendent security and transcendent eternity. He who participates in God participates in eternity. But in order to participate in him you must be accepted by him and you must have accepted his acceptance of you.

Luther had experiences which he describes as attacks of utter despair ("Anfechtung"), as the frightful threat of a complete meaninglessness. He felt these moments as satanic attacks in which everything was menaced: his Christian faith, the confidence in his work, the Reformation, the forgiveness of sins. Everything broke down in the extreme moments of this despair, nothing was left of the courage to be. Luther in these moments, and in the descriptions he gives of them, anticipated the descriptions of them by modern Existentialism. But for him this was not the last word. The last word was the first commandment, the statement that God is God. It reminded him of the unconditional element in human experience of which one can be aware even in the abyss of meaninglessness. And this awareness saved him.

It should not be forgotten that the great adversary of Luther, Thomas Munzer, the Anabaptist and religious socialist, describes similar experiences. He speaks of the ultimate situation in which everything finite reveals its finitude, in which the finite has come to its end, in which anxiety grips the heart and all previous meanings fall apart, and in which just for this reason the Divine Spirit can make itself felt and can turn the whole situation into a courage to be whose expression is revolutionary action. While Luther represents ecclesiastical Protestantism, Munzer represents evangelical radicalism. Both men have shaped history, and actually Munzer's views had even more influence in America than Luther's. Both men experienced the anxiety of meaninglessness and described it in terms which had been created by Christian mystics. But in doing so they transcended the courage of confidence which is based on mystical union. This leads to a last question: whether the two types of the courage to accept acceptance can be united in view of the all-pervasive presence of the anxiety of doubt and meaninglessness in our own period . . . .

We have avoided the concept of faith in our description of the courage to be which is based on mystical union with the ground of being as well as in our description of the courage to be which is based on the personal encounter with God. This is partly because the concept of faith has lost its genuine meaning and has received the connotation of "belief in something unbelievable." But this is not the only reason for the use of terms other than faith. The decisive reason is that I do not think either mystical union or personal encounter fulfills the idea of faith. Certainly there is faith in the elevation of the soul above the finite to the infinite, leading to its union with the ground of being. But more than this is included in the concept of faith. And there is faith in the personal encounter with the personal God. But more than this is included in the concept of faith. Faith is the state of being grasped by the power of being-itself. The courage to be is an expression of faith and what "faith" means must be understood through the courage to be. We have defined courage as the self-affirmation of being in spite of nonbeing. The power of this self-affirmation is the power of being which is effective in every act of courage. Faith is the experience of this power . . . .

Faith is not a theoretical affirmation of something uncertain, it is the existential acceptance of something transcending ordinary experience. Faith is not an opinion but a state. It is the state of being grasped by the power of being which transcends everything that is and in which everything that is participates. He who is grasped by this power is able to affirm himself because he knows that he is affirmed by the power of being-itself. In this point mystical experience and personal encounter are identical. In both of them faith is the basis of the courage to be . . . .

Which courage is able to take nonbeing into itself in the form of doubt and meaninglessness? This is the most important and most disturbing question in the quest for the courage to be. For the anxiety of meaninglessness undermines what is still unshaken in the anxiety of fate and death and of guilt and condemnation. In the anxiety of guilt and condemnation doubt has not yet undermined the certainty of an ultimate responsibility. We are threatened but we are not destroyed. If, however, doubt and meaninglessness prevail one experiences an abyss in which the meaning of life and the truth of ultimate responsibility disappear. Both the Stoic who conquers the anxiety of fate with the Socratic courage of wisdom and the Christian who conquers the anxiety of guilt with the Protestant courage of accepting forgiveness are in a different situation. Even in the despair of having to die and the despair of self-condemnation meaning is affirmed and certitude preserved. But in the despair of doubt and meaninglessness both are swallowed by nonbeing.

The question then is this: Is there a courage which can conquer the anxiety of meaninglessness and doubt? Or in other words, can the faith which accepts acceptance resist the power of nonbeing in its most radical form? Can faith resist meaninglessness? Is there a kind of faith which can exist together with doubt and meaninglessness? These questions lead to the last aspect of the problem discussed in these lectures and the one most relevant to our time: How is the courage to be possible if all the ways to create it are barred by the experience of their ultimate insufficiency? If life is as meaningless as death, if guilt is as questionable as perfection, if being is no more meaningful than nonbeing, on what can one base the courage to be?

There is an inclination in some Existentialists to answer these questions by a leap from doubt to dogmatic certitude, from

243

meaninglessness to a set of symbols in which the meaning of a special ecclesiastical or political group is embodied. This leap can be interpreted in different ways. It may be the expression of a desire for safety; it may be as arbitrary as, according to Existentialist principles, every decision is; it may be the feeling that the Christian message is the answer to the questions raised by an analysis of human existence; it may be a genuine conversion, independent of the theoretical situation. In any case it is not a solution of the problem of radical doubt. It gives the courage to be to those who are converted but it does not answer the question as to how such a courage is possible in itself. The answer must accept, as its precondition, the state of meaninglessness. It is not an answer if it demands the removal of this state; for that is just what cannot be done. He who is in the grip of doubt and meaninglessness cannot liberate himself from this grip; but he asks for an answer which is valid within and not outside the situation of his despair. He asks for the ultimate foundation of what we have called the "courage of despair." There is only one possible answer, if one does not try to escape the question: namely that the acceptance of despair is in itself faith and on the boundary line of the courage to be. In this situation the meaning of life is reduced to despair about the meaning of life. But as long as this despair is an act of life it is positive in its negativity. Cynically speaking, one could say that it is true to life to be cynical about it. Religiously speaking, one would say that one accepts oneself as accepted in spite of one's despair about the meaning of this acceptance. The paradox of every radical negativity, as long as it is an active negativity, is that it must affirm itself in order to be able to negate itself. No actual negation can be without an implicit affirmation. The hidden pleasure produced by despair witnesses to the paradoxical character of self-negation. The negative lives from the positive it negates.

The faith which makes the courage of despair possible is the acceptance of the power of being, even in the grip of nonbeing. Even in the despair about meaning being affirms itself through us. The act of accepting meaninglessness is in itself a meaningful act. It is an act of faith. We have seen that he who has the courage to affirm his being in spite of fate and guilt has not removed them. He remains threatened and hit by them. But he accepts his acceptance by the power of being-itself in which he participates and which gives him the courage to take the anxieties of fate and guilt upon himself. The same is true of doubt and meaninglessness. The faith which creates the courage to take them into itself has no special content. It is simply faith, undirected, absolute. It is undefinable, since everything defined is dissolved by doubt and meaninglessness. Nevertheless, even absolute faith is not an eruption of subjective emotions or a mood without objective foundation.

An analysis of the nature of absolute faith reveals the following elements in it. The first is the experience of the power of being which is present even in the face of the most radical manifestation of nonbeing. If one says that in this experience vitality resists despair one must add that vitality in man is proportional to intentionality. The vitality that can stand the abyss of meaninglessness is aware of a hidden meaning within the destruction of meaning. The second element in absolute faith is the dependence of the experience of meaninglessness on the experience of meaning. Even in the state of despair one has enough being to make despair possible. There is a third element in absolute faith, the acceptance of being accepted. Of course, in the state of despair there is nobody and nothing that accepts. But there is the power of acceptance itself which is experienced. Meaninglessness, as long as it is experienced, includes an experience of the "power of acceptance." To accept this power of acceptance consciously is the religious answer of absolute faith, of a faith which has been deprived by doubt of any concrete content, which nevertheless is faith and the source of the most paradoxical manifestation of the courage to be.

This faith transcends both the mystical experience and the divine-human encounter. The mystical experience seems to be nearer to absolute faith but it is not. Absolute faith includes an element of skepticism which one cannot find in the mystical experience. Certainly mysticism also transcends all specific contents, but not because it doubts them or has found them meaningless; rather it deems them to be preliminary. Mysticism uses the specific contents as grades, stepping on them after having used them. The experience of meaninglessness, however, denies them (and everything that goes with them) without having used them. The experience of meaninglessness is more radical than mysticism.

Therefore it transcends the mystical experience.

Absolute faith also transcends the divine-human encounter. In this encounter the subject-object scheme is valid: a definite subject (man) meets a definite object (God). One can reverse this statement and say that a definite subject (God) meets a definite object (man). But in both cases the attack of doubt undercuts the subject-object structure. The theologians who speak so strongly and with such self-certainty about the divine-human encounter should be aware of a situation in which this encounter is prevented by radical doubt and nothing is left but absolute faith. The acceptance of such a situation as religiously valid has, however, the consequence that the concrete contents of ordinary faith must be subjected to criticism and transformation. The courage to be in its radical form is a key to an idea of God which transcends both mysticism and the person-to-person encounter . . . .

The courage to be in all its forms has, by itself, revelatory character. It shows the nature of being, it shows that the self-affirmation of being is an affirmation that overcomes negation. In a metaphorical statement (and every assertion about being-itself is either metaphorical or symbolic) one could say that being includes nonbeing but nonbeing does not prevail against it . . . . Nonbeing belongs to being, it cannot be separated from it. We could not even think "being" without a double negation: being must be thought as the negation of the negation of being. This is why we describe being best by the metaphor "power of being." Power is the possibility a being has to actualize itself against the resistance of other beings. If we speak of the power of being-itself we indicate that being affirms itself against nonbeing. In our discussion of courage and life we have mentioned the dynamic understanding of reality by the philosophers of life. Such an understanding is possible only if one accepts the view that nonbeing belongs to being, that being could not be the ground of life without nonbeing. The self-affirmation of being without nonbeing would not even be self-affirmation but an immovable self-identity. Nothing would be manifest, nothing expressed, nothing revealed. But nonbeing drives being out of its seclusion, it forces it to affirm itself dynamically . . . .

Nonbeing (that in God which makes his self-affirmation

dynamic) opens up the divine self-seclusion and reveals him as power and love. Nonbeing makes God a living God. Without the No he has to overcome in himself and in his creature, the divine Yes to himself would be lifeless. There would be no revelation of the ground of being, there would be no life.

But where there is nonbeing there is finitude and anxiety. If we say that nonbeing belongs to being-itself, we say that finitude and anxiety belong to being-itself. Wherever philosophers or theologians have spoken of the divine blessedness they have implicitly (and sometimes explicitly) spoken of the anxiety of finitude which is eternally taken into the blessedness of the divine infinity. The infinite embraces itself and the finite, the Yes includes itself and the No which it takes into itself, blessedness comprises itself and the anxiety of which it is the conquest. All this is implied if one says that being includes nonbeing and that through nonbeing it reveals itself. It is a highly symbolic language which must be used at this point. But its symbolic character does not diminish its truth; on the contrary, it is a condition of its truth. To speak unsymbolically about being-itself is untrue.

The divine self-affirmation is the power that makes the self-affirmation of the finite being, the courage to be, possible. Only because being-itself has the character of self-affirmation in spite of nonbeing is courage possible. Courage participates in the self-affirmation of being-itself, it participates in the power of being which prevails against non-being. He who receives this power in an act of mystical or personal or absolute faith is aware of the source of his courage to be.

Man is not necessarily aware of this source. In situations of cynicism and indifference he is not aware of it. But it works in him as long as he maintains the courage to take his anxiety upon himself. In the act of the courage to be the power of being is effective in us, whether we recognize it or not. Every act of courage is a manifestation of the ground of being, however questionable the content of the act may be. The content may hide or distort true being, the courage in it reveals true being. Not arguments but the courage to be reveals the true nature of being-itself. By affirming our being we participate in the self-affirmation of being-itself.

247

There are no valid arguments for the "existence" of God, but there are acts of courage in which we affirm the power of being, whether we know it or not. If we know it, we accept acceptance consciously. If we do not know it, we nevertheless accept it and participate in it. And in our acceptance of that which we do not know the power of being is manifest to us. Courage has revealing power, the courage to be is the key to being-itself.

4. THE RELATION OF RELIGION AND SCIENCE

Physicist <u>Henry</u> <u>Margenau</u> marvels at the order and consistency of the simple constructs of scientific methodology, but recognizes that there is an existential depth to the data of experience which cannot be analyzed by the method of science in its current state. While he believes that it would be possible to extend science beyond its present methodology so as to include an analysis of religious experience there is no conflict between science and religion as conceived by an Existential Theist. In that view science is limited to an objective, rational interpretation of perceived data while religion opens up those subjective depths in our immediate experience which are necessary for full meaning and which are closed off to scientific experience. In this way science and religion stand in a relation of complimentarity.

<u>Truth</u> <u>in</u> <u>Science</u> <u>and</u> <u>Religion</u>

Henry Margenau

This discussion falls naturally into two sections, the first dealing with matters of science, of which I am reasonably sure, and the second with problems of religion. That I am not an expert in theology I need not emphasize, for it will be abundantly evident from what I am about to say. More to the point is the admission that I have no strong doctrinal views upon matters of religion, and that the voicing of thoughts in the second section is essentially indicative of the struggle for enlightenment and truth on my own part.

Some claim that there is no method of science: there are only sciences, each evolving its own method as it proceeds. This work-aday view of the toiling scientist is a natural reflection of his daily experience. The specialist is concerned with a multitude of diverse tasks requiring different methods for their solution. Unless his mind soars above his daily pursuits, it is fairly natural that the working scientist should characterize his business as a welter of different techniques. In the same spirit the woodsman might claim that there are only trees but no forests.

Even for the generalist and the philosopher of science, common features among the various scientific disciplines are not easy to perceive. They will continue to escape one's view so long as it is focused solely upon the substance or the subject matter of the disciplines. The factual field covered by physics is entirely different from that of biology, that of biology entirely different from that to which psychology applies its methods of inquiry, and so forth. So long as <u>subject</u> <u>matter</u> is made a principle of classification, there will indeed be only sciences. However, when one asks the more general questions, what is a scientific problem and when does science regard its problems to be solved, certain features common to physics, biology, and psychology spring into view. A measure of unity arises in this <u>methodological</u> <u>approach</u> to the meaning of science. It is this approach which I now wish to sketch, an approach that allows science to be seen as a part of our human concern for the validity of knowledge or, some would hold, as that phase of the cognitive process which to date has achieved its highest perfection.

Features Common to All Sciences

Science in its truest sense is precisely what the etymology of its name suggests; it comprises what we know, that is to say, everything we "really" know. How often have we uttered in conversation the simple phrase, "Yes, I know." To lay bare its meaning is our present task, for the meaning of this innocent sentence reveals the method of science.

Since science describes the process of knowing, and since knowing is only part of human experience, science is limited. For our total experience includes, besides knowledge, such components as feeling, judging, willing, and acting as well. To recognize the peculiar relevance of science for knowledge, however, is not tantamount to admitting that science has no application to the fields of feeling, judging, and acting. It may well be that purely affective experiences, insofar as they become objects of knowledge, thus become indirectly tractable by the methods of science. But I wish to ignore this nest of problems at the present time, so that the central features of scientific method shall not be obscured by too much inessential detail.

Let us denote by the term "experience" the broad expanse of all matters that can possibly enter our consciousness. Experience thus means more than it does in the sense of the strict empiricist, who wishes to limit the term to that which is sensorily perceived. Its present usage includes sensing, knowing, reasoning, feeling, judging, acting, and all the rest. From this universe of experiences we now select what is known as the cognitive component. While it may be difficult to define it clearly (the contents of our experience do not fall into neat pigeonholes, and to define an isolated part of it is always an arbitrary procedure), we all know what is meant by the ingredients of the process of knowing. It involves having some sort of sense impression, remembering similar impressions, interpreting the impression or awareness in terms of some object or objects, relating these objects to other objects of a similar kind, reasoning about that class of objects, etc. In another form, the process of knowledge may start with a question which is heard or read, a question which sets us to thinking, to recalling facts, to analyzing a situation in order to arrive at an answer. Loosely, the faculties which bring about cognition are known as the senses, memory, and reasoning. But these are psychological terms which suggest distinctions that are not altogether clear in the facts of experience.

Two Extreme Types of Knowledge

Among the elements that go into what is called knowledge, two extreme types can be recognized. Representative of one type is a mathematical idea such as that of a number or a function or a group, a pure concept, very abstract and rationally manipulable, whose meaning does not flow from whether or not it "exists." The

251

other type is represented by what is usually known as fact. Pure concepts and pure facts are the names which common language attributed to these two polar types of experience. Yet I hesitate to use these words, pure concepts and facts, because they convey an impression of obviousness and of finality which obscures many of the intricate details and problems of science. This is particularly true about the word "fact," which covers too many sins. At the expense of annoying you, therefore, I shall introduce a different terminology which I will now proceed to explain.

What is factual about a fact is that it is independent of our control: it is simply there; it clamors to be recognized by us as such. A fact is what cannot be denied, what obtrudes itself into the process of knowledge whether we wish it there or not; it is the last instance of our rational or cognitive appeal. A fact is spontaneous in our experience, often unexpected and practically never merely the consequence of some chain of reasoning. It is often in the form of an immediate perception, or a sensory datum, or an observation. At any rate, facts function as protocols against which all other kinds of conjectures are ultimately tested. Let me simply use the letter P (which may stand for perception, or for protocol, if you please) to designate this kind of experience. As examples I offer the seeing of some shape, the hearing of a sound, the awareness of a pain, or indeed that combination of many such immediacies which we call an observation in science.

What are Concepts ?

Contrasted with these P-elements are thoughts, ideas, mental images, fancies, in general all that goes by the more sober name of concepts. Concepts are the results of human processes of abstraction, sifting, reasoning; they emerge at the end of a long chain of activity in which man feels himself intelligently involved and responsible. Their genesis is perhaps best described by the term "construction." I therefore propose to call them constructs in order to indicate the active part which our reason plays in their production. Whether and in what sense they are pure constructs having no relevance at all for more factual types of experience is not of interest at this moment.

252

The polarity of constructs and P-data should not be construed as implying that these two classes of entities never mix. In fact, any cognitive experience involves elements of both classes, but it is only through an effort at methodological reduction that the two ingredients can be separated. Almost any statement, any sentence about a factual experience, already involves interpretation, conceptualization, and thereby constructional elements. In fact, the latter abound in our experience, and it is difficult to point to a kind of experience of which it may be said that it is pure P-fact.

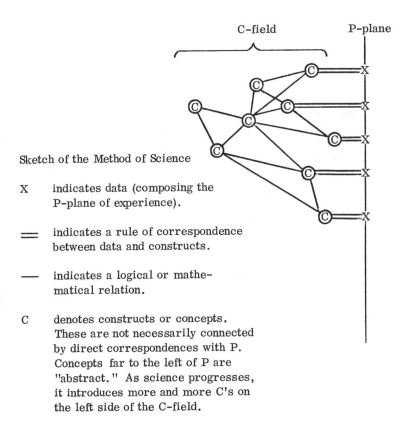

Sketch of the Method of Science

X   indicates data (composing the P-plane of experience).

=   indicates a rule of correspondence between data and constructs.

—   indicates a logical or mathematical relation.

C   denotes constructs or concepts. These are not necessarily connected by direct correspondences with P. Concepts far to the left of P are "abstract." As science progresses, it introduces more and more C's on the left side of the C-field.

253

There is a sense in which facts are immune to treatment by reasoning; they are simply there and have to be reckoned with. Indeed, it is their lack of internal order, their refusal to follow an obvious rational pattern, which constrains our mind to engage in the process of constructing rational counterparts for them, counterparts which are manipulable by rational rules and can be made to fulfill our desire for order and coherence in experience. A heard noise at once suggests the presence of a sound source somewhere in space; we look for it, and if this search ends in another P-type experience in which we see the object, our desire for rational coherence in our experience is satisfied. Coherence has not been established directly between the two P-facts; an essential third element within this coherent scheme is the constructed object.

Necessity of Distinctions

To speak of the intervening object as a construct may be offensive to many. But it is very important for us to learn to recognize the germ of the difference between P-type facts or data, and constructs, even in so simple an experience as this, for if we go blindly ignoring this distinction, we shall never be able to understand fully the more recondite and involved excursions of science.

If practically any cognitive experience already contains constructs, what can possibly be meant by a pure P-datum? My answer is it probably does not exist. Yet whenever we analyze a scientific experience, we sooner or later come to a place where we say: "This we accept," or, "This is incontrovertibly true." Here we have reached the P-domain. It forms a sort of limiting plane bounding the unlimited domain of constructional experience. Because of this I like to speak of the P-facts as lying on the P-plane, and to look upon the P-plane as forming a boundary, as it were, of the constructional domain to which I shall henceforth refer as the C-field. The latter contains most of the things of which we talk in science, excluding only that "direct appeal to nature" called observation or empirical verification which the scientist uses to validate his notions about the world.

From the point of view of the psychologist, a P-plane fact is neither simple nor unanalyzable, but it is a necessity for every science to regard certain data as incontrovertible; if it gives up this premise, every science loses the very basis of its competence. Let us remember, however, that a P-fact for one science may not be a P-fact for another. The point is that our experience confronts us with a P-plane which in its complete lack of organization and coherence defies our understanding. To alleviate our bafflement we set up correspondence between these factual experiences and certain constructs.

Berkeley and "Logical Fertility"

The business of science might be supposed to be the mapping of individual P-experiences in a unique and simple way upon the field of constructs, a mapping which is regulated by principles of convenience and of economy of thought. If this were the entire truth, then the simplest and most acceptable scientific theory would probably be one proposed by Berkeley, who believed that every factual experience is but the manifestation of a thought in the mind of God. His thesis creates a simple and indeed convenient correspondence between the points on the P-plane and the constructs of the C-field. Yet it is unsatisfactory. The reason is not that it is wrong; its fault lies in its very generality. For it lacks a property which I like to call logical fertility. The whole scheme is logically sterile, there is nothing which the scientist can derive from it, nor anything which he can test by empirical means. The theory states its case and is done, its acceptance or rejection makes no difference in our experience and our thoughts.

The lesson we may draw from this consideration is that scientific theories must contain constructs which are in some sense logically fertile, and I shall mean by this the deductive quality which the Berkelian theory so obviously lacks. Scientific theories differ in the degree to which they are logically fertile, some having a great deal of logical power, others very little. But in general, scientific constructs strive for a maximum of logical fertility; science avoids the use of ideas leading to sterile situations in which predictions cannot be made.

When the information drawn from many examples is systematized, it entails the following conclusion: Scientific constructs are regarded as valid representations of (P-plane) facts if they satisfy two large sets of requirements. The first set may be called methodological, or indeed metaphysical. It has to do with the native fitness of the constructs themselves, with the manner in which they place themselves in formal relations, with their coherence and their logical sweep. It is possible to name the different criteria; I have tried to present a list of them in my book, THE NATURE OF PHYSICAL REALITY. Metaphysical requirements which the constructs of science have to satisfy are: logical fertility, extensibility, multiple connection, simplicity, elegance, and several others. This enumeration should not be taken as naming a set of basic axioms, of unchanging categories of thought in the Kantian sense. It is simply an assortment of metaphysical principles of science which has grown through application and use throughout the history of science, principles which have proved their power and have now come to be generally accepted by working scientists, who perhaps without knowing it employ them in their researches. They are not necessary principles of knowledge, and they may change in time. But a survey of the history of science shows that changes in them proceed very slowly, and that a modification of the metaphysical requirement, when it occurs (e.g., the present changing attitude with respect to the principle called causality), induces profound and extensive changes in the structure of science itself.

Hypothesis Into Theory

A set of constructs which obeys the metaphysical requirement does not for that reason alone become acceptable. Theories, i.e., sets of constructs, must also satisfy the requirement of empirical verification. The scientist starts with an observation; this observation is then interpreted in terms of the constructs that are associated with it. These constructs allow him to reason, and he finally emerges with a prediction which says that if the original observation was true, then something else must also be true on the P-plane. This something else can usually be investigated by empirical means. If it is found to be true, the circuit is declared successful. Now the requirement of empirical verification demands that a set of constructs be traversable in many ways by circuits of the type I have described. If all these circuits have been found successful, that is to say, if the theory has been tested in many ways, the scientist regards the constructs forming the theory as valid. What was originally an hypothesis has now become a satisfactory theory, the former constructs have transformed themselves into verifacts, and insofar as the constructs had the character of tentative entities, these entities have now become realities, and they are said to exist.

The method of science is nothing more than an elaboration of procedures of common sense. Even the simplest instances of gaining knowledge are examples of the scientific process just described.

The first part of this discussion has concerned itself with some very general features of scientific method, features so general as to be applicable to almost any kind of science, past and present. The treatment, though induced by contemporary developments of physical science, did not take them into explicit consideration. It behooves us, therefore, to comment briefly upon the novel aspects of physical science and upon the way in which they facilitate passage from the strict field of science to the more amorphous domains that lie around science. These include religion.

Common Sense in Error

Fifty years ago a physicist would have been amazed, or shall I say dismayed and shocked, at the remark that the ultimate constituents of the physical world, like electrons, may not have definite positions at all instants of time. How can we conceive of particles that are nowhere in particular? Does not this allegation contradict the most fundamental tenets of common sense? It does indeed, and insofar as it conflicts with common sense, common sense is in error. We have learned with some pain, perhaps, that the ultimates of nature need not have picturable attributes. Common sense once thought that every object, no matter how small, would have to occupy a definite region of space. This insistence was a facile generalization based upon observations in the molar world of ordinary experience. But clearly when an object like an electron is far too small ever to be grasped or be experienced in kinesthetic or tactile fasion, the attribute of localizability may very well disappear.

There is no logical difficulty in supposing that something which is too small to be seen may not have a position at all. At this point we simply have to ignore the bidding of common sense, free ourselves of its beguilement, and proceed on the basis of logical and mathematical rules alone. When this is done, we arrive at the science of quantum mechanics, which provides a very successful set of constructs in terms of which atomic experience can be understood.

From many changes in the concepts of modern atomic physics there has resulted a freer and more tolerant view of the requirements of scientific explanation. Science now acknowledges as real a host of entities that cannot be described completely in mechanistic or materialistic terms. For these reasons the demands which science makes upon religion when it examines religion's claim to truth have become distinctly more modest; the conflict between science and religion has become less sharp, and the strain of science upon religion has been greatly relieved. In fact, a situation seems to prevail in which the theologian can seriously listen to a scientist expounding his methodology with some expectation that the latter may ring a sympathetic chord. It is not altogether out of the question that the rules of scientific methodology are now sufficiently wide and flexible to embrace some forms of religion within the scientific domain. At any rate, science has become a wide and open field and, as I see it, there are several ways in which it can adjust itself to the concerns of religion. In the following I shall point to three such ways.

The Scientist Amazed

The open-minded and perceptive scientist, even if he has no desire to ask religious questions, cannot help but marvel at the success of his own method. As he ponders over the infinite and unruly mass of his factual experience, as he contrasts it with the striking simplicity and elegance of the constructional scheme whereby he is able to explain the formidable contingency of P-facts, he succumbs to a feeling of surprise. His amazement concerns the circumstance that it should be possible at all for man to comprehend so vast a domain of unorganized happenings. Scientists feel wonder and awe at the realization that our experiences are not a chaotic welter but display that measure of order and consistency which expresses itself in the use of simple constructs.

Paradoxically such amazement does not spring from the occurrence of breaches in natural order which are often called miracles; on the contrary, it attaches to what seems to be the greatest miracle of all, namely, the lack of interruption of the natural order which expresses itself in the continued and perhaps expanding simplicity of human explanations. The theologian Schleiermacher phrased this sentiment concerning the one supreme miracle, namely, natural order, with unforgetable beauty in his speeches to the German nation. If this sentiment be religious, science does indeed engender it.

Yet I doubt if this form of religion, cosmic religion, if you please, will satisfy the desires of the theologian. He may wish to take it as a basis and go on from there, postulating a cause for order and perhaps a Deity to maintain it. In doing so he goes, of course, beyond the confines of science; his religion becomes what I should like to call a metascience; but I see nothing in the methodology of science which forbids this expansion, this extrapolation upon the method of science. Most scientists readily admit that their methods have limits, and that beyond these limits procedures controlled by other principles may well take hold. It is this transcendence out of the domain of science into a region from which science as a whole can be surveyed that I wish to designate by applying the word metascience.

Freedom and Limitation

Further examination leads to another interesting conjecture. A given P-phenomenon can be explained by a series of steps that has apparently no end. Thus, for example, in answering the question why an object falls near the surface of the earth, one may refer to the Galilean theory of free fall which says merely that all bodies fall with equal and constant acceleration. This takes us to a set of constructs not far removed from the P-plane. But this law of free fall is nothing more than a special instance of a more general set of constructs known as the theory of universal gravitation, which in our symbolic sense of distance lies further away from the P-plane. Again we need not stop there. It is possible to view the theory of universal gravitation as a special case of Einstein's law of general relativity. We have thus taken a third step back to the left away from the P-plane. To be sure, at present it is necessary for us to stop at this stage. But there is nothing to block further progress into the more abstract. Indeed, if the past development of science holds a lesson, it is that we shall someday doubtless find an even more general law in terms of which the law of Einstein and others can be jointly comprehended. No limit seems to be set to man's progress to the left in the C-field. But as we reverse this procedure, going from the general to the more particular, we end up by saying that the stone simply falls. This is a brute fact, grotesque, final, and meaningless.

Thus arise two questions. The first has often been asked in the history of philosophy as follows: If the P-plane limits experience, is there anything beyond experience? If so, and if science is limited to experience, then the affirmative answer transcends science. But I doubt if it is necessarily religion. What lies beyond may be the Kantian thing in itself, that essence which, being no part of experience, is never knowable. Or there may be some mystical kind of non-scientific reality which, lying by definition beyond experience, can never be fathomed. If it is thought that we may encounter the divine in this passage beyond the P-plane, that divine, since it excludes the possibility of experience, is not likely to interest the theologians.

The Existentialist View

But the closure of the field of experience raises still another question. Perhaps closure arises from the circumstance that in our entire epistemology we have limited ourselves to vehicles which are rational procedures. We have used induction and deduction in traveling back and forth to examine the P-plane. Could it not be that, in order to fathom and probe the fullness of what is actually present on or near the P-plane, we are required to abandon reason and to give ourselves to basking without restraint in the sensation of the immediately given? Here we encounter a new emphasis, different from what we call intuition. The fundamental essence of the ebb and flow of sensations, the richness of the immediacy of our direct experience, the metaphysical substance of what assails our being in the act of sensation and affection, may after all escape the net of rational analysis. This is the view of the existentialist, who feels that our representation of the P-plane merely as the limiting surface of the scientific domain cannot do it justice, and that much greater emphasis upon the purely existential, upon the contingent and spontaneous features of our total experience are necessary.

There are questions which science with its present methodology will probably never answer; the full drama of existence cannot be enacted on the stage of science with its contemporary setting. Questions like those raised by Kierkegaard and Heidegger-- why am I, why is there anything at all, why the phenomenon of experience which science analyzes--questions such as these appear as idle vaporings when viewed as problems of science. Yet they bespeak an intense human concern and contain a powerful appeal that defies the positivistic insistence that they are meaningless or insignificant. If science does not answer them, is it not reasonable that at this point we resign ourselves to other hands? This is indeed affirmed by those who see religion as an extension of experience into the existential domain. They feel that the P-plane must somehow be opened up by a new kind of analysis, an analysis not scientific, an analysis for which science offers no help. What happens when this extension is permitted can hardly be predicted in detail. One can go the way of Sartre and dwell in nonreligious fashion upon the nausea of existence. Or one can go the way of Kierkegaard and Gabriel Marcel and couple the existential affirmation with an excursion into the domain of religion. At any rate, the P-plane quite obviously is an area of contact between science and religion, as the widespread acceptance of existentialist philosophy today clearly shows. As I see the situation, there appears to be no conflict between science and existentialism; rather, they stand in a relation of complementarity.

A Formal Structure for Theology

My own hope lies in the direction of amalgamating religion with science by an extension of the latter. For it is by no means out of the question that a theory of religion, i.e., theology, when fully developed, may exhibit the same formal structure as science

261

itself.

If such an approach is to be started, the first question to be answered is: What is the P-plane of religious experience? A possible and probably correct answer appears to be: The kind of immediate experience which is often regarded as distinctly religious. I mean such things as the feeling of gratitude that springs up in man's heart on a joyous day, the monitoring awareness of a conscience that regulates the lives of most of us, the feeling of awe in the face of overwhelming beauty, the guiltful contrition that follows a sinful experience, the sentiments of misery and abandon at the insufficiency of human power before fate, the longing for grace and for redemption. To say that these are peculiarly religious experiences is not to argue that they are exclusively religious. For they are also P-plane facts for several of the so-called social sciences, and it is far from my intention to suggest that psychology, psychiatry, sociology, and anthropology should not be concerned with them and endeavor to show how they can be organized in the constructional schemes of these sciences. This, however, does not cast out the possibility of an analysis in religious terms, nor does it show it to be illegitimate. For any simple sensation may well be the starting point of an inquiry into a physical or biological or a psychological domain of constructs. The fact that a given experience can be P-datum for a variety of sciences must be very clearly recognized and is no argument against the validity of the various explanatory schemes. And in this sense religion, too, can claim its due.

What follows next in the development of a "science" of religion is a little difficult to predict, though probably not more difficult than it would have been to predict the structure of modern science in Aristotle's day. Sciences grow when people become convinced of their importance and their necessity, and they develop their methodology as they mature. There are those who believe that theology already provides a C-field in terms of which a concatenation and a logical nexus between the experiences I have named can be achieved. If this is to be accepted, the ideas of theology must be subjected to the same metaphysical requirements which we impose on scientific theories. That is to say, they must partake of logical fertility, multiple connection, extensibility, simplicity,

262

etc. Nor is this often denied by workers in the field.

Religion Subjected to Tests

Moreover, if religion is to have the structure of science, it must also expose itself to tests in the manner of our circuits of empirical verification. This forces us to reject at once certain peculiar kinds of theology, such as the deism of the Enlightenment and probably also predetermination of the Calvin type. For these theories could never be tested. Any tests man could devise would be foreordained, would have been included in the Creator's foresight at the very beginning. It would, therefore, be futile to regard the outcome of the tests as significant. But such criticisms do not affect most major theological systems.

It appears that natural science is not wholly without suggestions as to the structure of a religion based on the grounds of its own methodology. But it offers no detailed material aid. Least of all does it require the slavish adherence of theological doctrine to the constructs of physics and chemistry. Not even the social sciences, notably psychology, deem it necessary any longer to ape the physicist. This does not imply contrasts or contradictions--for surely, if a concept applicable in one field has no application in another, it does not contradict it. The notion of temperature is entirely in harmony with that of an atom, although it has no relevance for a single atom. It is the methodological structure of science that might be transferable; I do not advocate "physicalism" in religion.

Whatever else these vague considerations may imply, they are utterly damaging to the tired old slogan that soulless science conflicts with the spirit of religion.

Martin Buber believes that the awareness of the real self
does not appear until we make an absolute moral judgment in relation to conduct and action. When that absolute judgment is made it
is not basically a judgment about the conduct and action themselves,
but really about what we are "in truth." The moral judgment,
therefore, opens up and affirms our essential personal being. The
absolute moral judgment, however, cannot be made without an
awareness of our relation to the Absolute, that mysterious being
who manifests Himself in our essential human being. Thus, the
moral experience is the end of the religious experience. Both make
possible a mode of existing with being in the world which is authentically human and "holy," I-Thou rather than I-It. An interesting
comparison with Humanism can be made at this point. In Humanism religious experience is essentially moral while in Existential
Theism moral experience is essentially religious.

Religion and Ethics

Martin Buber

All religious reality begins with what Biblical religion calls
the "fear of God." It comes when our existence between birth and
death becomes incomprehensible and uncanny, when all security is
shattered through the mystery. This is not the relative mystery of
that which is inaccessible only to the present state of human knowledge and is hence in principle discoverable. It is the essential
mystery, the inscrutableness of which belongs to its very nature;
it is the unknowable. Through this dark gate (which is only a gate

---

and not, as some theologians believe, a dwelling) the b
steps forth into the everyday which is henceforth hallo
place in which he has to live with the mystery. He ste
rected and assigned to the concrete, contextual situatio
existence . . . .

An important philosopher of our day, Whitehead, asks how
the Old Testament saying that the fear of God is the beginning of
wisdom is to be reconciled with the New Testament saying that God
is love. Whitehead has not fully grasped the meaning of the word
"beginning." He who begins with the love of God without having
previously experienced the fear of God, loves an idol which he himself has made, a god whom it is easy enough to love. He does not
love the real God who is, to begin with, dreadful and incomprehensible. Consequently, if he then perceives, as Job and Ivan Kara-
mozov perceive, that God is dreadful and incomprehensible, he is
terrified. He despairs of God and the world if God does not take
pity on him, as He did on Job, and bring him to love Him Himself.
This is presumably what Whitehead meant when he said that religion
is the passage from God the void to God the enemy and from Him to
God the companion. That the believing man who goes through the
gate of dread is directed to the concrete contextual situation of his
existence means just this: that he endures in the face of God the
reality of lived life, dreadful and incomprehensible though it be.
He loves it in the love of God, whom he has learned to love . . . .

That one accepts the concrete situation as given to him does
not, in any way, mean that he must be ready to accept that which
meets him as "God-given" in its pure factuality. He may, rather,
declare the extremest enmity toward this happening and treat its
"givenness" as only intended to draw forth his own opposing force.
But he will not remove himself from the concrete situation as it
actually is; he will instead, enter into it, even if in the form of
fighting against it. Whether field of work or field of battle, he
accepts the place in which he is placed. He knows no floating of
the spirit above concrete reality; to him even the sublimest spirituality is an illusion if it is not bound to the situation. Only the
spirit which is bound to the situation is prized by him as bound to
the "Pneuma," the spirit of God . . . .

For man the existent is either face-to-face being or passive object. These essence of man arises from this twofold relation to the existent. These are not two external phenomena but the two basic modes of existing with being. The child that calls to his mother and the child that watches his mother--or to give a more exact example, the child that silently speaks to his mother through nothing other than looking into her eyes and the same child that looks at something on the mother as at any other object--show the twofoldness in which man stands and remains standing. Something of the sort is sometimes even to be noticed in those near death. What is here apparent is the double structure of human existence itself. Because these are the two basic modes of our existence with being, they are the two basic modes of our existence in general--I-Thou and I-It. I-Thou finds its highest intensity and transfiguration in religious reality, in which unlimited Being becomes, as absolute person, my partner. I-It finds its highest concentration and illumination in philosophical knowledge. In this knowledge the extraction of the subject from the I of the immediate lived togetherness of I and It and the transformation of the It into the object detached in its essence produces the exact thinking of contemplated existing beings, yes, of contemplated Being itself . . . .

The religious reality of the meeting with the Meeter, who shines through all forms and is Himself formless, knows no image of Him, nothing comprehensible as object. It knows only the presence of the Present One. Symbols of Him, whether images or ideas, always exist first when and insofar as Thou becomes He, and that means It. But the ground of human existence in which it gathers and becomes whole is also the deep abyss out of which images arise. Symbols of God come into being, some which allow themselves to be fixed in lasting visibility even in earthly material and some which tolerate no other sanctuary than that of the soul. Symbols supplement one another, they merge, they are set before the community of believers in plastic or theological forms. And God, so we may surmise, does not despise all these similarly and necessarily untrue images, but rather suffers that one look at Him through them. Yet they always quickly desire to be more than they are, more than signs and pointers toward Him. It finally happens ever again that they swell themselves up and obstruct the way to Him, and He removes Himself from them . . . .

266

We grasp an essential element of the path of the human spirit known to history if we regard it from the standpoint of the changes in the relationship between the ethical and the religious. But we must consider each, both the ethical and the religious, not in one or another of its manifestations, but in its basic form.

We mean by the ethical in this strict sense the yes and no which man gives to the conduct and actions possible to him, the radical distinction between them which affirms or denies them not according to their usefulness or harmfulness for individuals and society, but according to their intrinsic value and disvalue. We find the ethical in its purity only there where the human person confronts himself with his own potentiality and distinguishes and decides in this confrontation without asking anything other than what is right and what is wrong in this his own situation. The criterion by which this distinction and decision is made may be a traditional one, or it may be one perceived by or revealed to the individual himself. What is important is that the critical flames shoot up ever again out of the depths, first illuminating, then burning and purifying. The truest source of this is a fundamental awareness inherent in all men, though in the most varied strengths and degrees of consciousness, and for the most part stifled by them. It is the individual's awareness of what he is "in truth," of what in his unique and non-repeatable created existence he is intended to be. From this awareness, when it is fully present, the comparison between what one actually is and what one is intended to be can emerge. What is found is measured against the image, no so-called ideal image, nor anything imagined by man, but an image arising out of that mystery of being itself that we call the person. Thus the genius bearing his name confronts the demonic fullness of the possible conduct and actions given to the individual in this moment. One may call the distinction and decision which arises from these depths the action of the <u>pre-conscience</u>.

We mean by the religious in this strict sense, on the other hand, the relation of the human person to the Absolute, when and insofar as the person enters and remains in this relation as a whole being. This presupposes the existence of a Being who, though in Himself unlimited and unconditioned, lets other beings, limited and conditioned indeed, exist outside Himself. He even allows them to enter into a relation with Him such as seemingly can only exist between limited and conditioned beings. Thus in my definition of the religious "the Absolute" does not mean something that the human person holds it to be, without anything being said about its existence, but the absolute reality itself, whatever the form in which it presents itself to the human person at this moment. In the reality of the religious relation to Absolute becomes in most cases personal, at times admittedly, as in the Buddhism which arose out of a personal relation to the "Unoriginated," only gradually and, as it were, reluctantly in the course of the development of a religion. It is indeed legitimate to speak of the person of God within the religious relation and in its language; but in so doing we are making no statement about the Absolute which reduces it to the personal. We are rather saying that it enters into the relationship as the Absolute Person whom we call God. One may understand the personality of God as His act. It is, indeed, even permissible for the believer to believe that God became a person for love of him, because in our human mode of existence the only reciprocal relation with us that exists is a personal one.

We cannot, on the other hand, speak of the religious in the strict sense meant here where there is no relation and cannot be one. This is the case when a man means by his concept of God simply all that is, outside of which he himself can no longer in any way exist as a separate being who is able as such to enter into relationship with God, even though it be to lose himself ever anew in it. But this is also the case when a man means by the concept of God his own self, no matter under what complicated disguise he hides his meaning. What happens here in the pseudo-mystical chamber of ghosts and mirrors has nothing to do with the real relation or even with the real self. The real self appears only when it enters into relation with the Other. Where this relation is rejected, the real self withers away--an event which at times, indeed, can evoke most phosphorescent effects . . . .

The essence of the relationship between the ethical and the religious cannot be determined by comparing the teachings of ethics and religion. One must rather penetrate into that area within each sphere where they become solidified in a concrete, personal situation. Thus it is the factual moral decision of the individual on the one hand and his factual relationship to the Absolute on the other that concerns us. In both cases it is not a mere faculty of the person that is involved, whether it be his thought or his feeling or his will, but the totality of these faculties, and more than this, the whole man. A third sphere overlying these two is not given us; we can only let the two confront each other, and in such a way that in this meeting each of them determines its relationship to the other. If from the point of view of the religious we look in such concreteness at the relation between the two spheres, we shall see its strong tendency to send forth its rays into the whole life of the person, effecting a comprehensive structural change. Living religiousness wishes to bring forth living ethos. Something essentially different meets our view if we seek to examine the connection between the two fields from the standpoint of the ethical. The man who seeks distinction and decision in his own soul cannot draw from it, from his soul, absoluteness for his scale of values. Only out of a personal relationship with the Absolute can the absoluteness of the ethical coordinates arise without which there is no complete awareness of self. Even when the individual calls an absolute criterion handed down by religious tradition his own, it must be reforged in the fire of the truth of his personal essential relation to the Absolute if it is to win true validity. But always it is the religious which bestows, the ethical which receives.

It would be a fundamental misunderstanding of what I am saying if one assumed that I am upholding so-called moral heteronomy or external moral laws in opposition to so-called moral autonomy or self-imposed moral laws. Where the Absolute speaks in the reciprocal relationship, there are no longer such alternatives. The whole meaning of reciprocity, indeed, lies in just this, that it does not wish to impose itself but to be freely apprehended. It gives us something to apprehend, but it does not give us the apprehension. Our act must be entirely our own for that which is to be disclosed to us to be disclosed, even that which must disclose each individual to himself. In theonomy the divine law seeks for your own, and true revelation reveals to you yourself . . . .

It is customary to see the connection between the ethical and the religious in Israel exclusively in the form of a heavenly command accompanied by a threat of punishment. To do this is to miss

269

what is essential. For the giving of the law at Sinai is properly understood as the body of rules which the divine Ruler conferred upon His people in the hour of His ascension to the throne. All the prescriptions of this body of rules, both the ritual and the ethical, are intended to lead beyond themselves into the sphere of the "holy." The people's goal was set not by their being bidden to become a "good" people but a "holy" one. Thus every moral demand is set forth as one that shall raise man, the human people, to the sphere where the ethical merges into the religious, or rather where the difference between the ethical and the religious is suspended in the breathing-space of the divine. This is expressed with unsurpassable clarity in the reason given for the goal that is set: Israel shall become holy, "for I am holy." The imitation of God by man, the "following in His way," can be fulfilled naturally only in those divine attributes turned towards the human ethos, in justice and love, and all the attributes are transparent into the Holiness above the attributes, to be reproduced in the radically different human dimension. The absolute norm is given to show the way that leads before the face of the Absolute.

The presupposition for this connection between the ethical and the religious, however, is the basic view that man, while created by God, was established by Him in an independence which has since remained undiminished. In this independence he stands over against God. So man takes part with full freedom and spontaneity in the dialogue between the two which forms the essence of existence. That this is so despite God's unlimited power and knowledge is just that which constitutes the mystery of man's creation. In this is founded the lasting reality of the distinction and decision which man consummates in his soul.

6. HUMAN DESTINY

The existential theist bases his belief in the existence of God upon his longing for being. Unamuno conforms to this methodology in his belief in the immortality of the soul. There are no rational proofs for the immortality of the soul, but it is reasonable to believe that there is something immortal in us which longs for immortality. We cannot believe ourselves to have real existence without believing this existence to be immortal. The alternative is the belief in the absurdity that we are nothing. Unamuno's acceptance of the tragic sense of life wherein we must base our beliefs upon desires which are unfulfilled in earthly life is characteristic of the existential theist. Unlike the pantheist he does not desire union with God in eternity, but fulfillment of his own existence as an immortal being.

The Hunger of Immortality

Miguel de Unamuno

It is impossible for us, in effect, to conceive of ourselves as not existing, and no effort is capable of enabling consciousness to realize absolute unconsciousness, its own annihilation. Try, reader, to imagine to yourself, when you are wide awake, the condition of your soul when you are in a deep sleep; try to fill your consciousness with the representation of no-consciousness, and you will see the impossibility of it. The effort to comprehend it causes the most tormenting dizziness. We cannot conceive ourselves as not existing.

Reprinted with permission of Macmillan Publishing Co., Inc. from THE TRAGIC SENSE OF LIFE by Miguel de Unamuno. Translated by J. E. Crawford Flitch (New York: Macmillan, 1921).

The visible universe, the universe that is created by the instinct of self-preservation, becomes all too narrow for me. It is like a cramped cell, against the bars of which my soul beats its wings in vain. Its lack of air stifles me. More, more, and always more! I want to be myself, and yet without ceasing to be myself to be others as well, to merge myself into the totality of things visible and invisible, to extend myself into the illimitable of space and to prolong myself into the infinite of time. Not to be all and for ever is as if not to be—at least, let me be my whole self, and be so for ever and ever. And to be the whole of myself is to be everybody else. Either all or nothing!

All or nothing! And what other meaning can the Shakespearean "To be or not to be" have, or that passage in Coriolanus where it is said of Marcius "He wants nothing of a god but eternity"? Eternity, eternity!—that is the supreme desire! The thirst of eternity is what is called love among men, and whosoever loves another wishes to eternalize himself in him. Nothing is real that is not eternal . . . .

Everything passes! Such is the refrain of those who have drunk, lips to the spring, of the fountain of life, of those who have tasted of the fruit of the tree of the knowledge of good and evil.

To be, to be for ever, to be without ending! thirst of being, thirst of being more! hunger of God! thirst of love eternalizing and eternal! to be for ever! to be God! . . .

The tragic Portuguese Jew of Amsterdam wrote that the free man thinks of nothing less than of death; but this free man is a dead man, free from the impulse of life, for want of love, the salve of his liberty. This thought that I must die and the enigma of what will come after death is the very palpitation of my consciousness. When I contemplate the green serenity of the fields or look into the depths of clear eyes through which shines a fellow-soul, my consciousness dilates, I feel the diastole of the soul and am bathed in the flood of the life that flows about me, and I believe in my future; but instantly the voice of mystery whispers to me, "Thou shalt cease to be!" the angel of Death touches me with his wing, and the systole of the soul floods the depths of my spirit with the blood of divinity.

Like Pascal, I do not understand those who assert that they care not a farthing for these things, and this indifference "in a matter that touches themselves, their eternity, their all, exasperates me rather than moves me to compassion, astonishes and shocks me," and he who feels thus "is for me," as for Pascal, whose are the words just quoted, "a monster."

It has been said a thousand times and in a thousand books that ancestor-worship is for the most part the source of primitive religions, and it may be strictly said that what most distinguishes man from the other animals is that, in one form or another, he guards his dead and does not give them over to the neglect of teeming mother earth; he is an animal that guards its dead. And from what does he thus guard them? From what does he so futilely protect them? The wretched consciousness shrinks from its own annihilation, and, just as an animal spirit, newly severed from the womb of the world, finds itself confronted with the world and knows itself distinct from it, so consciousness must needs desire to possess another life than that of the world itself. And so the earth would run the risk of becoming a vast cemetery before the dead themselves should die again.

When mud huts or straw shelters, incapable of resisting the inclemency of the weather, sufficed for the living, tumuli were raised for the dead, and stone was used for sepulchres before it was used for houses. It is the strong-builded houses of the dead that have withstood the ages, not the houses of the living; not the temporary lodgings but the permanent habitations.

This cult, not of death but of immortality, originates and preserves religions. In the midst of the delirium of destruction. Robespierre induced the Convention to declare the existence of the Supreme Being and "the consolatory principle of the immortality of the soul," the Incorruptible being dismayed at the idea of having himself one day to turn to corruption.

A disease? Perhaps; but he who pays no heed to his disease is heedless of his health, and man is an animal essentially and substantially diseased. A disease? Perhaps it may be, like life itself to which it is thrall, and perhaps the only health possible may be death; but this disease is the fount of all vigorous health. From the depth of this anguish, from the abyss of the feeling of our mortality, we emerge into the light of another heaven . . . .

Although this meditation upon mortality may soon induce in us a sense of anguish, it fortifies us in the end. Retire, reader, into yourself and imagine a slow dissolution of yourself--the light dimming about you--all things becoming dumb and soundless, enveloping you in silence--the objects that you handle crumbling away between your hands--the ground slipping from under your feet-- your very memory vanishing as if in a swoon--everything melting away from you into nothingness and you yourself also melting away --the very consciousness of nothingness, merely as the phantom harbourage of a shadow, not even remaining to you.

I have heard it related of a poor harvester who died in a hospital bed, that when the priest went to anoint his hands with the oil of extreme unction, he refused to open his right hand, which clutched a few dirty coins, not considering that very soon neither his hand hor he himself would be his own any more. And so we close and clench, not our hand, but our heart, seeking to clutch the world in it.

A friend confessed to me that, foreseeing while in the full vigour of physical health the near approach of a violent death, he proposed to concentrate his life and spend the few days which he calculated still remained to him in writing a book. Vanity of vanities!

If at the death of the body which sustains me, and which I call mine to distinguish it from the self that is I, my consciousness returns to the absolute unconsciousness from which it sprang, and if a like fate befalls all my brothers in humanity, then is our toilworn human race nothing but a fatidical procession of phantoms, going from nothingness to nothingness, and humanitarianism the most inhuman thing known . . . .

No! The remedy is to consider our moral destiny without

flinching, to fasten our gaze upon the gaze of the Sphinx, for it is thus that the malevolence of its spell is discharmed.

If we all die utterly, wherefore does everything exist? Wherefore? It is the Wherefore of the Sphinx; it is the Wherefore that corrodes the marrow of the soul; it is the begetter of that anguish which gives us the love of hope . . . .

I must confess, painful though the confession be, that in the days of the simple faith of my childhood, descriptions of the tortures of hell, however terrible, never made me tremble, for I always felt that nothingness was much more terrifying. He who suffers lives, and he who lives suffering, even though over the portal of his abode is written "Abandon all hope!" loves and hopes. It is better to live in pain than to cease to be in peace. The truth is that I could not believe in this atrocity of Hell, of an eternity of punishment, nor did I see any more real hell than nothingness and the prospect of it. And I continue in the belief that if we all believed in our salvation from nothingness we should all be better . . . .

The greater part of those who seek death at their own hand are moved thereto by love; it is the supreme longing for life, for more life, the longing to prolong and perpetuate life, that urges them to death, once they are persuaded of the vanity of this longing.

The problem is tragic and eternal, and the more we seek to escape from it, the more it thrusts itself upon us. Four-and-twenty centuries ago, in his dialogue on the immortality of the soul, the serene Plato--but was he serene?--spoke of the uncertainty of our dream of being immortal and of the risk that the dream might be vain . . . .

Faced with this risk, I am presented with arguments designed to eliminate it, arguments demonstrating the absurdity of the belief in the immortality of the soul; but these arguments fail to make any impression upon me, for they are reasons and nothing more than reasons, and it is not with reasons that the heart is appeased. I do not want to die--no; I neither want to die nor do I want to want to die; I want to live for ever and ever and ever. I want this "I" to

275

live--this poor "I" that I am and that I feel myself to be here and now, and therefore the problem of the duration of my soul, of my own soul, tortures me.

I am the centre of my universe, the centre of the universe, and in my supreme anguish I cry with Michelet, "Mon moi, ils m'arrachent mon moi!" What is a man profited if he shall gain the whole world and lose his own soul? (Matt. xvi. 26). Egoism, you say? There is nothing more universal than the individual, for what is the property of each is the property of all. Each man is worth more than the whole of humanity, nor will it do to sacrifice each to all save in so far as all sacrifice themselves to each. That which we call egoism is the principle of psychic gravity, the necessary postulate. "Love thy neighbour as thyself," we are told, the pre-supposition being that each man loves himself; and it is not said "Love tyself." And, nevertheless, we do not know how to love ourselves.

Put aside the persistence of your own self and ponder what they tell you. Sacrifice yourself to your children! And sacrifice yourself to them because they are yours, part and prolongation of yourself, and they in their turn will sacrifice themselves to their children, and these children to theirs, and so it will go on without end, a sterile sacrifice by which nobody profits. I came into the world to create my self, and what is to become of all our selves? Live for the True, the Good, the Beautiful! We shall see present-ly the supreme vanity and the supreme insincerity of this hypo-critical attitude.

"That art thou!" they tell me with the Upanishads. And I answer: Yes, I am that, if that is I and all is mine, and mine the totality of things. As mine I love the All, and I love my neighbour because he lives in me and is part of my consciousness, because he is like me, because he is mine.

Oh, to prolong this blissful moment, to sleep, to eternalize oneself in it! Here and now, in this discreet and diffused light, in this lake of quietude, the storm of the heart appeased and stilled the echoes of the world! Insatiable desire now sleeps and does not even dream; use and wont, blessed use and wont, are the rule of

276

my eternity; my disillusions have died with my memories, and with my hopes my fears.

And they come seeking to deceive us with a deceit of deceits, telling us that nothing is lost, that everything is transformed, shifts and changes, that not the least particle of matter is annihilated, not the least impulse of energy is lost, and there are some who pretend to console us with this! Futile consolation! It is not my matter or my energy that is the cause of my disquiet, for they are not mine if I myself am not mine--that is, if I am not eternal. No, my longing is not to be submerged in the vast All, in an infinite and eternal Matter or Energy, or in God; not to be possessed by God, but to possess Him, to become myself God, yet without ceasing to be I myself, I who am now speaking to you. Tricks of monism avail us nothing; we crave the substance and not the shadow of immortality.

Materialism, you say? Materialism? Without doubt; but either our spirit is likewise some kind of matter or it is nothing. I dread the idea of having to tear myself away from everything sensible and material, from all substance. Yes, perhaps this merits the name of materialism; and if I grapple myself to God with all my powers and all my senses, it is that He may carry me in His arms beyond death, looking into these eyes of mine with the light of His heaven when the light of earth is dimming in them for ever. Self-illusion? Talk not to me of illusion--let me live!

They also call this pride--"stinking pride" Leopardi called it--and they ask us who are we, vile earthworms, to pretend to immortality; in virtue of what? wherefore? by what right? "In virtue of what? you ask; and I reply, In virtue of what do we now live? "Wherefore?--and wherefore do we now exist? "By what right?"--and by what right are we? To exist is just as gratuitous as to go on existing for ever. Do not let us talk of merit or of right or of the wherefore of our longing, which is an end in itself, or we shall lose our reason in a vortex of absurdities. I do not claim any right or merit; it is only a necessity; I need it in order to live.

And you, who are you? you ask me; and I reply with

Obermann, "For the universe, nothing; for myself, everything!"
Pride? Is it pride to want to be immortal? Unhappy men that we
are! 'Tis a tragic fate, without a doubt, to have to base the affirmation of immortality upon the insecure and slippery foundation
of the desire for immortality; but to condemn this desire on the
ground that we believe it to have been proved to be unattainable,
without undertaking the proof, is merely supine. I am dreaming
. . . ? Let me dream, if this dream is my life. Do not awaken
me from it. I believe in the immortal origin of this yearning for
immortality, which is the very substance of my soul. But do I
really believe in it . . . ? And wherefore do you want to be immortal? you ask me, wherefore? Frankly, I do not understand
the question, for it is to ask the reason of the reason, the end of
the end, the principle of the principle.

7. EXISTENTIAL THEISM AND THE PROBLEMS OF HUMAN SOCIETY

The existential theist believes that the problems of human society are caused by the failure to achieve a truly authentic personal existence. That failure results in a dehumanization of life which is characterized by anonymity, inner isolation, manipulation by impersonal forces, the treating of each other as objects only and a general sense of meaninglessness. Most other problems of society originate in these existential problems and all are subordinated to them. The loss of authentic personal existence is caused by a loss of the awareness of mysterious personal presence which emerges only in the awareness of mysterious being-itself.

Gabriel Marcel believes that scientific and technological progress have caused a desacrilization of human life. While there are some human problems that can be aided by technology a total reliance upon it as a means to the solution of all human problems leads to a manipulation of human life which is degrading. If we are to be authentically human we must realize that we are mediators of being rather than creators of it. Our essential being cannot be created, only received as a gift from reality beyond our comprehension. Our essential, inward freedom is a transcendence which has its source in transcendent being. Human life becomes sacred only in that awareness. It remains sacred only when we relate ourselves to each other in such a way as to recognize and preserve our unique essential inwardness as individuals.

While Marcel believes that the loss of personal existence is caused by overemphasis upon technological progress, Ralph Harper believes its principal cause is the complexity of modern life which confuses ideals and virtues and makes them difficult to achieve. The basic solution is not to seek fulfillment in an order of justice which may have existed in the past or might exist in the future. In these cases fulfillment is denied in the present. The solution is to be found in the ideal longing for fulfillment which makes us aware of our true being. This "homesickness" allows us to achieve the presence of being in an imperfect world and overcome the anonymity and alienation of "homelessness." This "poetic justice" is dependent upon our awareness of finitude in the face of transcendent being and is complete when it brings us into presence with others in love.

The Sacral in the Era of Technology

Gabriel Marcel

What do I mean when I say the people around me have entered the era of technology? I certainly want to do more than simply reiterate that in recent times technology has made remarkable progress. What I particularly want to stress is man's growing tendency to understand the world around him--and even himself--in terms of technology. But then of course, I should specify what I mean by technology. I consider it a specialized and rationally elaborated skill that can be improved and taught to others. When we speak of technology we do not have in mind the cumulative sum of a variety of different skills. Technology is not a unity we can amass. It is human reason insofar as it strives to manage, so to speak, the earth and everything living within it. Today it might even extend to the management of other planets, although this is still only a possibility, and no one really knows whether it is destined to become reality or not.

To maintain as I do that man is being misled to understand the world and himself in reference to technology, postulates that man is under the impression he can modify the world methodically by his own industry in such a way as to satisfy his needs in an increasingly perfect manner. Some time ago I called attention to the

280

fact that this kind of thinking gives rise to a genuine anthropocentrism. Man tends to look upon himself as alone being capable of giving meaning to an otherwise meaningless world. Doubtless this will have a remarkable effect on man's ability to admire the things around him; there will be an increased tendenncy to admire the products of his own technology--as they appear to afford a matchless measure of perfection and precison. The German critic Günther Anders, in an outstanding book published some time ago entitled Die Antiquiertheit des Menschen (The Antiquatedness of Man), tried to show how eventually man will see himself as something of a nuisance, almost refuse, for being nothing more than human. And then he will set about rectifying the evident shortcomings in what he understands by "nature." . . .

Are not the most enlightened spirits of our age intent upon organizing the earth as scientifically as possible? Would we be able to alleviate the hunger of the world, for instance, if this enterprise should fail? Obviously not; for the solution first and foremost entails the distribution of raw materials and disclosing the world's vast larder of untouched resources. A major problem like that of developing entire nations can be solved only with the assistance of technological progress. Again, we could cite any number of examples, and they could only be denied by unprogressive spirits who are amateurish in their thinking and hardly comprehend the imminent danger of the situation. In fact it seems that we have gotten to the point where we are faced with a categorical necessity we cannot avoid without regressing to a state of unparalleled barbarity.

By and large, the characteristic attitude of technocratic thinking does not consist solely in propounding the principles we elucidated above, but also in considering as somehow futile everything that would obstruct the forward movement of technology. Precisely this latter attitude conjures up the problem I would like to consider at length . . . . (I)t is in reference to the development of contraceptives.

We simply have to understand the opposition of many faithful believers, especially Catholics, to their general use. The employment of such devices seems to imply a misunderstanding, if not an outright denial, of the sacred character of life. For reasons we ought to be aware of, believers see procreation as something very much more than a purely biological function. Even the word "procreation" would seem out of place in this context insofar as it intimates a process of generating life that actually degrades the act of propagation to some extent; it does away with that very element which, in the eyes of the believer, gives it its particular value as well as its transcendence. Naturally, the biologist has no other alternative but to call this value and transcendence into question; he finds it foolish to draw a distinction of nature between conception and any other physiological process. But what is particularly--if not solely--important is the fact that a husband and wife as procreators are limited to fulfilling the conditions according to which a human being, an image of God, becomes flesh. It is extremely important to realize that this entails a gift of God; and man has to place himself in God's service. If we proceed from the acknowledgement of this gift, and from this acknowledgement alone, it definitely is possible to attribute a sacral character to life. The indiscriminate manipulation of human life, on the other hand, to which any kind of contraceptive practice might lead, would seem to imply a disregard for the fact that the power of procreation is a gift. Man tends to function as though he were the actual producer and not merely a mediating agent. Furthermore, mediation is closely associated with the act of producing; in fact every activity looked upon by man as creative actually has to be understood as mediative.

Therefore, I think everyone will agree that because of scientific and technological progress, man has come to look upon himself as a creator rather than an agent. And I will admit that in a world that is (or is becoming) ours everything is apparently proceeding as though this substitution were sanctioned by reason. Consequently, we will have to make a strenuous effort if we are going to extricate ourselves and restore the forgotten reality of mediation.

Doubtless others will think we are foolish. After all, as they see it, it means swimming against the inexorable tide of progress. In other words we are being asked to reject our rather "theocentric" explanation of reproduction and be courageous enough to acknowledge that the reproductive act is no one's business but man's.

While we are on the subject of reproduction, it should be obvious enough that the industrial notion of reproduction hardly fits into our present context. Procreation is not the same thing as fabrication. The seed, or more precisely the semen, transmits a past that is literally unbounded. Consequently man can never be wholly conscious of what he is about when performing the procreative act; the full implications of the deed infinitely exceed his powers of consciousness. In effect he is implementing a procedure he cannot possibly explain. This is just the opposite of what happens in the industrial process, where the materials are not only completely understandable, but actually have to be understood if the process is to meet with any success . . . . The act by which life is transmitted . . . is fundamentally inscrutable.

Several questions are in order: Is it not completely arbitrary to interpret this obscurity as indicating some form of the sacral? Would it not be more normal simply to regard it as witnessing to the fact that man, rooted as he is in a darkened nature, has to consider that he is called to liberate himself as far as possible and eventually gain access to the light of reason?

Actually I hardly think we can dismiss this objection or even substantially modify it; but if such a thing is possible, I think it will have to be reached by way of a very long and circuitous route and on condition that the sacral be regarded as transcending experience. In other words, even granting that someday we might be able, with the help of paleontological discoveries, to go back in time to what we call our origin, this would still not provide us with any substantial illumination, for the further we penetrate into pre-history, the more faint our understanding becomes. This is not to say that our origin cannot be illuminated at all, but if it is to be illuminated the light will have to come from some other quarter.

We have to keep in mind that there is a fundamental difference between production and propagation: the begetter is essentially a go-between the past and the future, both of which elude him. But to the measure we approach our debut into the world, it becomes possible to locate a point where the sacral has its proper place--as exemplified, perhaps, by those religions that practice ancestor worship . . . .

Today life is rarely thought of as a benefaction. People are more inclined to underscore what life implies in the way of revealing absurdity and precipitating despair. Hence, parents look upon themselves as having unjustifiably destined someone who did not ask for life to share the same unintelligible and too often disastrous gamble in which they themselves are implicated. Philosophically speaking, this is the most important aspect of the problem we dealt with a moment ago in our discussion of contraception. If we proceed from a completely desacralized, pessimistic view of life we tend to treat life simply as a power we have to control if we are going to minimize its baneful effects. But in effect this pessimistic outlook is a definite component of the technological notion of the world. It leads us to arrogate to itself the right to manipulate life--simply because it has none of those sacral qualities we discover through a theocentric perspective.

It would be similarly fitting to meditate on man's conduct in the face of death. I am speaking, of course, about the death of someone else, not one's own. For a long time it was noticeable in France how people preserved their respect for death long after their own personal faith had disappeared. But now I think we have a right to ask if even this respect is about to disappear, and, if so, can we attribute its disappearance to any particular kind of thinking. It would seem that life is regarded as entirely useless; consequently, one can estinguish it like a candle. Murder is gradually losing that stigma proper to it in light of the Ten Commandments; we hardly recognize it as a crime anymore. Doubtless we can trace the trend to the terrible mass murders that were perpetrated during the two World Wars and the pogroms. But what I particularly have in mind is the statistical presentation of the facts that ultimately and unnoticeably infects those who have never killed and who doubtless remain true to the traditional view on the subject in their manner of judging. I am almost tempted to speak in stock market jargon about a devastating "drop" in the price of life. Here as anywhere else in business life numbers have an important function. But the number factor operates in absolute opposition to the sacral. The very act of counting itself, I would think, is the beginning of desecration. And if this is so, it is all the more true of statistical evaluation, though, admittedly, those entrusted with the preservation of genuine religious values often condescend to this kind of reckoning--just so much more proof of how far along the process of desacralization actually is. And, conversely, it perhaps helps us grasp the true essence of the sacral in itself.

This is an opportune moment for me to refer to some of my earlier writings. In notes I wrote in 1930 on the prevailing lack of religion, I pointed out that the feeling for the sacral belongs to a realm where the subject finds himself face to face with something beyond his comprehension. Nothing, I said at the time, is more characteristic than the behavior of the believer who folds his hands and by this very gesture declares that there is nothing to be done and nothing to be changed; he simply resigns himself. His gesture is one of dedication and worship.

But conceivably I have still not made the case for the inviolability of the sacral plainly enough. I want to show it to be there where we face whatever is in itself defenseless. For a person who has not been totally absorbed by the technical and, let us say, dehumanized world, contemplation of the most frail of creatures is better suited than anything else to incite him to adoration. Think of the toddler when he suddenly ceases to be a squirming something and his face lights up in a smile. The very presence of the defenseless creature disarms us of all the instruments that would have enabled us to take the actualities in hand and alter them. In my opinion we can best understand "transcendence" within this framework. But it is equally certain that what we have said will be branded as sickly, and perhaps even disastrous, sentimentality by those who look upon themselves as the shock troops of the latest forms of technology--in particular psychoanalysis, at least when it adheres to a naturalistic philosophy (as seems true in the case of Freud, in his earliest writings at least). The psychoanalyst will no doubt cede us the right, though grudgingly, to be touched by the little child; but he will generally deny that the compassion involved--if we may call it that--has anything to do with truth. Now, this is important, for the word sacral ceases to have any meaning; as soon as one ceases to accept that it refers to an actuality that absolutely transcends the level of simple emotion, it degenerates into a nondescript epithet. Moreover, if we were to emphasize in the sacral that element which can in no way be attributed to states of consciousness and still less to kinds of behavior, we would certainly be led to discover the hidden, intimate relationship between the sacral and holiness . . . . It is not impossible that the sacral, on condition it retains its full meaning, has its foundation in a conviction concerning the holiness of God. And, conversely, I feel it is extremely probable that once we impugn this conviction in the name of a "theodicy in reverse," so to speak, we will eventually do away with the sacral altogether.

We are now in a position to recognize that in a world where technology enjoys absolute primacy, a desacralizing process inevitably sets in that it is directed against life and all its manifestations, and particularly against the family and everything connected with it. On the other hand, experience indicates that in totalitarian countries, at least, a strongly nationalized society is attempting to take over and reinstate precisely those elements the family has lost--and that to their own advantage. But we also know that this only leads to the formation of nothing more than the "pseudo-sacral." This is destined to arouse criticism, and a totalitarian society can only defend itself by having recourse to force, coercion and terror.

There are those who would reject both alternatives: the sacral that is only a relic of the past and which depends on a Weltanschauung sufficiently refuted by science, as well as the "pseudo-sacral" that is introduced by tyrannical governments at the expense of the individual's right to mold his own conscience. In their stead they would propose that the world be based on contractual, that is to say, voluntarily approved, relationships; a democracy worthy of the name is actually nothing else. While their attitude appears reasonable enough, I fear it reflects a profound ignorance of the authentic human condition. Agreement, by its nature, requires an oath, that is to say, the sacral. But at the same time experience clearly proves that a contract actually tends to desacralize itself and eventually degenerates into an agreement that each party tries to use to his own best advantage. Or it may simply become a bureaucratic adjustment that no one actually observes; instead everyone tries to circumvent it as far as possible. This malignancy--the core of bureaucracy almost everywhere--is only possible on the basis of the kind of degradation we described above, and it is very difficult, if not impossible, to see how it can be avoided. At best we can try to gloss it over. But how can we overlook the fact that there is a reverse side to the phenomenon: human profiteering is growing more and more complicated, and to the extent I exert myself to discover solutions for the countless practical problems resulting from and posed by numbers, I will have recourse to the domain of statistics. And I find it extremely difficult to believe that statistics can at all be sacral, for they postulate a lack of consideration for, or implicit indifference to, the individual. The only way to rediscover the path to the sacral is to turn away from the world and recapture simplicity, which is perhaps only another word for uniqueness and inwardness, the favorite abode of the sacral.

It is vain to hope that human reality as it is comprehended by statistical methods could ever admit the sacral. It is completely foreign to grace. Grace can only reach the individual, and if it reaches the masses through the individual then it will only happen if the masses arouse themselves from the stupor that made them masses in the first place . . . .

All these considerations lead to a single conclusion: in the technical era the sacral can only reveal itself on condition we are converted (taking of course the word conversion in its usual sense). It seems unreasonable to presume the sacral will ever reveal itself of a sudden in the sweep of development that we constantly have before our eyes. On the contrary, the development itself is aimed at a general and fundamental rejection of the sacral, and this to the degree it encourages ever more explicitly a Promethean attitude--with its attendant hubris, or pride.

But what exactly do we mean by conversion? I do not think we should place the emphasis on one's particular religious confession, although admittedly conversion does usually have a confessional character. But the very least we can say is that conversion can reveal itself in different ways. Conversion is first of all the movement by which the consciousness turns away from

287

the oppressive and distressing spectacle that the technocratic view of the world offers, or--and this amounts to the same thing--by which consciousness transcends the obsession with numbers through the same thing--by which consciousness transcends the obsession with numbers through the numberless. It is the inwardness we regain through an action which is not only free, but in fact is freedom itself. But we have to remember that in its essence inwardness is not tantamount to restriction, and it would be gravely deceptive to think so. And it is just as wrong to imagine the individual who becomes a unity all to himself on account of his conversion. The exact opposite is true; inwardness must be reciprocal; it is a relationship of one individual to another, of an 'I' to a "Thou," as both Martin Buber and I have tried to prove in our writings.

Poetic Justice

Ralph Harper

Poetic justice is a sentiment, not a fact. The fact, if there is one is an order of justice. And since we know little of any order of justice beyond the casual justice of courts and human relations, it is the sentiment of justice that we must deal with first. Poetic justice is the literary expression of someone's longing for justice. Some human being has wanted things to come right in the end so badly that he has put justice into a story. And so many others have wanted the same that no one can now identify the author of the tale. The author need not have believed in justice coming to him, but he must at least have been convinced that that is what he needed most. Perhaps he was defiant rather than

---

From NOSTALGIA (pp. 18-32) by Ralph Harper. Published by The Press of Western Reserve University, copyright (c) 1966. Used by permission of the author.

288

optimistic. Perhaps longing and conviction came out of disillusion-
ment. He knew the world is not just, but that is how he would have
it if it were possible.

The question for the reader of a fairy story is: "Can I admit
that this is how I would have life be, if it were possible?" . . .
Poetic justice convinces only when one can believe in the deserving: good and evil must be easily recognizable . . . .

Not all fairy stories are equally enchanting. None is more
so than the tale of The Sleeping Beauty . . . . In it a beautiful
princess is imprisoned in an enchanted sleep of a hundred years.
She is awakened only at the end of this time when a foreign prince
passes through the briar hedge surrounding the castle, past the
sleeping princess who awakes at the touch. To those who were
contemporaneous with the enchantment, the prince's coming was
unexpected, but to those in the know, like the hearers of a tale,
the prince had come at the only time, the right time, and in coming fulfilled a promise made long before. In coming he had brought
to life the past itself as if no time at all had gone by. Few can
read this without feeling the sentiment in the poetic justice, the
longing for fulfilment of all that is best in life. We do ourselves
injustice if we pretend that this longing is not worth knowing more
about . . . .

There is no faltering in a fairy story, no question of its
values, the deserving or the end. For the fairy story represents
permanent longings and convictions rather than history and change.

So much anyone can see easily. But what one does not
usually see is that these longings and convictions relate to a world
which is within our grasp, which is actually experienced. We have
had the habit of putting this justice in heaven--which, being unseen, is presumed also not real--away from experience. The
truth is, we respond delightedly to such a tale as that of The
Sleeping Beauty because it is in some way familiar to us. Not
only is the longing familiar, the fulfilment is also. This is because we know more of fulfilment that we realize. We know as
much about fulfilment as about longing. Contrary to the usual

opinion, one can say that the only reason we have and understand longing is that we have and can understand fulfilment.

We cannot long for something we do not know; we know only what is in some way already experienced. However new an experience seems to be, if it fulfils longing it is recognized as familiar as well as new. Fulfilment is in some sense a return. This is illustrated by the tale of The Sleeping Beauty. The princess returns to life; the prince himself comes out of nowhere. And yet to the princess the prince is familiar. To the prince the princess is beyond expectation. There is this paradox in the fairy story that matches the paradox in experience. A fairy story is the story of enchantment. Enchantment is a mixture of the familiar and the unexpected; so is the fulfilment of longing in the story. In experience we know that only something new can fill the emptiness, the frustration, the loss, and yet what we actively look forward to, in longing, is like something we have met somewhere before.

On this fact of experience mankind is disposed to deceive itself by looking for obvious large-sized evidence of fulfilment, and also by not really knowing what the signs of fulfilment are. The signs and experience of fulfilment are usually small, insignificant in a world which puts quantity and material advantage before the less visible achievements of character and sensitivity. Perhaps never before has mankind been so demoralized by the suppression of the second.

It is not easy to characterize the twentiety century, not because we are in the middle of it or because we do not know all that can be said of it. The difficulty is that one is depressed by a multiplicity of evidence that all is not going well. Perhaps the most significant fact of the times is the curious intermixture of success and failure. This is a century of homelessness and exile, of nervous disorder and persecution, of actual enslavement and barbaric cruelty. It is also a century of the highest advances in technology and comfort, of the profoundest social and critical sensitiveness. The greater the wisdom and the more widespread the social aspirations, the greater the disillusion with false leaders and false movements. When things go wrong, as they so often do, disillusion then matches expectation. It may not be true that more has gone wrong in this century than in any other; it is certainly true that mankind is more conscious now of its failure, just because it knows so much more surely what it ought to be able to accomplish. For this reason the twentieth century has to be judged in terms of the opposites which make up its power. It is just as false to speak of its homelessness without speaking first of its belief in social and economic justice, as it would be to speak of its technology without speaking of the wars which absorb so much of that technology. And yet it is proper that we should think first of the homelessness that is expressing itself in personal homesickness and longing for lands never seen. If fulfilment must somehow precede longing, it is nevertheless fitting that an understanding of homelessness must precede an understanding of longing and fulfilment.

In the midst of our affluence we should not underestimate certain threats to civilization. Some people, of course, do not like being reminded of them, because they have the nineteenth-century illusion that if the human race is not improving it ought to be, and they resent any implication that life is more complicated than it was when they were children. But however much men suppress or ignore depressing appraisals of our situation, we all experience the same realities. The most obvious of these is the reality of tightly controlled police states in which political and other social freedoms are subservient to economic ends. Old injustices long delayed in old countries have changed chairs with new injustices. And in the new and developing nations the need to plan the future, while sustaining life in the present against odds from without as well as from within, brings instability which over-zealous leaders too often pacify by suppressing liberties.

With this all around them, the prosperous respond as usual with fear and hostility, resenting non-conformity of all kinds, castigating dissent and intelligence unless obviously useful. Some excuse perhaps can be found in the continuing acceleration of modern life which all must contend with, psychologically as well as practically. The fact that most of the demands made on us are trivial does not make them less effective or less noticeable.

There is so much to learn, so much to do, see, hear about, so much that changes even while we watch, that life sometimes seems like getting a mailbag full of third-class matter which we dare not throw away unopened. The effect of these pressures on us is to make us feel we do not know who we are, without names which can live on in the memory or affection of others. Whoever feels this kind of anonymity feels himself ceasing to be a real person . . . .

Isolation was the nineteenth century's answer to anonymity. Today isolation itself must be regarded as the chief symptom of the pressures on man. To-day isolation and anonymity are synchronous. The resolution of the problem will have to be more positive than isolation, for isolation is now part of the problem. What this resolution is we will not know until we know more surely the problem set in terms of anonymity.

Is anonymity just another word for homelessness? No, it is not. A man who feels anonymous, loney in a crowd, feels he is missing the distinctness from his neighbour that a name would give him. This distinctness--or distinction, when brought to flower--would matter less if there were not the question of time. With only a few years to maintain or achieve distinctness from other creatures, there is an urgent need to find oneself. But to find oneself is also to find one's place, to belong somewhere, to be part of some space called home. Only at home, only when one is at home with some part of life, does the spectre of anonymity cease to hover. And as long as pressures make anonymous units out of beings who should be persons, these men will feel homeless. The truth is they are rendered anonymous when they are driven from their homes. Anonymity is a special form of homelessness. The worst that can be said of it is that the more anonymously mankind is treated, the less man feels his homelessness. As long as home is remembered, as long as a man is homesick, he still knows what it is to be a person, even if displaced. And so long will he know the simple, if impracticable way back home. That way is the recognition by the home that matches one's own recognition of the place, the family, and the beauty of their own presence together. Even without this double recognition, homeless men may at least realize that the key to the passage from anonymity to homelessness is the understanding of non-recognition.

What is it like to be not-recognized? Psychologically speaking, it means that a man is not known as familiar; one has never seen him before. Morally speaking, it means that he is a stranger to others, not familiar. There are occasions when a man is not recognized by someone who has known him. We say that he has been cut and, we might say, cut from a familiar or familial relationship. To be cut is to be betrayed, to have evil done deliberately to one. There is no more embittering experience than this. On the other hand, to be recognized is, at least, to be acknowledged, to have one's presence registered. At best, it means to be taken for what one is. Whichever way one is recognized, the aspect of familiarity is the determinant. Unless a man is taken for or allowed to be familiar in some way, he is not recognized; he is then forgotten. When a man is cut, he is betrayed, and it is as if he were forgotten. No wonder he feels anonymous and homeless. But when he is recognized, he is remembered, and is glad and grateful that someone else has remained loyal to him.

In the twentieth century there are four kinds of pressure which encourage non-recognition, homelessness, and anonymity. We have mentioned three of these already: the reality of totalitarian government, bourgeois indifference, the acceleration and overwhelming complexity of modern life. Their effects are seen on both the physical and the psychological levels. Some men are actually herded from their homes to cattle cars; others feel as if they had no homes at all. But the fourth kind of pressure, which we have not mentioned, is the perennial pressure of affliction. Mankind has always suffered, often past endurance. But now suffering is less easily borne than before, for people have every right to expect to be spared suffering by the precautions and therapies of their technology. In addition, most men have no consoling belief in a heavenly justice that will make everything come right, even the most outrageous suffering. Modern values do not encourage stoicism, and modern police techniques make stoicism almost impossible. Thus in the present century men are more prone to the suffering that desolates, that cuts them off from everything familiar, and are less able to bear suffering when it does come.

Only one hundred years ago almost any member of the bourgeoisie could say confidently: "Others are anonymous but not I." And although he might be mistaken, from the point of view of Kierkegaard or Nietzsche, at least we can say for him that there were then many exceptional men, artists, thinkers, writers, scientists, statesmen, of whom no one could have the right to use the epithet anonymous. And yet at that very time the conquest by anonymity was being advanced. By the end of the century Nietzsche was speaking openly of homelessness, for his situation was, as we can now see, a transition from the emphatic self-confidence of exceptionally sensitive men like Stendhal and Kierkegaard, to the metaphysical solitude which obsessed Kafla. Nietzsche was not himself homesick, however clearly he saw the possibility of homesickness for others, for he had no memory of a paradise lost. Homesickness reflects another and better time. The most contrary individualisms of the nineteenth century looked to the future rather than the past. And individualism broke apart just because it wore itself out chasing the future while it lacked a true present. The homesick man, on the other hand, looks to the past not because he does not want the future, but because he wants a true present. The past with which alone he is familiar offers itself to him as a model. Much nonsense has been written about turning the clock back, of burying oneself in days that are well gone, of ignoring what one has or should grasp for the sake of regrets and illusions. However just these fears may often be, they keep one from seeing the utility of homesickness, as a sign in man of his need for a true present.

To be homesick can mean more than to want to go back to the scenes of one's childhood, or even to one's family. "Home is where the heart is," and one's heart can be almost anywhere. The lines of Burns, "My heart is in the Highlands, my heart is not here," tell us poignantly of the element of distance between a man and the homeland which is elsewhere. The more anonymous life becomes, the more disquieted a man becomes, the more frequently will homesickness fall upon him, unless he has surrendered to the many demands to depersonalize himself. Homesickness or nostalgia is an involuntary conscience, a moral conscience, positive rather than prohibitory. It reminds a person, by way of giving

294

him the experience, of the good he has known and lost. Nostalgia is neither illusion nor repetition; it is a return to something we have never had. And yet the very force of it is just that in it the lost is recognized, is familiar. Through nostalgia we know not only what we hold most dear, but the quality of experiencing that we deny ourselves habitually. This is why nostalgia is a moral sentiment. It is also the moral sentiment of the present century.

As long as mankind was sure of its ideals and virtues, as long as men knew where they belonged and lived as if they knew, as long as they could believe that there was an order of justice transcending their own mistakes, nostalgia was but one sentiment among many others. But when the ideals and virtues were forgotten or discredited, when the gods died and men themselves were forced into wandering and exile, then nostalgia stood out as a light-house to wave the way back to the homeland. Unfortunately, nostalgia is still misconceived by a remnant of shallow optimism, as sickly, illusory, unprogressive. Actually, it is the very opposite, understood by stout souls who, being homesick, are yet not sickly, being realistic, have no illusions, and who, while searching for something abiding, have no use for change for change's sake.

Nostalgia should be valued for the same reason that a fairy story's poetic justice is superior to that of a thriller; it is not deliberately contrived. It is evidence given to persons who need reassurances and direction. Because it is not contrived, we can distinguish it from the more conscious longing that is the open turning away from homelessness to homesickness. Without this evidence one would be justified, as some in our time have believed they were, in waiting for justice to come to them. They have wanted but have not dared to long for fulfilment, and lacking nostalgia have wasted their time. It is not to be doubted that those who wait have been homesick too. We may guess that they too have surrendered to the habit of ignoring the implications of nostalgia. This natural sentiment lives in between waiting and longing, and appears, in the midst of wretchedness and failure, to recall the soul to its inner unity and value. The soul shudderingly draws itself up and offers to the depressed consciousness a psychic experience of presence. In nostalgia one smells and tastes, one responds from the darkest corners of oneself, as a renewed whole, to some reality one loves, a person or a place or even an idea. No longer is there any excuse for waiting; nostalgia is regenerative and requires the starting of life all over again.

This is why it is mistaken to think of homesickness as sickly or unprogressive. On the contrary, it is the soul's natural way of fighting the sickness of despair. And if one understands what is required of one, the effect of nostalgia should be a progress toward presence. But there is no denying that the way of this progress is the way of a return. The way to paradise is at the same time a journey from paradise. This is not as pessimistic as it may sound, for to have come from a paradise is a guarantee of paradise. There are two distinct notions in the phrase "journey from paradise," a phrase suggested to me by Proust's remark that "the only true paradise is the paradise we have lost." The first is the notion that life is a pilgrimage, voyage, or wandering--and the last is certainly the least desirable. The second is the idea of a return. But one can see both ideas in the phrase without being sure what direction the journey is taking. At first glance, one would suppose that he who journeys from paradise is travelling in and towards misery and surely it would be hard to deny that misery is implied, or that the world does not provide it. A second glance gives one a chance to wonder whether a journey from paradise may not be different from a journey to misery. Can the memory of paradise help to characterize the journey as well as the hardship of the journey itself? If so, is it certain that paradise cannot be regained?

In lingering homesickness just as in short intense nostalgic flashes, paradise is, as it were, regained. One feels as if one were there, except--and this is the other side of nostalgia--one knows one is not there. The gain and the loss are inextricably mixed, and the effect on the soul is to remind one that one misses and has missed chances to be and see as one should. Without nostalgia a man would have no way of telling himself what life ought to be like, for no purely rational plan or decision can include the principal character of happiness and fulfilment, namely, presence. Nostalgia makes presence, theatrically, but convincingly, for it represents the thing or person or place we care for as an oasis of presence in a desert of loss. It is this juxtaposition of the negative with the positive, this enveloping of the negative, of change, of disappearance, of our having lost touch, of our having diminished, which seems to isolate the good for us and momentarily stop time. If you say that nostalgia is not the only means of achieving presence, we should have to admit that love does this also. But love and possibly certain artistic and contemplative experiences are defined by their sense of a presence which wells up through the surrounding, shifting, arbitrariness of consciousness and environment. We are not talking of essences, with which a man cannot be totally identified, but with presences which seem to meet him halfway. There is no question here of distance, of objectivity. That has its place, but not where justice and paradise are concerned. Anonymity, homelessness, waiting and longing are not to be satisfied except by counter-currents which sweep them along. To journey from paradise, in this sense, means to journey towards the end that was the beginning. This is a return, therefore, to what has been known and loved. If one objects to this, one must first prove that there is nothing worth having known and loved, and then that it is impossible to be made happy by returning. Perhaps such a sceptic should also wonder whether his diagnosis of human restlessness is thorough enough to let him be satisfied with restlessness itself as the only mode of existence. For there is no alternative. The choice is between yielding completely to time and change or trying in some way to find that principle of identity and integrity and satisfaction which the restlessness itself tells us we need but do not have. Platonists and Christians alike have assumed in this manner that man is meant to have unity, integrity, peace, and a true present. But none has realized that the model and the instinct is nostalgia, the sentiment of presence, which phoenix-like springs from the ashes of disquietude, sentiment of emptiness and alienation.

At this point, if not before, some people cannot help asking, out of their restlessness, whether nostalgia can possibly be thought of as a way of life. Should one be nostalgic? The answer is, one is already nostalgic if one is sensitive to one's failure to achieve the presence that signifies the reality of justice and happiness. The problem is to understand the nostalgia, not make it. And there is no doubt that true understanding is itself a way to happiness. For how can one search for presence if one does not know what to search for ? And how can one know what presence is, what it feels like to be near it, unless one has been near it and has reflected enough on it to know it ? The search and then the practice of presence are further steps and stories, but the understanding of the direction and the end is the necessary beginning of the ascetic journey. Asceticism need not and should not imply starvation or self-laceration; it is simply the concentration, the recollection, of all the energies of body as well as spirit, on some high task. The task nostalgia sets man again and again is the need and beauty of presence.

Presence is not a familiary philosophical term, for it is only since the first world war that it has been deliberately used by some European philosophers. This is an interesting fact, because presence is the new ontological expression spontaneously put to use in response to the longing arising out of homelessness. It has always had several different but allied usages. Before all others it has meant "being. " It is, in fact, the concrete way of denoting being or existence. But it cannot be adequately explained only as the equivalent of being and/or existence. It suggests that some being is actively, almost vibratingly related to one. And it is not much of a jump from here to the psychic presences that are known as ghosts. A presence is a being which is intimate with us. Wordsworth's "presence that disturbs me" says much the same thing. But whether physical or spiritual, palpable or purely psychic, a presence is something which moves one. Perhaps we should remark that of a presence it is impossible to say whether the moving is exclusively physical or spiritual, the two are so confused.

If the presence is friendly, something in us is moved in return, and we are fulfilled. Justice is done. The sleeping beauty awakes. If the presence disturbs as a source of hurt or panic, one might have to ask whether justice has not been done here too. Who knows just what one deserves ? Who knows also when the final decision on one's case has been handed down ? But however sceptical, however we hold ourselves in suspense or are held down by circumstances, we do meet presences if we have not inured ourselves to their influence. And whether or not we are educated to appreciate their importance, we feel instinctively at the time that we are experiencing something special. Of all these experiences,

that of love, with its mixture of giving and wanting, is the proto-
type. The more anonymous and homeless men become, the less
they experience love in its fullness. As love recedes, only nostalgia remains to recall them before they accept their rejection. That
kind of acceptance makes men into barbarians and slaves. An
understanding of homesickness is their last chance to return to the
world of presence before they are lost forever in a world ruled by
hate and alienation.

There is no word for "being" that has so many implications
as "presence": metaphysical, moral, psychological, religious.
And we expect this of a word which, in English at least, has several undertones. "The present" is temporal. The present is what
we never fully attain except in recollection, memory and reflection,
and in longing. "A present" is a gift from elsewhere to us. A
present is what a person needs who knows he is not self-sufficient,
and who can respect the presence of another. "The presence" of
another is the available intimacy which promises to give what we
need for fulfilment. Wherever there is this awareness of intimacy,
of the chance that one may be given what one longs for and needs,
one can be sure there is a "real presence." There are unreal
presences, evil, empty, deceiving. There are also the substantial presences which admit us to their intimacy in the fullness of
time. It is appropriate that the Christian religion, a religion
depending so much on an encounter of eternity with history, should
speak of the sacramental incarnation as a real presence which the
faithful approach in prayer and expectation. Prayer is the religious equivalent of longing. Whenever longing approaches fulfilment, it is approaching a real presence, in loving as in praying.

These four undertones of presence correspond to the four
implications, the metaphysical, the moral, the psychological, the
religious. They define the shape of the world that nostalgia dreams
of. In this world where anonymity and noise and change reign,
where every day homelessness is confirmed rather than diminished,
it has, paradoxically, become possible to see more clearly than
ever before the life that mankind probably enjoys less than at any
other time. Never before has the world wanted presence enough
to make clear what it is. Can we practise it once we too know it

again? That is the problem for further searching and exercising. But there is no need for searching and exercising until we begin to recognize the presence that is lost to us in our homelessness and anonymity. The tale of The Sleeping Beauty is a tale of just such a recognition.

PART FIVE

NEW DIRECTIONS

Paul M. Van Buren
John F. Miller, III
Peter L. Berger
Jürgen Moltmann

1. INTRODUCTION

The religious perspectives which we have examined represent four clearly distinct ways in which religion can be understood basically, consistently and comprehensively. Though Pantheism and Natural Theism have ancient origins both continue to attract serious and able interpreters who attempt to bring them into focus and dialogue with modern knowledge. Humanism and Existential Theism, in their philosophical formulation, are largely products of the modern age. Yet, their interpreters often believe that they have found the best way to understand ancient religious truths. All four of them have established themselves so firmly as to be "live options" in the contemporary world.

Religious perspectives, however, rarely remain static and never are without challenge from those who are seeking "new directions." New directions, when they come, are never so new as to ignore well established views. They are usually made by interpreters who are seeking to challenge some dimension of a well established view, make a bridge between two established views or change an old view in light of new knowledge, conditions and insights.

The four articles which follow represent such attempts. While they have received serious attention in the contemporary world it remains to be seen whether they will form the nucleus of a new perspective or the older perspectives will prevail against them. This should not, however, be the only criterion by which we judge new directions. They can be the "life blood" by which the older perspectives are given transfusions and kept dynamically alive.

Paul Van Buren's article describes the cultural condition in the contemporary world with which any meaningful religion must come to terms. In a relativistic world language about the Absolute is no longer meaningful. This view is also held by the Humanists, but Van Buren's world is not structured solely by the methods of science. It is much more pluralistic. His emphasis upon a tolerant, secular spirit as being the one out of which religious commitments should be fashioned is compatible with what has sometimes been called "Secular Religion."

A significant religious phenomenon in the contemporary world is the development in the West of numerous religions of Eastern origins. Most of these religions usually seek to use Eastern methodologies to accomplish those goals which have been identified with Western culture. John Miller's article is a philosophical formulation of such an attempt. His "New Humanism" bears certain similarities to the humanistic perspective, in its emphases of individualism, naturalism, social action and historical development. Yet, his emphases of freedom of conscious control, unity of all conscious life and oneness with Nature are clearly pantheistic. The "New Age Science" which he advocates has much in common with pantheistic Eastern religions, while the goals to be attained by it seem quite humanistic.

Peter Berger attempts to construct a new "Natural Theology." He accepts the existential theist's methodology of basing his theism upon an analysis of tendencies toward transcendence in the finite human condition. Unlike existential theism, however, faith is not based upon a longing for the infinite but trust that the universe really is as we project it to be in our natural human experiences. Thus his faith is "inductive," beginning in "empirical" data about human nature and pointing to an ultimate reality which is, itself, not experienced. The similarity to Natural Theism is obvious, but there is one notable divergence. The God hypothesis is not based upon the knowledge that we have about the world, but upon the natural tendencies toward faith that are rooted in human experience. This, perhaps, makes his view a little more subjective than most natural theists would accept. It seems clear that while Berger is speaking to those who have been "disillusioned about the Absolute" he is somewhat influenced by that condition as well as by Existential Theism.

Jürgen Moltmann's new direction of transcendence can be seen in its relation to the nature of religious experience. Religious experience for the natural theist is the experience of God as

304

revealed in the natural order of the created world. It grows out of a condition of alienation of the self from the finite, transitory things of the world and transcends toward an immutable, fixed and benevolent infinite reality. For the existential theist religious experience begins in the experience of alienation of the subjective being of the finite self from the objective being of the world and transcends toward the mysterious being-in-itself which breaks through into personal existence and authenticates it. Moltmann rejects both of these on the grounds that modern human alienation is not from the order of the natural world or the objective world which the subject transcends. Modern alienation is from the social and political systems which are the work of human hands but now are out of control and seek to enslave their creators. While the transcendence of Natural Theism enhances the acceptance of the natural order and that of Existential Theism enhances the preservation of inner subjectivity neither overcomes modern alienation. A new transcendence is needed. It must be a transcendence over the conditions of society in history and directed toward a future wherein these conditions are transformed. This is the only transcendence which promises liberation from alienation. It is not the future itself which brings liberation, however, but hope which transforms the social and political conditions of the present. Hope is dependent upon faith that the ultimate has been revealed in the historical Christ "eschatologically," that is, as the end toward which history is to be redeemed. Religious experience is, therefore, a revolutionary consciousness which continually seeks to liberate the conditions of alienation and suffering in human society. In this respect it bears some resemblance to Humanism, except that for Moltmann this future transcendence is dependent upon a hope which transcends history itself.

2. THE DISSOLUTION OF THE ABSOLUTE

Paul M. Van Buren

. . . The world in which I live, and apparently not alone, is a world which I should like to describe as following upon, or in the late stages of, a major socio-psychological shift in our culture, which I shall label "The Dissolution of the Absolute." It seems to have been the case, prior to this shift, that thoughtful men spoke not infrequently, and as though they had no thought of not being understood by their peers, of the Absolute, the Highest Good, or of Reality (with a capital R). This characteristic of language and thought has become increasingly difficult to maintain or recapture. The change has come about, so far as I can see, not as a result of a frontal assult on the idea of the Absolute, but by a process of dissolution or decay. The Absolute was not murdered, Zarathustra not withstanding; it died of neglect.

The dissolution of the Absolute, the passing of a world view and a habit of thought, or its quiet displacement by another and different habit of thought, is a phenomenon that I have called a socio-psychological fact. With that label I wish to indicate how broad and basic a shift I have in mind, and how many ways there are of exploring and describing this change. One can, for example, ask about the causes and timing of the dissolution of that pattern of thought in which differing views about the Absolute were held to be of such importance that these differences could lead to heresy trials and burnings at the stake, not to speak of wars. I take this question about the causes and timing of the change to be a historical question which it is the proper business of the historian of Western culture to explore. Setting dates for this sort of cultural shift is a rather arbitrary business, but let me just suggest, as an illustration of the historical aspect of the problem, that if one were

---

to write a history of Western Christianity, it might be more accurate to locate the fundamental turning point not in the Reformation, as is so often the case with Protestant histories of Christianity, but somewhere nearer the French Revolution. After all, Luther and Calvin stand in one world with Augustine and Aquinas, no matter how they may disagree about the details; whereas none of them fit easily, if at all, into the world of Enlightenment. The gap between the Reformers and the Scholastics is small indeed compared with the gap between them all and such men as Rousseau, Voltaire, or Jefferson.

One can also ask about the extent of the dissolution, to what extent it is the case that people no longer seem to operate on the assumption of an absolute. This is a question which the sociologist might be in as good a position as any to explore. Or, if they were willing to study our society with the penetration shown in their study of some other societies, perhaps cultural anthropologists could help us to see the extent to which our values, attitudes, and patterns of thought betray a departure from those in which words such as "God," "providence," "destiny," and "absolute" seemed to function powerfully. The social sciences could help us see to what extent the Absolute has been dissolved out of our operative images of life and the world.

Or one can ask about the shape of this changed situation, how it looks when the dissolution has taken place. This can be opened up to some extent by the social sciences, but it can also be exposed by the works of writers, poets, and artists. The question of shape is in part an aesthetic question, and insofar as a quantifiable answer seems to fall short of satisfying our questions, the artists, writers, literary and art critics, and aestheticians can help us to see where we are today.

Further, there is a task of clarifying the dissolution and the logic of our new situation, which is, from one point of view, a philosophical question. Metaphysics I take to be not some sort of superscience which might provide us with new information about the universe or "Reality" of a rather esoteric or subtle kind. I know that there are theologians who speak as if ontology were some sort of penetration of the "structure of being," but I gather that few if any philosophers are impressed by this. A metaphysics or ontology, as I gather it would be taken by most philosophers today, consists rather of a proposal, one might say an invitation, to see what we already know in a particular way. Metaphysics does not give us something new to see (such as "being itself" or "the ground of being") in any other way than by giving us a new way to see what we have been looking at all along.

From this point of view, then, to speak of the dissolution of the Absolute is one way of indicating a shift which has occurred in our metaphysical assumptions. At this point, however, I find that philosophers seem to withdrawn from what I take to be a serious and worthwhile enterprise: the attempt to formulate and clarify the logic of the commonsense metaphysics of our society. They say, quite correctly, that a major piece of this job is not their business: namely, the careful empirical study of what people in our society think and the way in which they think. That would properly be the business of the behavioral and social sciences to discover. Yet when it comes to the task of formulating and analyzing the workings of our commonsense attitudes, it would seem to me that the philosopher need not be so retiring. The disdainful remark that the common sense of today is only the poor leavings of the best thinking of yesterday and beneath the dignity of philosophical investigation, which I have heard from several philosophers, bothers me a bit. After all, the common sense of today is the pattern of thinking in which we do our major arguing and debating of the great issues of our society. I notice that philosophers appear just about as frequently as theologians among the lists of those thinkers called upon by government and industry to assist in dealing with the major issues of our time. Could it be that philosophers as well as theologians, admittedly for different reasons, have simply opted out of the society of common sense? If theologians are the more irrelevant to life today, it is because they have been even more disdainful of the realm of ordinary language and ordinary common sense. Be that as it may, I would still wish to urge that there is a philosophical task to be performed in our attempts to get clear about the commonsense understandings of our time, and if this task is not well done by competent philosophers, then it will be poorly and sloppily done by others.

The dissolution of the Absolute, then, is a broad cultural shift which may be investigated and documented from a number of angles. It is a change that has affected our thought and language in ways so fundamental that they are not always noticed. Few have taken as little account of this shift as have the theologically inclined, although it should be evident that religion and theology are as much or more touched by the dissolution of the Absolute as any area of human activity. One consequence of failing to see this change that has taken place has been a certain degree of linguistic and logical confusion, resulting from attempting to operate in a world without absolutes while using ideas and languages drawn from a world in which the idea of the Absolute had an important place. The confusion is not unlike that of the substitute player in a football game rushing onto the field firmly clutching a baseball bat.

A prime example of this sort of confusion may be seen in the use of the word "reality." Now on any showing, this is a tricky word, an odd sort of noun, like "sadness" or "beauty," which is derived from a reasonably clear usage in the adjectival form of the word. That is to say, we do not seem to have much difficulty when we use the word "real." There is little difficulty knowing what we say that a mirage, the appearance of water on the road ahead on a hot summer day, is not real. Or in doing an elementary experiment in refraction, we may see that a stick half immersed in water looks bent; but we know, or so we say without confusion, that the stick is really straight, in spite of appearances. In these cases the words "real" and "really" serve the purpose of touching base in or reminding us of a commonly agreed frame of reference. Empirically minded though we may be, we are also aware of the limitations of sense experience. Our senses are not infallible, we say. Things are not always what they seem; skim milk masquerades as cream. But we do have words such as "seem," "appear," and "masquerade," and we do have the working distinction between the uses of these words and the use of the word "real," because we do have that common network of ground rules to which we are able to appeal with the word "real." If this, then, is how we use

309

the word "real," what would be the meaning of "reality"? Well, in a great many cases "reality" is a word that refers to the whole of our understandings of how things are according to this same network of ground rules. So we might say that a man who is insane is a man who has "lost touch with reality." We mean that he no longer plays life's game according to the common rules. Or we say that a hypothesis seems "to conform to reality," by which we mean that it seems to fit fairly well into how we take things to be according to our commonly held understandings.

So far so good. That is, nothing is at all airtight about any of this, but we get along all right; we understand each other fairly well. Now along comes the knight of faith and speaks of "reality breaking in upon us!" Or he speaks to us in the name of "absolute reality," or, even more confusing, his faith is placed in "an objective reality." And here I would suggest that language has gone on a wild binge, which I think we should properly call a lost weekend.

This knight of faith is presumably speaking English, and so we take him to be using words which we have learned how to use. Only see what he does with them. "Reality," which is ordinarily used to call our attention once more to our agreements about how things are, is used now to refer to what the knight of faith must surely want to say is radically the opposite of all of our ordinary understandings. Why not better say, "Unreality is breaking in upon us"?

I think we can say something about what has gone wrong here. There was a time when the Absolute, God, was taken to be the cause of a great deal of what we would today call quite real phenomena, from rain and hail to death and disease. God was part of what people took to be the network of forces and factors of everyday existence, as real and as objective as the thunderbolts he produced. But today we no longer have the same reference for the word "reality." The network of understandings to which the word points has undergone important changes. The word "reality" has taken on an empirical coloration which makes it now a bit confusing to speak of "reality breaking in upon us," unless we are referring to, for example, a sudden and unexpected visit from the police or a mother-in-law.

There is, however, another source of unclarity or confusion here, and that is the very fact of the dissolution of the Absolute itself. In the eleventh century the great theologian Anselm of Canterbury wrote a little essay containing an argument for the existence of God which continues to this day to occupy philosophers and theologians. I do not intend to explore Anselm's argument, but there is one contextual aspect of it which bears on our problem. Anselm was asking a certain question, the question about God, in such a way that he understood himself to be asking the one question which included and summed up every human question. Indeed, I believe that this observation is true for all of the great traditional arguments for the existence of God. Those arguments were not trying to make a case for simply one entity, namely God, but for that which was the basis for and foundation of everything that is. Take away this frame of reference, this approach to these argument, and they all become a bit silly.

Now the reason why most people today do regard these arguments as silly, the reason why we have difficulty accepting the answers or conclusions of these arguments, is because we simply do not know how to ask Anselm's question. We do not conceive it possible that there could be one answer which would entail and provide the answer to every question man can ask, in such diverse areas as, for example, politics, physics, mathematics, and aesthetics; so we are unable to ask after "God" in the way in which Anselm could. That being the case, we find it hard to accept his, or any of the arguments for the existence of God, as being persuasive. To speak of Absolute Reality is to speak in Anselm's world, not ours, both with respect to the word "Absolute" and to the word "Reality."

The change which I have called the dissolution of the Absolute has led to a pluralistic society and a pluralism of values and understandings. We are not in this world in one way; we live in our world in many ways, and it hardly seems to make sense to try to pull everything together under one heading. The sociologists call this differentiation, I believe, and another way of putting it would be to say that we have become relativists as well as pluralists. I am not saying, however, that we think everything is of the same or equal importance, or that we inhabit our various worlds or parts thereof in always the same and equal ways. Plurality does not entail equality of all the parts. It does mean, however, that life and the world are for us many different things, and that when we talk in a manner which convinces ourselves, we talk about "the whole" of life by talking in more detail or with more care about the various parts.

I touched on this in connection with Anselm's question and our inability to ask his question. The fact that Anselm and his word are part of our past may be taken as a clue to what I would call our monistic hangover, which, when it is particularly acute, makes our pluralist waking an agony. The monistic images of our past haunt us in the most unexpected and sometimes unwanted places. We may find, for example, when we try to think or speak of the universe, that we do not honestly want to spell "universe" with a capital "U." If we are asked about the extent of our small "u" universe, we may mention the rule of thumb which gives it a radius twice the range of the most powerful telescope, under the assumption that any presumed sources of light beyond that range are moving away from us at so nearly the speed of light that for all practical purposes (and isn't that a revealing phrase!) we can ignore them. And if we come closer to home, it is only out of habit that we speak of a "universe" at all. It really depends on how you approach it, we might say, for the "universe" of one discipline is but the background or a detail for another. All things considered, it appears to be more appropriate to speak of a poly-verse.

But then that old monistic hangover begins to creep over us and tempts us to ask if there is not something fundamental to the human mind which leads us to keep on trying to pull things together, to see everything in some sort of interrelatedness, to devise laws and hypotheses in the hope of seeing how it all fits together into one whole. Perhaps at this point we need a bit of aspirin. Does the human mind actually do this, or is it more accurate to say that the human mind indeed tended to do this in the past out of which we have come? Perhaps we need to recall, for example, that historical study is one way of going at things, and it has developed and continues to develop its own methods. And physics is another way of going at things, with its own methods. And literary critics and biologists and painters also have their appropriate ways of exploring the world. Do we honestly think we shall come to understand any one of these ways, with its results, or indeed the whole of life, by somehow pulling them all together into one great system? When human knowledge was conceived of hierarchically--say on the model of a Gothic arch--it made sense to build comprehensive systems, and there could also be one queen of the sciences. But since the Gothic arch has been displaced by the marketplace as a model for human understanding, comprehensive systems have become strangely out of place, just as royalty finds itself out of a job in the context of the marketplace.

Pluralism means that we have granted that there are many ways of looking and seeing, many points of orientation, and that attempts to pull these all together into one grand scheme do not bring us closer to understanding how things are. The generalist has been displaced by the specialist in our society, in area after area of our common life. Insofar as this is true, insofar as this is how we think, we lose interest in Anselm's answer because we are not convinced he was asking the right question.

Relativism means that we appear to be coming more and more to a consensus that there is more than one way to look at any matter, and that what is said can be called true or false only in the terms provided by the particular point of reference. The student of art, for example, is encouraged to look at a given work of art in the light of the problems which the artist set for himself or were set for him by his situation. It is not a serious question for the student of art to ask what is the single greatest painting of all time.

Pluralism and relativism do not mean, however, that there are no distinctions to be made. One may have reasons for preferring one scale of values to another, one way of looking at a problem to another. But it is, I think we should agree, a mark of education and good sense to refrain from dogmatic statements which necessarily deny all merit to all other positions and points

313

of view. One can hold serious commitments without universalizing them and without insisting that all who disagree are either knaves or fools. If relativism has an unpleasant sound, then let us call it tolerance. By whatever name, it is an important feature of the (secular) spirit of our age; and when we run into its denial, as in McCarthyism or Goldwaterism, most of us are at least uncomfortable. Somehow extremism has lost status, and if at moments it seems to make headway again, I think most of us regard this as a step backward, as a betrayal of what little progress civilization has made.

To ask theology and religion to accept the dissolution of the Absolute, to open their eyes to the world in which they live, is admittedly to ask much. It means that religion must not only become much more guarded in speaking of God (if not give this up altogether) it means also that more care be exercised in speaking of "unique revelation," "absolute commitment," and some single "ultimate concern." It is to ask of the life of faith that it be lived as a certain posture, involving commitments, but held in balance with many other commitments; a certain willingness to see things in a certain way without feeling obliged to say that this is the only way in which they can be seen. The question may fairly be asked whether theology and faith can survive this shift of focus; whether Christianity, for example, which has for so long proclaimed a monistic view of the universe, a single and unique point of reference as the only valid one, with a single and unique revelation of this truth, can learn to live in a world from which the Absolute has been dissolved. However one may choose to answer this in theory, we are in fact in the actual process of finding this out, for living when we do and as we are is not exactly a matter of choice. What are the values and dangers of this? Well, what are the values and dangers of being alive? They are the values and dangers of being who we are.

3. HUMANISM IN THE NEW AGE

John F. Miller, III

Whether or not many of us are even aware of it, and whether we will accept its metaphysics or its philosophical ramifications, a "New Age" is breaking upon the West . . . .

Just as we are entering a New Age, so too there is emerging a New Humanism . . . . The value and dignity of man are very much the focal point, with man as the measure of reality and human nature the proper study of man. Man is viewed as part of both Nature and History, and the importance of the liberal arts education is not to be underestimated as man develops those capacities and powers which elevate him above the animals . . . .

The New Age freedom is fundamentally a freedom in consciousness. No longer need one believed that consciousness is limited to the narrow confines traditionally prescribed by Western philosophy and psychology. As William James noted, normal rational consciousness is but one kind of awareness of which man is capable. With biofeedback machines, man is learning how to control processes of his body which have long been believed to lie beyond conscious control. It has now been demonstrated that the functions of the central and autonomic nervous systems, the immunological system, and the endocrine system are within the conscious and deliberate exercise of man's mind. Health, then, is within his freedom; and he is free to avail himself of the freedom from disease of which he is now recognized to have been largely the cause. Fifty to eighty percent of disease is psychosomatic, according to Stanley Krippner--others would place the estimate even higher--so health and sickness are not a matter of chance, luck, or germs, operating beyond man's freedom. Through

From PHILOSOPHIC RESEARCH AND ANALYSIS (Vol. VI, No. 12, Late Winter, 1978), pp. 10-13. Used by permission of the publisher and the author.

imagination the central nervous system and the immunological system can be harnessed in the healing process. Self-healing usually requires relaxation, and alpha states of brain consciousness are capable of being learned through various techniques. Moreover, although perhaps as much as 90 per cent of psychic healing is not "paranormal," there are some instances of such healing which are not easily explained on the standard model currently accepted within Western medicine. This leaves open the possibility that the potential for healing can be activated by those who choose to do so. Of course, the distinction between "normal" and "paranormal" is not one which will long persist in the New Age, for in both esoteric and Oriental metaphysics there is no place for such distinctions. Both philosophies recognize powers of healing as natural within the human capabilities, though it may require deprogramming or de-hypnotization to reawaken these siddhis.

Freedom of consciousness is possible in other remarkable ways, as known within the esoteric and Yogic traditions. In the Vibhuti Pada of Patanjali's Yoga-Sutras such "altered states of consciousness" are described: knowledge of past and future; communication with all living beings; direct awareness of one's previous lives; direct perception of the content of others' minds; knowledge of one's time of death as well as the reasons for the events which are happening to one in his life; solar and lunar knowledge; knowledge of the organization of the body; ability to control hunger and thirst; ability to see into the higher planes, as well as the ability to sense with all the faculties on the higher levels of consciousness. In addition, one can gain the freedom to walk upon water or to pass through fire without being burned. These kinds of Yogic and esoteric powers enable one to be as free as a god-on-earth, with virtually unlimited power and knowledge, developed through non-attachment, perhaps the greatest freedom of all. Man is free to understand his place within Nature and History, to perceive the unity of Truth within all religions and philosophies, no matter how distorted or exaggerated, and the oneness of religion, philosophy, and true science, from which emerges love and tolerance for all ideas and beings, though attachment to none.

This New Age freedom is inseparable from individualism. In the New Humanism, each person is an individual, unique and different, yet forming a harmony in union with all other individuals. Each person is a particular expression and combination of universal characteristics, which, though calculable astrologically and numerologically, are nevertheless unique. One is free to rise above his environment and heredity, his parochial world view or provincial conceptual framework to take his place as a citizen of the world. Rising above personality, the mask through which the individuality expresses itself, one frees himself from the source of conflict and is capable of integration and harmonious unity. As with the fourteenth century humanists, the New Humanists emphasizes wisdom, the gnostic heritage, his trust that through knowledge man has the ability to become a god. With Nietzsche, the New Humanist realizes his calling to be a bridge beyond normal humanity. Confidence in man's ability as man, in his ability to exceed even himself: this is the foundation of the freedom and indivduality of the New Age Humanism . . . .

It is part of the New Humanism to emphasize man's relation to Nature and his essential naturalness. Indeed, man feels himself an integral part of Nature, realizing that what occurs in his natural environment has a pronounced influence upon him. It is in this light that we must understand the importance which environmental issues play in the New Age. Both astrology and astronomy make clear man's relationship to Nature. As Dr. Burr (H. S. Burr, The Fields of Life, 1973) has demonstrated in his experiments with "L-fields," the electro-magnetic environment, influenced by the Sun, Moon, and Earth's own gravitational fields, is a definite causal factor in man's life. Bio-rhythm charts are increasingly employed by individuals to determine the appropriateness (or naturalness) of activities at certain times. In health and preventive medicine the importance of a diet consisting of natural foods becomes an essential ingredient; and the use of natural supplements, rather than artificial chemical substances, to treat illness emphasizes man's oneness with Nature.

In the New Humanism, a natural balance is preferred between

317

activity and contemplation. Many people who but a few years ago prided themselves on their sedentary contemplative life are now jogging to work or at regularly scheduled times during the day. Social action has become more marked in recent times, intellectuals no longer being content merely to write about social life. And as activism, participation, and involvement become watchwords of the New Age, moral action takes its rightful place in the New Humanism.

Through participating in bio-feedback, meditation, and yoga, the New Age man has expanded the very concept of Nature. What used to be considered unnatural and even physically impossible has now been demonstrated to be within human capacity. Experiences of calmness and peace, tranquility and joy, have become part of the experiences of hundreds of thousands who practice meditation or mind-control. So many have experienced "altered states of consciousness" that now a New Age Humanist will find himself at home in a Nature which has been enlarged so as to contain an enhanced conception of the potentials of man, wherein activity, contemplation, meditation, moral action, science, religion, and philosophy are all equally natural . . . .

It is in the legitimacy of social action and participatory involvement that the importance of the historical perspective may be understood. The individual is important in history, his actions do count, and he is the center of the historical arena. We cannot doubt the effects of protesting against the Vietnamese War, we cannot ignore the influence of civil rights demonstrations, and we cannot deny the results of causes which range from environmental interests to citizen's lobbies. The individual does count, his voice is heard, and he does make a difference. This is an increasingly important feature of the New Age Humanism . . . .

The religion of the New Age and the New Humanism is not the narrowly paraochial religion of the past millenia. Rather it is an expansive, experiential, experimenting, daring religion of the individual as he seeks the experience and exercise of the freedom and the potentials of his own soul. Daring not dogmatic, experimental not theoretical, based on experience not faith, the new religious attitude encompasses East and West, esoteric and exoteric, mysticism and animism, spiritualism and spiritism, communication with Nature and communication with the gods or Masters. It is participatory, involved, active: mind-control, meditation, mantras, astral projection, soul travel, healing by the laying on of hands, and the conscious communication with the Nature spirits. Ten years ago who would have believed a Findhorn possible, who would have suggested that the death-of-God theologies would spawn a spiritual engagement with Oriental religions, and who would have anticipated the eight-thousand ways to awaken spiritually which would appear on the continent of North America. From Silva Mind Control to the Indian groups such as Transcendental Meditation, Yoga, Vendanta Societies, Ananda Margo, and Self-Realization Fellowship; from the Sufis, Buddhists, Tiebetans, Vajardhatu Association, Myingma Institute, Zen Integral Yga Institute, and the International Society for Krishna Consciousness to the Arica Institute, Dr. Assogioli's Psychosynthesis, the National Training Laboratories Institute for Applied Sciences, Esalen Institute and Synanon; and from the Rosicrucian groups, the Builders of the Adytum, and the theosophical organizations to those who study in the privacy of their homes, astrology, tarot, kaballah, and the mystery teachings of Greece, Egypt, and Tibet: there are hundreds of thousands of Americans involved in one way or another in a spiritual reawakening.

Christian authors such as James Sire (The Universe Next Door, 1976) and Os Guiness (The Dust of Death, 1973) reluctantly admit that Christian culture is disintegrating and the old humanism has failed to provide an alternative. Many writers talk of a post-Christian West, where meditation replaces prayer, where verification is through participation, where integration and a feeling of oneness replace the alienation of isolation, and where the goal is freedom from personality and emergency into genuine individuality.

The increase in interest in the mystery teachings heralds a new dawning of a New Age gnosticism, the importance of knowing truth and experiencing it in one's life, a definite movement toward the Western religious path, and a rising above the conventional and traditional morality. Knowledge is the way to salvation, but this knowledge is lived-knowledge or wisdom, not merely intellectual and theoretical knowledge. Man's salvation is his own problem, not thrown on the shoulders of a Saviour whose death some two thousand years ago is somehow, miraculously and mysteriously, to save one from his sins. Not wallowing in sin but rising above sin is the goal; one is to become a Buddha or a Christos. As the death-of-God theologians recognized, the Church has become demonic and Satanic, blocking the very revelation for the New Age. What is called for is sacrifice, sacrifice which takes the form of social action, sacrifice which walks the path of love and service. In his odyssey, the New Age Humanist has no place for Christianity's exclusive claims to final validity and full truth. For Hermes, Orpheus, Krishna, Buddha, Pythagoras, Christ, and Baha'ullah all taught the same truth: the path of crucifixion of personality and resurrection of the divine human nature so that a life of love and service might be rendered to the brotherhood of man in the name of the Unity of the One. . . .

This last point is illustrative of the importance of tolerance in New Age Humanism, which is based on the firm conviction of the fundamental unity of all religions and of Truth itself. Properly seen in the right hierarchical perspective, empiricism and rationalism, theism and atheism, monism and dualism, materialism and Absolution all point to the same truth: the One in the Many, and the Many in the One. Though it may take the eye of the abstract thinker to discern the unity, it is this vision which fosters the atmosphere of tolerance in the New Age. Moreover, there is the recognition of the age-old wisdom, expressed in the symbols of Yin/Yang and the philosophy of the I Ching, that coversion takes place only when one is ready, in which case exhortation and evangelizing are unnecessary, or worse, counter-productive. As in Nature each thing has its place and own rhythm and tempo. It is as foolish to try to persuade someone of or convert him to a truth which he is not ready to receive as it is to attempt to force a tree to bear fruit in the dead of winter. . . .

The science of the New Age will be decidely humanistic. Its emphasis will be on man, on his health, both physical and psychological, both mental and spiritual, and on his relation with nature. New Age science will then contain both an ecological/environmental awareness as well as a magic-oriented consciousness. In short, the science of the New Age will be holistic.

If New Age science is to reflect the growing humanism, it will have to extend beyond its present exclusive concern with classes and concentrate more of its attention upon the individual. Of course, science will continue to deal with universal qualities and characteristics, but these will be applied to individuals, not merely to classes or groups. If the proper study of man is man, then the particular man must be the object of investigation, not merely the group-man. This is why Marshall McLuhan ("The McLuhan Dew Line," Time, March 21, 1969) can say that astrology, clairvoyance, and mysticism will become part of the science of tomorrow. This is why, too, we see the growing interest in those ancient sciences such as palmistry, astrology, tarot card reading, handwriting analysis, and numerology, all of which analyze the particular human subject. Again, interest in such phenomena as bio-rhythms may be attributed to the search for scientific data pertaining to the individual.

The New Age science will involve its investigators in an experiential, rather than merely a theoretical, way. The New Age scientist will be encouraged to become a participant; and, as in the East, verification will increasingly become through participation . . . .

Rather than accepting the dogma and authoritative pronouncements of those scientists who disparage the New Age and who always have been the sort of scientists who have stood in the way of progress, the growing breed of New Age scientists will be open to experiment, experience, and testing, thereby embodying what is truly the scientific attitude.

If what we are suggesting is true, we can expect significant developments in two important areas, psychology and medicine. It is not that there will not be advances in other scientific fields, but rather that for the humanist these two fields are among the most significant. In psychology, trans-personal, Jungian, and oriental/esoteric models will continue to emerge, replacing the more naive and single-dimensionsed models implicit in materialism, behaviorism, and determinism. With these new models will awaken the awareness of new possibilities for humanity, new vistas of perception, new levels of awareness, new levels of consciousness. These will enhance the understanding of the nature of man and will offer an added dimension to the New Age humanism. In medicine, too, great strides will be taken, as indicated by those who have already pushed ahead of their colleagues. Preventive medicine will expand; and natural techniques for self-healing such as relaxation, visualization, imagination, and meditation will become increasingly popular . . . . One can expect, further, a growing sensitivity to music and color, as the populace becomes more sensitive to vibrations. Music will play an essential part in life, spreading its healing power to the masses; and color will become a common source of general healing and energizing as psychological studies are corrolated with medical data. If any of this seems incredible, one need only check his local bookstore for the hundreds of books which have already appeared on these subjects . . . .

This, then, is what the humanism of the New Age holds out to us. There are many models of human nature which could be offered to account for the possibilities which we will see emerging in the New Age; but above all, we must recognize that whatever model is offered is tentative, hypothetic, helpful to some but not to all, and certainly a model, not the reality itself. In this way, whatever model is offered, esoteric, oriental, trans-personal, Jungian, Gestalt, or whatever, it is still only one model out of many. More important than the map is the reality to which it refers; and more important than any "ism" are the real possibilities which New Age Humanism holds out to all mankind in the New Age.

4. FROM ANTHROPOLOGY TO THEOLOGY

Peter L. Berger

If anthropology is understood here in a very broad sense, as any systematic inquiry into the constitution and condition of man, it will be clear that any kind of theology will have to include an anthropological dimension. After all, theological propositions only very rarely deal with the divine in and of itself, but rather in its relations to and significance for man. Even the most abstract speculations concerning the nature of the Trinity were much more salvation-oriented than theoretical in their underlying impetus, that is, they derived not from disinterested curiosity but from a burning concern for the redemption of man. The real question, then, is not so much whether theology relates to anthropology--it can hardly help doing so--but what kind of relation there will be . . . .

The suggestion that theological thought revert to an anthropological starting point is motivated by the belief that such an anchorage in fundamental human experience might offer some protection against the constantly changing winds of cultural moods. In other words, I am not proposing a "more relevant" program or a new dating of our intellectual situation ("post-X" or "neo-Y"). Instead, I venture to hope that there may be theological possibilities whose life span is at least a little longer than the duration of any one cultural or socio-political crisis of the times.

What could an anthropological starting point mean for theology ? . . .

I would suggest that theological thought seek out what might be called <u>signals of transcendence</u> within the empirically given human situation. And I would further suggest that there are <u>prototypical human gestures</u> that may constitute such signals. What does this mean?

By signals of transcendence I mean phenomena that are to be found within the domain of our "natural" reality but that appear to point beyond that reality. In other words, I am not using transcendence here in a technical philosophical sense but literally, as the transcending of the normal, everyday world that I earlier identified with the notion of the "super-natural." By prototypical human gestures I mean certain reiterated acts and experiences that appear to express essential aspects of man's being, of the human animal as such. I do not mean what Jung called "archetypes"—potent symbols buried deep in the unconscious mind that are common to all men. The phenomena I am discussing are not "unconscious" and do not have to be excavated from the "depths" of the mind; they belong to ordinary everyday awareness.

Any historical society is an order, a protective structure of meaning, erected in the face of chaos. Within this order the life of the group as well as the life of the individual makes sense. Deprived of such order, both group and individual are threatened with the most fundamental terror, the terror of chaos that Emile Durkheim called anomie (literally, a state of being "orderless").

Throughout most of human history men have believed that the created order of society, in one way or another, corresponds to an underlying order of the universe, a divine order that supports and justifies all human attempts at ordering. Now, clearly, not every such belief in correspondence can be true, and a philosophy of history may . . . be an inquiry into the relationship of true order to the different human attempts at ordering. But there is a more basic element to be considered, over and above the justification of this or that historically produced order. This is the human faith in order as such, a faith closely related to man's fundamental trust in reality. This faith is experienced not only in the history of societies and civilizations, but in the life of each individual—indeed, child psychologists tell us there can be no maturation without the presence of this faith at the outset of the socialization process. Man's propensity for order is grounded in a faith or trust that, ultimately, reality is "in order," "all right," "as it should be." Needless to say, there is no empirical method by which this faith can be tested. To assert it is itself an act of faith. But it is possible to proceed from the faith that is rooted in experience to the act of faith that transcends the empirical sphere, a procedure that could be called the argument from ordering.

In this fundamental sense, every ordering gesture is a signal of transcendence. This is certainly the case with the great ordering gestures that the historian of religion Mircea Eliade called "nomizations"--such as the archaic ceremonies in which a certain territory was solemnly incorporated into a society, or the celebration, in our own culture as in older ones, of the setting up of a new household through the marriage of two individuals. But it is equally true of more everyday occurrences. Consider the most ordinary, and probably most fundamental, of all-the ordering gesture by which a mother reassures her anxious child.

A child wakes up in the night, perhaps from a bad dream, and finds himself surrounded by darkness, alone, beset by nameless threats. At such a moment the contours of trusted reality are blurred or invisible, and in the terror of incipient chaos the child cries out for his mother. It is hardly an exaggeration to say that, at this moment, the mother is being invoked as a high priestess of protective order. It is she (and, in many cases, she alone) who has the power to banish the chaos and to restore the benign shape of the world. And, of course, any good mother will do just that. She will take the child and cradle him in the timeless gesture of the Magna Mater who became our Madonna. She will turn on a lamp, perhaps, which will encircle the scene with a warm glow of reassuring light. She will speak or sing to the child, and the content of this communication will invariably be the same--"Don't be afraid--everything is in order, everything is all right." If all goes well, the child will be reassured, his trust in reality recovered, and in this trust he will return to sleep.

All this, of course, belongs to the most routine experiences of life and does not depend upon any religious preconceptions. Yet this common scene raises a far from ordinary question, which immediately introduces a religious dimension: Is the mother lying to the child? The answer, in the most profound sense, can be "no" only if there is some truth in the religious interpretation of human existence. Conversely, if the "natural" is the only reality there is, the mother is lying to the child--lying out of love, to be sure, and abviously not lying to the extent that her reassurance is grounded in the fact of this love--but in the final analysis, lying all the same. Why? Because the reassurance, transcending the immediately present two individuals and their situation, implies a statement about reality as such.

To become a parent is to take on the role of world-builder and world-protector. This is so, of course, in the obvious sense that parents provide the environment in which a child's socialization takes place and serve as mediators to the child of the entire world of the particular society in question. But it is also so in a less obvious, more profound sense, which is brought out in the scene just described. The role that a parent takes on represents not only the order of this or that society, but order as such, the underlying order of the universe that it makes sense to trust. It is this role that may be called the role of high priestess. It is a role that the mother in this scene plays willy-nilly, regardless of her own awareness or (more likely) lack of awareness of just what it is she is representing. "Everything is in order, everything is all right" --this is the basic formula of maternal and parental reassurance. Not just this particular anxiety, not just this particular pain--but everything is all right. The formula can, without in any way violating it, be translated into a statement of cosmic scope--"Have trust in being." This is precisely what the formula intrinsically implies. And if we are to believe the child psychologists (which we have good reason to do in this instance), this is an experience that is absolutely essential to the process of becoming a human person. Put differently, at the very center of the process of becoming fully human, at the core of humanitas, we find an experience of trust in the order of reality. Is this experience an illusion? Is the individual who represents it a liar?

If reality is coextensive with the "natural" reality that our empirical reason can grasp, then the experience is an illusion and the role that embodies it is a lie. For then it is perfectly obvious that everything is not in order, is not all right. The world that the child is being told to trust is the same world in which he will eventually die. If there is no other world, then the ultimate truth about

326

this one is that eventually it will kill the child as it will kill his mother. This would not, to be sure, detract from the real presence of love and its very real comforts; it would even give this love a quality of tragic heroism. Nevertheless, the final truth would be not love but terror, not light but darkness. The nightmare of chaos, not the transitory safety of order, would be the final reality of the human situation. For, in the end, we must all find ourselves in darkness, alone with the night that will swallow us up. The face of reassuring love, bending over our terror, will then be nothing except an image of merciful illusion. In that case the last word about religion is Freud's. Religion is the childish fantasy that our parents run the universe for our benefit, a fantasy from which the mature individual must free himself in order to attain whatever measure of stoic resignation he is capable of.

It goes without saying that the preceding argument is not a moral one. It does not condemn the mother for this charade of world-building, if it be a charade. It does not dispute the right of atheists to be parents (though it is not without interest that there have been atheists who have rejected parenthood for exactly these reasons). The argument from ordering is metaphysical rather than ethical. To restate it: In the observable human propensity to order reality there is an intrinsic impulse to give cosmic scope to this order, an impulse that implies not only that human order in some way corresponds to an order that transcends it, but that this transcendent order is of such a character that man can trust himself and his destiny to it. There is a variety of human roles that represent this conception of order, but the most fundamental is the parental role. Every parent (or, at any rate, every parent who loves his child) takes upon himself the representation of a universe that is ultimately in order and ultimately trustworthy. This representation can be justified only within a religious (strictly speaking a supernatural) frame of reference. In this frame of reference the natural world within which we are born, love, and die is not the only world, but only the foreground of another world in which love is not annihilated in death, and in which, therefore, the trust in the power of love to banish chaos is justified. Thus man's ordering propensity implies a transcendent order, and each ordering gesture is a signal of this transcendence. The parental role is not based on a loving lie. On the contrary, it is a witness to the ultimate truth of man's situation in reality. In that case, it is perfectly possible (even, if one is so inclined, in Freudian terms) to analyze religion as a cosmic projection of the child's experience of the protective order of parental love. What is projected is, however, itself a reflection, an imitation, of ultimate reality. Religion, then, is not only (from the point of view of empirical reason) a projection of human order, but (from the point of view of what might be called inductive faith) the ultimately true vindication of human order.

Since the term "inductive faith" will appear a number of times, its meaning should be clarified. I use induction to mean any process of thought that begins with experience. Deduction is the reverse process; it begins with ideas that precede experience. By "inductive faith," then, I mean a religious process of thought that begins with facts of human experience; conversely, "deductive faith" begins with certain assumptions (notably assumptions about divine revelation) that cannot be tested by experience. Put simply, inductive faith moves from human experience to statements about God, deductive faith from statements about God to interpretations of human experience.

Closely related to, though still distinct from, the foregoing considerations is what I will call the argument from play . . . . When one is playing, one is on a different time, no longer measured by the standard units of the larger society, but rather by the peculiar ones of the game in question. In the "serious" world it may be 11 A. M., on such and such a day, month, and year. But in the universe in which one is playing it may be the third round, the fourth act, the allegro movement, or the second kiss. In playing, one steps out of one time into another . . . .

This is true of all play. Play always constructs an enclave within the "serious" world of everyday social life, and an enclave within the latter's chronology as well. This is also true of play that creates pain rather than joy. It may be 11 A. M., say, but in the universe of the torturer it will be thumbscrews time again. Nevertheless one of the most pervasive features of play is that it is usually a joyful activity. Indeed, when it ceases to be joyful and becomes misery or even indifferent routine, we tend to think of this as a perversion of its instrinsic character. Joy is play's intention. When this intention is actually realized, in joyful play, the time structure of the playful universe takes on a very specific quality--namely, it becomes eternity. This is probably true of all experiences of intense joy, even when they are not enveloped in the separate reality of play . . . . The playful universe has a temporal dimension that is more than momentary and that can be perceived as a distinct structure. In other words, in joyful play it appears as if one were stepping not only from one chronology into another, but from time into eternity. Even as one remains conscious of the poignant reality of that other, "serious" time in which one is moving toward death, one apprehends joy as being, in some barely conceivable way, a joy forever. Joyful play appears to suspend, or bracket, the reality of our "living towards death" (as Heidegger aptly described our "serious" condition).

It is this curious quality, which belongs to all joyful play, that explains the liberation and peace such play provides. In early childhood, of course, the suspension is unconscious, since there is as yet no consciousness of death. In later life play brings about a beatific reiteration of childhood. When adults play with genuine joy, they momentarily regain the deathlessness of childhood. This becomes most apparent when such play occurs in the actual face of acute suffering and dying. It is this that stirs us about men making music in a city under bombardment or a man doing mathematics on his deathbed . . . .

Some little girls are playing hopscotch in the park. They are completely intent on their game, closed to the world outside it, happy in their concentration. Time has stood still for them--or, more accurately, it has been collapsed into the movements of the game. The outside world has, for the duration of the game, ceased to exist. And, by implication (since the little girls may not be very conscious of this), pain and death, which are the law of that world, have also ceased to exist. Even the adult observer of this scene, who is perhaps all too conscious of pain and death, is momentarily drawn into the beatific immunity.

In the playing of adults, at least on certain occasions, the

329

suspension of time and of the "serious" world in which people suffer and die becomes explicit. Just before the Soviet troops occupied Vienna in 1945, the Vienna Philharmonic gave one of its scheduled concerts. There was fighting in the immediate proximity of the city and the concertgoers could hear the rumbling of the guns in the distance. The entry of the Soviet army interrupted the concert schedule--if I'm not mistaken, for about a week. Then the concerts resumed, as scheduled. In the universe of this particular play, the world-shattering events of the Soviet invasion, the overthrow of one empire and the cataclysmic appearance of another, meant a small interruption in the program. Was this simply a case of callousness, of indifference to suffering? Perhaps in the case of some individuals, but basically, I would say not. It was rather an affirmation of the ultimate triumph of all human gestures of creative beauty over the gestures of destruction, and even over the ugliness of war and death.

The logic of the argument from play is very similar to that of the argument from order. The experience of joyful play is not something that must be sought on some mystical margin of existence. It can be readily found in the reality of ordinary life. Yet within this experienced reality it constitutes a signal of transcendence, because its intrinsic intention points beyond itself and beyond man's "nature" to a "supernatural" justification. Again, it will be perfectly clear that this justification cannot be empirically proved. Indeed, the experience can be plausibly interpreted as a merciful illusion, a regression to childish magic (along the lines, say, of the Freudian theory of wishful fantasy). The religious justification of the experience can be achieved only in an act of faith. The point, however, is that this faith is inductive--it does not rest on a mysterious revelation, but rather on what we experience in our common, ordinary lives. All men have experienced the deathlessness of childhood and we may assume that, even if only once or twice, all men have experienced transcendent joy in adulthood. Under the aspect of inductive faith, religion is the final vindication of childhood and of joy, and of all gestures that replicate these.

Another essential element of the human situation is hope, and there is an _argument from hope_ within the same logic of inductive

330

faith . . . .

Human existence is always oriented toward the future. Man exists by constantly extending his being into the future, both in his consciousness and in his activity. Put differently, man realizes himself in projects. An essential dimension of this "futurity" of man is hope. It is through hope that men overcome the difficulties of any given here and now. And it is through hope that men find meaning in the face of extreme suffering. A key ingredient of most (but not all) theodicies is hope. The specific content of such hope varies. In earlier periods of human history, when the concept of the individual and his unique worth was not as yet so sharply defined, this hope was commonly invested in the future of the group. The individual might suffer and die, be defeated in his most important projects, but the group (clan, or tribe, or people) would live on and eventually triumph. Often, of course, theodicies were based on the hope of an individual afterlife, in which the sufferings of this earthly life would be vindicated and left behind. Through most of human history, both collective and individual theodicies of hope were legitimated in religious terms. Under the impact of secularization, ideologies of this worldly hope have come to the fore as theodicies (the Marxist one being the most important of late). In any case, human hope has always asserted itself most intensely in the face of experiences that seemed to spell utter defeat, most intensely of all in the face of the final defeat of death. Thus the profoundest manifestations of hope are to be found in gestures of courage undertaken in defiance of death.

Courage, of course, can be exhibited by individuals committed to every kind of cause--good, bad, or indifferent. A cause is not justified by the courage of its proponents. After all, there were some very courageous Nazis. The kind of courage I am interested in here is linked to hopes for human creation, justice, or compassion; that is, linked to other gestures of humanitas--the artist who, against all odds and even in failing health, strives to finish his creative act; the man who risks his life to defend or save innocent victims of oppression; the man who sacrifices his own interests and comfort to come to the aid of afflicted fellow men. There is no need to belabor the point with examples. Suffice it to say that it is this kind of courage and hope that I have in mind in this argument.

We confront here once more, then, observable phenomena of the human situation whose intrinsic intention appears to be a depreciation or even denial of the reality of death. Once more, under the aspect of inductive faith, these phenomena are signals of transcendence, pointers toward a religious interpretation of the human situation. Psychologists tell us (correctly no doubt) that, we may fear our own death, we cannot really imagine it. Our innermost being shrinks from the image and even theoretical detachment seems to be caught in this fundamental incapacity. It is partly on this basis that Sartre has criticized Heidegger's concept of "living unto death" arguing that we are fundamentally incapable of such an attitude. The only death we can experience, Sartre maintains, is the death of others; our own death can never be part of our experience, and it eludes even our imagination. Yet it is precisely in the fact of the death of others, and especially of others that we love, that our rejection of death asserts itself most loudly. It is here, above all, that everything we are calls out for a hope that will refute the empirical fact. It would seem, then, that both psychologically (in the failure to imagine his own death) and morally (in his violent denial of the death of others) a "no!" to death is profoundly rooted in the very being of man.

This refusal is to be found in more than what Karl Jaspers called the "marginal situations" of human life--such extreme experiences as critical illness, war, or other natural or social catastrophes. There are, of course, trivial expressions of hope that do not contain this dimension--"I hope that we will have good weather for our picnic." But any hope that, in whatever way, involves the individual as a whole already implicitly contains this ultimate refusal--"I hope to finish my work as a scientist as well as I can"--"I hope to make a success of my marriage"--"I hope to be brave when I must speak up against the majority." All these contain an ultimate refusal to capitulate before the inevitability of death. After all, even as I express these limited hopes, I know that I may die before my work is finished, that the woman I marry may even now be afflicted by a fatal disease, or that some majorities, if outraged enough, may kill me. The denial of death implicit in hope becomes more manifest, of course, in the extreme cases--

"I hope to finish my work as well as I can, despite the war that is about to destroy my city"--"I shall marry this woman, despite what the doctor has just told me about her condition"--"I shall say my piece, despite the murderous plans of my enemies."

It is again very clear that both the psychological and moral aspects of such denial can be explained within the confines of empirical reason. Our fear of death is instinctually rooted and presumably has a biological survival value in the process of evolution. The psychological paralysis before the thought of our own death can be plausibly explained in terms of the combination of the instinctual recoil before death and the peculiarly human knowledge of its inevitability. The moral refusal to accept the death of others can equally plausibly be explained as nothing but a "rationalization" (in the Freudian sense) of instinctual and psychological forces. In this perspective, the denial of death and any manifestation of hope (religious or otherwise) that embodies this denial is a symptom of "childishness." This, indeed, was the burden of Freud's analysis of religion. Against such "childish" hopes there stands the "mature" acceptance of what is taken to be final reality . . . . It hardly needs to be said that this kind of stoicism merits the deepest respect and, in fact, constitutes one of the most impressive attitudes of which man is capable. Freud's calm courage in the face of Nazi barbarity and in his own final illness may be cited as a prime example of this human achievement.

Nevertheless the twin concepts of "childishness" and "maturity" are based on an a priori metaphysical choice that does not follow of necessity from the facts of the matter. The choice does not even necessarily follow if we are convinced (which, let it be added, I am not) by the Freudian interpretation of the psychological genesis of death-denying hope. Man's "no!" to death--be it in the frantic fear of his own annihilation, in moral outrage at the death of a loved other, or in death-defying acts of courage and self-sacrifice--appears to be an intrinsic constituent of his being. There seems to be a death-refusing hope of the very core of our humanitas. While empirical reason indicates that this hope is an illusion, there is something in us that, however, shamefacedly in an age of triumphant rationality, goes on saying "no!" and even says "no!" to the ever so plausible explanations of empirical reason.

In a world where man is surrounded by death on all sides, he continues to be a being who says "no!" to death--and through this "no!" is brought to faith in another world, the reality of which would validate his hope as something other than illusion . . . .

Inductive faith acknowledges the omnipresence of death (and thus of the futility of hope) in "nature," but it also takes into account the intentions within our "natural" experience of hope that point toward a "supernatural" fulfillment. This reinterpretation of our experience encompasses rather than contradicts the various explanations of empirical reason (be they psychological, sociological, or what-have-you). Religion, in justifying this reinterpretation, is the ultimate vindication of hope and courage, just as it is the ultimate vindication of childhood and joy. By the same token, religion vindicates the gestures in which hope and courage are embodied in human action--including, given certain conditions, the gestures of revolutionary hope and, in the ultimate irony of redemption, the courage of stoic resignation.

A somewhat different sort of reasoning is involved in what I will call the argument from damnation. This refers to experience in which our sense of what is humanly permissible is so fundamentally outraged that the only adequate response to the offense as well as to the offender seems to be a curse of supernatural dimensions. I advisedly choose this negative form of reasoning, as against what may at first appear to be a more obvious argument from a positive sense of justice. The latter argument would, of course, lead into the territory of "natural law" theories, where I am reluctant to go at this point. As is well known, these theories have been particularly challenged by the relativizing insights of both the historian and the social scientist, and while I suspect that these challenges can be met, this is not the place to negotiate the question. The negative form of the argument makes the intrinsic intention of the human sense of justice stand out much more sharply as a signal of transcendence over and beyond socio-historical relativities.

The ethical and legal discussion that surrounded, and still

334

surrounds, the trials of Nazi war criminals has given every thinking person, at least in Western countries, an unhappy opportunity
to reflect upon these matters. I will not discuss here either the
agonizing question "How can such things have been done by human
beings?" or the practical question of how the institution of the law
is to deal with evil of this scope . . . .

There are certain deeds that cry out to heaven. These deeds
are not only an outrage to our moral sense, they seem to violate a
fundamental awareness of the constitution of our humanity. In this
way, these deeds are not only evil, but monstrously evil. And it is
this monstrosity that seems to compel even people normally or
professionally given to such perspectives to suspend relativiza-
tions. It is one thing to say that moralities are socio-historical
products, which are relative in time and space. It is quite another
thing to say that therefore the deeds of an Eichmann can be viewed
with scientific detachment as simply an instance of one such mor-
ality--and thus, ultimately, can be considered a matter of taste.
Of course, it is possible, and for certain purposes may be very
useful, to attempt a dispassionate analysis of the case, but it
seems impossible to let the matter rest there. It also seems impossible to say something like, "Well, we may not like this at all,
we may be outraged or appalled, but that is only because we come
from a certain background and have been socialized into certain
values--we would react quite differently if we had been socialized
(or, for that matter, resocialized, as Eichmann presumably was)
in a different way." To be sure, within a scientific frame of
reference, such a statement may be quite admissible. The crucial point, though, is that this whole relativizing frame of reference appears woefully inadequate to the phenomenon if it is taken
as the last word on the matter. Not only are we constrained to
condemn, and to condemn absolutely, but, if we should be in a
position to do so, we would feel constrained to take action on the
basis of this certainty. The imperative to save a child from murder, even at the cost of killing the putative murderer, appears to
be curiously immune to relativizing analysis. It seems impossible to deny it even when, because of cowardice or calculation, it
is not obeyed.

The signal of transcendence is to be found in a clarification

335

of this "impossibility." Clearly, the murder of children is both practically and theoretically "possible." It can be done, and has been done in innumerable massacres of the innocent stretching back to the dawn of history. It can also be justified by those who do it, however abhorrent their justifications may seem to others. And it can be explained in a variety of ways by an outside observer. None of these "possibilities," however, touch upon the fundamental "impossibility" that, when everything that can be said about it has been said, still impresses us as the fundamental truth. The transcendent element manifests itself in two steps. First, our condemnation is absolute and certain. It does not permit modification or doubt, and it is made in the conviction that it applies to all times and to all men as well as to the perpetrator or putative perpetrator of the particular deed. In other words, we give the condemnation the status of a necessary and universal truth. But, as sociological analysis shows more clearly than any other, this truth, while empirically given in our situation as men, cannot be empirically demonstrated to be either necessary or universal. We are, then, faced with a quite simple alternative: Either we deny that there is here anything that can be called truth--a choice that would make us deny what we experience most profoundly as our own being; or we must look beyond the realm of our "natural" experience for a validation of our certainty. Second, the condemnation does not seem to exhaust its intrinsic intention in terms of this world alone. Deeds that cry out to heaven also cry out for hell. This is the point that was brought out very clearly in the debate over Eichmann's execution. Without going into the question of either the legality or the wisdom of the execution, it is safe to say that there was a very general feeling that "hanging is not enough" in this case. But what would have been "enough"? If Eichmann, instead of being hanged, had been tortured to death in the most lengthy and cruel manner imaginable, would this have been "enough"? A negative answer seems inevitable. No human punishment is "enough" in the case of deeds as monstrous as these. These are deeds that demand not only condemnation, but damnation in the full religious meaning of the word--that is, the doer not only puts himself outside the community of men; he also separates himself in a final way from a moral order that transcends the human community, and thus invokes a retribution that is more than human.

Just as certain gestures can be interpreted as anticipations of redemption, so other gestures can be viewed as anticipations of hell (hell here meaning no more or less than the state of being damned, both here and now and also beyond the confines of this life and this world). We have interpreted the prototypical gesture of a mother holding her child in protective reassurance as a signal of transcendence. A few years ago, a picture was printed that contains the prototypical countergesture. It was taken somewhere in eastern Europe during World War II at a mass execution--of Jews, or of Russians or Poles, nobody seems to know for sure. The picture shows a woman holding a child, supporting it with one hand and with the other pressing its face into her shoulder, and a few feet away a German soldier with raised rifle, taking aim. More recently two pictures have come out of the war in Vietnam that, as it were, separate the components of this paradigm of hell (and, when taken together, serve to remind us that damnation very rarely follows the political dividing lines drawn by men). One picture, taken at an interrogation of "Vietcong suspects," shows an American soldier holding a rifle against the head of a woman of indeterminate age, her face lined with anguish. Whether or not the rifle was eventually fired, the possibility is implied in the threatening gesture. The other picture was taken during the Tet offensive of the Vietcong in early 1968, in a military billet in Saigon where the Vietcong had massacred the families of officers of the South Vietnamese army. It shows an officer carrying his dead daughter in his arms. The lines on his face are like those on the face of the woman being interrogated. Only here we do not see the man with the rifle.

I would argue that both gesture and countergesture imply transcendence, albeit in opposite ways. Both may be understood, under the aspect of inductive faith, as pointing to an ultimate, religious context in human experience. Just as religion vindicates the gesture of protective reassurance, even when it is performed in the face of death, so it also vindicates the ultimate condemnation of the countergesture of inhumanity, precisely because religion provides a context for damnation. Hope and damnation are two aspects of the same, encompassing vindication. The duality, I am inclined to think, is important. To be sure, religious hope offers a theodicy and therefore consolation to the victims of in-

humanity. But it is equally significant that religion provides damnation for the perpetrators of inhumanity. The massacre of the
innocent (and, in a terrible way, all of history can be seen as this)
raises the question of the justice and power of God. It also, however, suggests the necessity of hell--not so much as a confirma-
tion of God's justice, but rather as a vindication of our own.

Finally, there is an <u>argument</u> <u>from</u> <u>humor</u> . . . . A good deal
has been written about the phenomenon of humor . . . .

I agree with Bergson's description: "A situation is invariably
comic when it belongs simultaneously to two altogether independent
series of events and is capable of being interpreted in two entirely
different meanings at the same time." But I insist upon adding that
this comic quality always refers to <u>human</u> situations, not to encounters between organisms and the non-organic. The biological
as such is not comic. Animals become comic only when we view
them anthropomorphically, that is, when we imbue them with human characteristics. Within the human sphere, just about any
discrepancy can strike us as funny. Discrepancy is the stuff of
which jokes are made, and frequently it is the punch line that
reveals the "entirely different meaning." The little Jew meets
the big Negro. The mouse wants to sleep with the elephant. The
great philosopher loses his pants. But I would go further than this
and suggest that there is one fundamental discrepancy from which
all other comic discrepancies are derived--the discrepancy between man and universe. It is <u>this</u> discrepancy that makes the
comic an essentially human phenomenon and humor an intrinsically
human trait. The <u>comic</u> <u>reflects</u> <u>the</u> <u>imprisonment</u> <u>of</u> <u>the</u> <u>human</u>
<u>spirit</u> <u>in</u> <u>the</u> <u>world</u>. This is why, as has been pointed out over and
over since classical antiquity, comedy and tragedy are at root
closely related. Both are commentaries on man's finitude--if
one wants to put it in existentialist terms, on his condition of
"thrown-ness." If this is so, then the comic is an objective
dimension of man's reality, not just a subjective or psychological
reaction to that reality . . . .

There is an additional point to be made. Humor not only
recognizes the comic discrepancy in the human condition, it also
relativizes it, and thereby suggests that the tragic perspective on

the discrepancies of the human condition can also be relativized. At least for the duration of the comic perception, the tragedy of man is bracketed. By laughing at the imprisonment of the human spirit, humor implies that this imprisonment is not final but will be overcome, and by this implication provides yet another signal of transcendence--in this instance in the form of an intimation of redemption, I would thus argue that humor, like childhood and play, can be seen as an ultimately religious vindication of joy.

Humor mocks the "serious" business of this world and the mighty who carry it out. There is a story that when Tamerlane conquered Persia he ordered the poet Hafiz to be brought before him and confronted him with one of his poems, in which he had promised all the glories of Samarkand for the mole on his sweetheart's cheek. "How dare you offer the splendor of my imperial capital for the shoddy attractions of a Persian whore?" Tamerlane angrily demanded. "Your majesty, it is from you that I have learned the habits of generosity," Hafiz is said to have replied. According to the story, Tamerlane laughed and spared the poet's life. He might well have reacted differently, conquerors and empire-builders not usually being endowed with much appreciation for humor. But whatever the outcome of such encounters between tyrants and poets, the question I would always ask is this: Who, in the end, is to be pitied--the one who holds the world in his powerful hands, or the one who laughs at him? The "serious" answer is, of course, that power is not to be pitied; that the pitiful are always the victims of power. Humor, at least for the instant in which it perceives the comic dimensions of the situation, gives the opposite answer. The one to be finally pitied is the one who has an illusion. And power is the final illusion, while laughter reveals the final truth. To a degree, this can be said without any reference to transcendence. Empirical reason knows that all power is precarious and that eventually even Tamerlane must die. But the revelation of laughter points beyond these empirical facts. Power is ultimately an illusion because it cannot transcend the limits of the empirical world. Laughter can--and does every time it relativizes the seemingly rocklike necessities of this world . . . .

There is by no means an exhaustive or exclusive list of

339

human gestures that may be seen as signals of transcendence. To provide one would entail constructing a philosophical anthropology and, on top of that, a theological system to go with it. I am not prepared to be quite as Quixotic as that! But I do want to go at least a few steps beyond setting up a program and suggest how it might be possible to theologize from an anthropological starting point. My choice of examples may not be convincing to everyone and, in any case, is fairly arbitrary. I could have chosen other examples, though I would contend that the ones just discussed are particularly useful because they all refer to very basic human experience. I have deliberately omitted any discussion of claims to direct religious experience (in the sense of experience of the supernatural). This is by no means intended to depreciate efforts to study and understand such phenomena; it merely follows from my earlier expressed belief that theological thought would do well to turn from the projections to the projector, and thus to empirical data about man. It is fairly clear that mysticism, or any other alleged experience of supernatural realities, is not accessible to everyone. Almost by definition, it partakes of the quality of the esoteric. My aim has been to explore theological possibilities that take as their starting point what is generally accessible to all men. I have therefore limited myself to a discussion of phenomena that can be found in everybody's ordinary life. Even the argument from damnation remains within the context of the "ordinary," in the sense that it does not presuppose any special illumination or intervention from beyond the human sphere. I make no claim for this method over any other, but, to repeat, it is a possible solution to the vertigo of relativity. It will appeal particularly, I think, to those who have passed through the "fiery brook" of sociological relativization . . . .

5. THE FUTURE AS NEW PARADIGM
OF TRANSCENDENCE

Jürgen Moltmann

"Transcendence" is a relative concept, for it concerns,
whenever and wherever it is employed, a transcendence of something and for something. By "transcendence" we ordinarily designate that which surpasses the present and experienceable "immanence," that which moved to a beyond. By "immanence" we
designate that which impinges upon us, the present, the here and
now. Just as the beyond is always the beyond of the here and now,
so also the here and now is always the here and now of a particular beyond. Both concepts belong together, reciprocally defining
each other and mutually relating to each other. The understanding
of transcendence is always dependent upon the experience of a
reality as immanence, and conversely, there is no concept of
immanence which does not already imply on the other side of the
coin, as it were, an understanding of transcendence. Between
immanence and transcendence there is no dichotomy, but only
distinction and relationship as we experience "the boundary." . . .

If something is experienced as limited and finite, there results at its boundaries the possibility of negation. Transcendence
is defined, then, in negative terms as the in-finite and un-limited.
If something is experienced as finite and limited, there results at
its boundaries, on the other hand, the possibility of advancing into
what is endless and boundless. Transcendence is defined then in
analogous terms as that which is trans-finite.

Historically, the experience of the "boundary" has been
quite diverse. But it was always this experience which first

---

evoked the possibility of speaking about "transcendence" and "immanence." If we no longer have an experience of the "boundary," transcendence is denied and the possibility of speaking about immanence no longer exists. The difference which is experienced at the "boundary" then vanishes: everything is one and the same, and Yes is No . . . .

The following presentation and comparison of the models of transcendence is perforce simplified and too neatly typologized. It does not present to be an exclusive answer suspending further inquiry but, rather, an orientation in the present . . . .

Greek metaphysics emerged as a way of perceiving reality (theoria) from the ground of ancient Greek religious cosmology . . . . Metaphysical thought interpreted the manifold of experienceable reality in terms of its one primordial source or in relationship to its most comprehensive horizon . . . .

Metaphysics is here the answer to the basic metaphysical question of all beings. Everything which exists is threatened by its finitude, transitoriness, and instability. Therefore, all beings strive for, and that being which is figted with consciousness asks for, an infinite, immutable, and fixed being . . . . If immanence is experienced at this "boundary" as finite, mutable, and threatened by chaos, then the corresponding transcendence takes the form of infinitude and immutability, of orderedness and oneness. Through participation in infinite being, finite being attains its transcendence, and in its correspondence this transcendence reclaims its immanence. "Physics" of finite being and "metaphysics" of the one ordering and prevailing being correspond to each other . . . .

Modern man no longer understands himself in terms of the world and as a part of finite being. Without having completely lost this view of self and world, man nevertheless understands the world more and more as the field of the constructive possibilities of his spirit. The world is for him no longer a "house of being" and a home in which he dwells. Increasingly, it becomes for him the material which he investigates for conversion into his own use. Having once felt cramped inside the eternal

342

orders of the cosmos, he now views himself as lord of nature, which stands over against himself. Indeed, the more the world becomes an object for man, the more he becomes in himself a world-transcending subject. As a result, he no longer finds transcendence in the outermost, all-encompassing periphery of the cosmos but in himself, for he has made himself the center of a world which is increasingly becoming his personal property for disposal as he sees fit. He no longer expects the heaven of metaphysics to unlock the physics of the earth for him. Now his world is made accessible to him through his own transcending subjectivity. Consequently, in modern times transcendence is more and more experienced in the inner dimension of human existence, in man's transcendental subjectivity. Man can objectivize and utilize all things; only his own self transcends all of the objectifications of his spirit. Because the "boundary" between immanence and transcendence runs through himself, man comes to know this boundary in his own existence. Existentially he experiences finitude and infinitude simultaneously. He understands himself as God present on earth. Hence in place of the old correlation of "physics and metaphysics" the modern correlation of "existence and transcendence" advanced to the foreground . . . .

As a result of this change in metaphysics the whole traditional conceptualization of God has collapsed . . . . Critical thinking insists that transcendence can no longer be expressed in objectifying language because the "objectivity" of the world has lost its old metaphysical framework. Only existentialist interruption can form a significant alliance between the Christian tradition as kerygma and man's new experience of transcendence.

To be sure, men always have the feeling that God is dead if a trusted concept of God is lost. They readily speak of the "end of metaphysics" if they lose the traditional sense for transcendence. But these are only surface phenomena. What is at stake is neither the "death of God in modern times," nor the end of metaphysics altogether, nor even the age of secularization and atheism but, rather, only the metamorphosis of transcendence and the transformation of the boundary experience of immanence. The experience of transcendence, the experience of boundary and religion and in a general sense just as real as in former times.

Only they are no longer to be found in those places where they once were . . . .

Today even the modern model of existence and transcendence has lost its formative power. Without doubt, man will continue to transcend nature both outside and within his own bodily existence, and through reflection intensify his possibilities for mastering the world. But instead of nature, there is revolving about him an increasingly impervious entaglement of his own works in social institutions, political organizations, and industrial enterprises, which in its own way constitutes a quasi-nature. . . . In place of the natural cosmos, which man ever more effectively colonizes and controls, there appears a new cosmos of his own objectifications which is consistently more difficult to penetrate and even more difficult to control. In this artificial cosmos of his scientific-technological civilization the old conditions, from which man freed himself, return in the form of the irrational coercion of his civilization: The opacity of destiny finds a new correspondence in the opacity of reticular bureaucratic manipulations; what once were natural catastrophes recur now in the guise of social and political catastrophes. The man who rules nature via society now becomes the slave of his own products. Man's creations become autonomous, "program" themselves out of his control and gain the upper hand over him. Since the beginning of the industrial revolution, the question of the liberation of man from the predominance of his own work has become the theme of the philosophy which is related to action.

In this situation man enters again into a new experience of boundary. It is no longer the experience of his inner subjectivity transcending the objective world but the experience of his own impotence in a strait-jacket of autonomous objectification and in a "closed society." The consciousness of transcendental subjectivity has, since the inception of the industrial world, become aware of its own impotence. Its own world becomes alient to it and it easily changes itself into the escapist form of romantic subjectivity . . . . The feeling of alienation through social thingification and the political impotence of the individual is growing, and out of these sufferings of man within his own world which enslaves its creator arise new ecstatic forms of seeing and experi-

encing transcendence. Where is there to be found a transcendence which does not alienate but, rather, liberates us from alienation?
. . .

Through many of these new forms of religiosity and search for transcendence, men are seeking that freedom which lies beyond the domain of necessity and need. Moreover, the alienation, through which man becomes aware of the "boundary," is now understood not so much as alienation but as unburdening . . . . The old relationship of immanence and transcendence is reversed. The immanence of man's own world, which makes itself independent and confirms its own autonomy while structuring an increasingly more stringent entaglement around man, released a free-floating transcendence of the soul which has become homeless in its own world. Because the modern subjectivity is no longer in a position to rule its own world, the inner transcendence of man becomes the play of an impotent escapism . . . . The abstract negation of the real world makes possible every sort of cynicism within the abandoned reality. Therefore, this new mysticism is frequently coupled with nihilism. These forms of modern romantic religiosity can be understood as epiphenomena of modern and existential transcendence, for they actually owe their existence to the fact that the soul has been unburdened by a stabilized immanence. Immanence, then, is no longer understood as immanence of a transcendence, as characterized, actuated, and transformed by that which surpasses it. It becomes the basis which sets free transcendence's abstract realm of play. This means that the character which is ascribed to immanence and transcendence is also changed.

In modern immanence where the production of foodstuffs is automated and the process of automation can be cybernetically controlled, "transcendence" has lost its job, as it were. It becomes the play of the unburdened spirit, free of necessity. The "realm of necessity" serves as the ground on which the realms of play, culture, and transcendence are constructed. Indeed, the more stable immanence becomes, the more unstable and open can transcendence be understood. Whereas transcendence had to be thought of earlier as a stabilizing factor of order--as "the highest star of being" (Nietzsche)--in a stabilized world, transcendence

345

can be thought of precisely in its boundless openness, as the inexhaustible fascination of new possibilities and fantasies . . . . But if the "kingdom of necessity" is automated and is increasingly converted into regulated processes, it forfeits the interest of man. For that which does not offer resistance, so that its creative appropriation requires the pain of work and disappointment, can no longer be experienced as "real." Therefore the unreal, the sphere of the not yet realized, of the not realizable and absolutely absured possibilities is increasingly capturing the interest of man and is experienced as "boundary." . . .

In a "post-industrial society" . . . industry becomes uninteresting and theology can become deadly serious play of man in previously unknown form. For then doxology and nihilism will be immediately confronted with one another, with the mediating work on that which is finitely negative being eliminated. Without such mediation, man has to seek the forms by which he can exist between God and nothingness. Intimations in this direction are found in modern literature and art. In his culture, man lives by such anticipations of "life." In play, in festivity, and in humor, he liberates himself from the rational, goal-regimentation of work and from moralistic coercion in order to change present conditions and improve society. If there were no such anticipation of the kingdom of freedom, play, and cheerfulness, no matter how insufficient in form, man would not experience suffering from the negatives, nor would he feel the necessities of life as pain . . . .

With the decline in the efficacy of existence-transcendence models, there now lies at hand a new realistic understanding of immanence as history. In the ancient conception of metaphysics, history had no particular significance. It was the incalculable and chaotic. Only the cosmos, with its recurring orders and the rule of destiny, had transcendence. In the models of transcendental subjectivity, history gained the significance of personal decision and encounter. Today, social, technical, and political history becomes the field of mediation between man and nature. Only in this field does man gain his identity and only in the context of history's mediation does he comprehend nature. It is here that nature becomes nature for man. If the context of this mediation becomes autonomous over against man, then the interrelationship between men and their objective world will increasingly become the theme of history. The "boundary" of transcendence lies no longer only in the finitude of all things and beings and also no longer in human subjectivity of his own objectifications and in the superiority of his own works over himself. In modern society, man's subjectivity and the objectivity of his works and relations appear so far separated that the products rule their producers and rationalized relationships exert a wholly irrational coercive force over men. This is a new "boundary" at which one inquires about transcendence. It is a transcendence over against a particular contemporary societal system. Therefore it is directed toward the "future." The present situation is experienced as a situation of antagonism between subjectivity and objectification . . . . This situation is characterized by the impotence of the individual and the superiority of those conditions which he himself creates.

If this characterizes the historical present in its strife-ridden totality, then it is clear that transcendence can be found neither on the subjective nor on the objective side, but only where this antagonistic situation finds a qualitatively different, transforming, and new future. If the "boundary" of the present immanence is experienced in such a way that man is alienated from his world and his world is alienated from man, then transcendence is experienced where critical perspectives on the divisions of the present are opened up, where new possibilities for a meaningful incarnation of man and new possibilities for a humanization of his alienated conditions are manifested, in brief: where a future of reconcilation and transformation attains the upper hand over this state of affairs.

But it is not only the understanding of "transcendence" which is subjected to the modern fissure within consciousness. Today the understanding of "future" suffers the same fate. On the one hand, "futre" in industrial society was identified with the progress and development of the present status quo. "Future" was objectified in the growth-rate of social products and the acceleration of the objective potencies of man. As long as the industrial system found itself in the process of construction, its objective progress exuded the fascinating spell of transcendence.

It promised the vanquishing of man's dependence on nature, the fulfillment of human longing, the subduing of economic alienation, and also the kingdom of political freedom. But the modern, "post-industrial," planned society defuturizes this kind of transcendental future. In the measure that the industrial society successfully completes its own edifice, its progress loses the fascination of transcendence. A planned and programed future has nothing more to do with transcendence . . . .

On the other hand, "future" was personalized and, as in Existentialism, became the inner extension of human existing, the openness of the heart and futurity of decision. Yet, this kind of personalization which develops from being unburdened from responsibility for present history owes its existence, on the other hand, to the objectification of the future. In this connection, the personalistic understanding of future as the possibility of existence is a product of the split in the modern spirit just as is the objectification of the future in the automatic progress of society.

In which sense, then, can "future" become a new paradigm of transcendence? It can become the new paradigm of transcendence only if it becomes the embodiment of the transcendence of present dissension and bondage in something qualitatively new. Future has the fascination of genuine transcendence it it promises something qualitatively new which stimulates the fundamental transformation of the "systems" of the present; if in it something different can be expected which leads to the basic transformation of the present, antagonistic conditions of immanence. This means in present-day language: if it becomes the occasion for the possibility of a revolutionary consciousness which seeks to transform an antagonistic into a nonantagonistic society and an unfree into a free society. Transcendence, then, in the manner of previous transformations of the concept of transcendence, is taken out of its substantival forms and put in the form of a verb. Transcendence becomes the embodiment of concrete, historical transcending of the concrete, historical "boundary." The substantive "transcendence" means, then, the space ahead of us in the open future where historical transformations take place. This implies that future as transcendence can no longer be understood as quantitative extension and development of the present, but must denote

348

qualitative transformation of the history which is experienced in conflicts. The "wholly other" . . . of transcendence, then, is conceived as the "wholly transforming" . . . and the "going beyond" as the transforming of history from the direction of its qualitatively new future.

The power of the existing status quo which wants only to sustain itself, or through various reforms adapt itself to the times, is confronted with the powers of a qualitatively new future and with a fundamental transformation. Today "transcendence" is sought and in many situations also experienced at this "boundary" or "front" of present history. What for Marxism is the leap from the quantitative into the qualitative and from the kingdom of necessity into the kingdom of freedom, what for many others is the transformation of an unfree into a free, a repressive into a human society is thought of by Christians as the qualitative difference between history and eschatology and is anticipated in concrete faith under the conditions of history . . . . It is precisely here that new experiences of the "boundary" and of transcendence are found in the shape of political responsibility. And while these new experiences of transcendence in a political context do not supplant the old ones, they differ decisively from the experiences of suffering within the conditions of finitude or of man's suffering within himself . . . .

In the models of metaphysical transcendence, reality was determined and ordered in definitions. The mode of viewing physical things combined the memory of eternal ideas with its act of perception . . . . The definitional concept became the image of true reality. If transcendence is the most perfect reality, the concept of transcendence is correspondingly the definition of all definitions, the epitome of all concepts. The hierarchy of definitional and subsumptive concepts corresponds to the hierarchy of being.

In the models of subjective transcendence we find another way of defining transcendence. Here the reflection of the subject connects objective experience with its own transcendental conditions of all possible experience . . . . In this situation, objective definitions are replaced by relational concepts which express the relationship of things to the human subject. Correspondingly, transcendence can no longer be grasped in definitions but only in relationships to the inner ground of the subject.

In the model "history and future," cognition and language are once again changed. The perception of a thing or a relationship combines with the experience of its reality the expectation of its future possibility. Things are perceived in their history and linked with the sought and hoped-for future of history. Things do not present themselves in an earthly mode of appearance before the transcendental heaven of their fixed ideas. Neither are they apprehended merely in the reflecting light of the perceiving subject. They are perceived on the foreground of an open future of history in its significance for the whole of reality . . . . Language does not simply make statements but knows that in the very act of speaking about that which is, it is already grasping and transforming it in the open process of history. Wherever cognition and language become aware of their own historicity, together with the historicity of things, constative language becomes a critical language, for everything which is historical is accompanied by its own negation. On the other hand, this historical language becomes a performative language . . . . Insofar as it brings things in history to expression, it changes history and the things in it. Historical language must be clear, therefore, for which purpose it wants to bring things to expression and for which it wishes to transform them. For this purpose, the objective, generic concept of species is replaced by the dynamic concept of function, and the concept of redemption which redeems a thing or a person from his fixity . . . .

Therefore, in the model of transcendence designated as "history and future," the representation of transcendence in the democratic network of interpersonal relationships is changed to new, revolutionary forms of transcending. In a society which is rivited to its status quo, this democratic transcendence, if it is not to fade into an empty, ideological sham, can be realized only if the oppressed and alienated groups in such a society are liberated and given an independent share in the shape of the society's future. Where fixed societies represent their transcendence in terms of their own fixity while excluding or outvoting others, true transcendence gains its representation in revolutionary groups that

350

ally themselves with those who are alienated, oppressed, or simply frustrated. Precisely for this reason, revolutionary movements in such societies have about them the fascination of transcendence. However, where they resume the old hierarchial form of transcendence through party machinery, etc., they betray the new experience of transcendence. If revolutionary movements end in bureaucratic hierarchies of functionaries, they represent no progress over against the democratic forms of transcendence, but actually a regression . . . .

Finally, by way of "experiment" alone, let us advance some reflections about a possible identification of "future" and "transcendence."

By "history" we understand here the experience of reality in conflicts. It is not simply the experience that everything is transitory. Neither is it simply the experience that all things find themselves in the river of time with the present standing between the no-more of the past and the not-yet of the future. Furthermore, it is not only the experience that man must ever and again make decisions. Rather, "history" is the impression that man together with his society and his world is an experiment and that not only he himself, but also his world, represents a risk. In situations of radical change and crisis he senses the constraint of Hamlet's "To be or not to be--that is the question." Involved in the experiment of history where the terrors of his failures always seize him, he must project visions of a successful solution. These visions also bear the character of being risks and projects. They must be authenticated through their critical power over against the present reality and through personal effort. They do not have the structure of projection into what is possible with the intent of changing the present necessity. It is in this sense that the following statements are to be understood.

"Future" has not as yet anything to do with "transcendence" if it is itself only a matter of historical future. To be sure, a vision of the future can be projected only from within history. Therefore, it is just as transient as history itself. "Boundless transcending" is not yet genuine transcendence . . . . Nevertheless, as regards the intention itself one can distinguish the idea of a future of history from future history.

Only a future which transcends the experiment of history itself can become the paradigm of transcendence and give meaning to the experiment "history." The "utopia of the beyond" explodes all known world conditions. It is the ultimate and also the most fundamental experience of transcendence and is usually expressed in religious symbols. If one can speak of reality as history, one can also speak of an "end of history." . . . With which eschatological symbols such an "end of history" can be expressed in the midst of history and under its conditions is another question. But here we can say at least this much: A "future of history" cannot be a merely quantitatively new future but must be a qualitatively new future. The future must be identified with a transformation of the conditions of history itself. Only if the conflicts which cause man to experience the present reality as history are abolished has future anything to do with transcendence. Only where these conflicts are transcended in the direction of their dissolution or reconciliation is something of this qualitatively new future present in history. Future prospects which do not meet these criteria reveal their psuedo-transcendency. They promise more than they can keep and impetuously exchange the fascination of transcendence for resignation.

But, on the other hand, the vision of a qualitatively new future of history can become the transcendent horizon which opens up and stimulates transcendence in a new historical future. If the relationship of history and eschatological future emerges in this way, then we encounter the relationship of difference and analogy. The future of history is something qualitatively different and new in the face of what is here experienced as history. But as future precisely of this historical reality it affects already here and now the experience and shape of history. In the qualitative difference, therefore, are correspondences, analogies, directions, and tendencies. They do not bring about the "new" in a different quality, but the vision of this necessary new departure influences the shape and also the suffering of history in the present.

In order to make the dialectic clearer, reference should be

352

made to two prejudices and seductions. If the qualitative distinction between history and eschatological future is overemphasized one falls into an abstract negation of the world and its history. The great failures in the experiment of history become, then, the circumstance for the meaninglessness of every event and action in history. The world is a "vale of tears." Radical evil dominates everything. The end is resignation. On the other hand, if the relationship of correspondence is stressed to the point of being the relationship of continuity, then transcendence is reviewed as the essence of history itself, that is, perpetual disclosure of the future in the present and permanent movement beyond the momentary present. The end is likewise resignation, for every attempt at transcending creates anew a preset which must be transcended. To what extent should that which is future be better than that which is present? A meaningful mediation seems to result only if the transcendence which is beyond history is linked with man's act of transcending within history; if in the midst of the critical difference one believes in the possibilities of correspondence, and is, conversely, in the possibilities of correspondence the qualitative difference is kept in mind. Then, "systematic transcendental criticism" joins itself with "systematic immanental criticism," and the openness of a qualitatively new future is linked with concrete steps for bringing about a qualitatively better correspondence. The Christian faith understand both history and eschatological future to be linked in the Christ in whom this qualitatively new future is present under the conditions of history. Therefore, it speaks of the historical Christ eschatologically and presently finds in him the end of history in the midst of history.

The Christian faith does not supplant history so that history would become an indifferent matter to believers. Because the Christian can hope in the new future through faith in Christ, he begins to suffer in the unredeemedness of the present and realized solidarity with all who suffer consciously or unconsciously in this unredeemedness. But neither does he become absorbed into history so that the future would become indifferent to faith. Because he can hope in this future, he begins to oppose the "scheme of this world" and the systems of the present and to change them. For a long time the Christian faith employed a metaphysical exegesis of the transcendence in which it believed through Christ.

Later, that faith interpreted it existentially. But today it is realizing that Christ is present where the "boundary" of immanence is experienced in suffering and transcended in active hope. The more it interprets Christian transcendence eschatologically, the more it will understand the boundary of immanence historically and surrender itself to the movement of transcending. But the more it interprets this eschatological transcendence in a Christian way, that is, in consideration of the crucified Jesus, the more it will become aware that the qualitatively new future of God has united itself with those who are dispossessed, denied, and oppressed in the present. Furthermore, it will become more sensitive to the fact that this future begins not from above at the point of the progress of an "advanced society," but from below with those who have been sacrificed to this progress. This means that the Christian faith will have to integrate hope in an eschatological future and love which realizes solidarity with the oppressed. In other words, the future of the new being which brings history to a close is allied with the dialectic of the negatives in the historical present. The transcendence of the future of a "wholly other" begins dialectically in establishing those who, in a settled present and in static societies, are "the others." Precisely this combination is, for the Christian faith, the "power of transformation." So the power of God, who transcends history, is experienced by Christians in the midst of history.